MORAL APOSTASY IN
RUSSIAN LITERATURE

MORAL APOSTASY IN RUSSIAN LITERATURE

GEORGE J. GUTSCHE

NORTHERN ILLINOIS UNIVERSITY PRESS

DEKALB, ILLINOIS

1986

Publication of this book was assisted
by a grant from the
Publications Program of the
National Endowment for the
Humanities, an independent
federal agency

Library of Congress Cataloging-
in-Publication Data
Gutsche, George J.
Moral apostasy in Russian literature.
Bibliography: p.
Includes index.
1. Russian literature—19th century—
History and criticism.
2. Russian literature—20th century
History and criticism.
3. Ethics in literature.
4. Values in literature.
5. Characters and characteristics in literature.
I. Title. PG3015.5.E74G88   1986
891.7'09'003   86–8513
ISBN 0-87580-118-8

*To Lorraine
Tania and Alex*

CONTENTS

PREFACE

THE STUDIES COLLECTED here share a preoccupation with moral issues as they are raised and depicted in literary works by major Russian authors. Although there is some sense of system to the arrangement of studies—they treat literary works chronologically, in the order in which they were written—they are not meant to cover the historical development of Russian literature from a moral perspective, or even to cover all of the major figures. Nor are they meant to exemplify a comprehensive new critical approach to literature. These studies are attempts to illuminate artistically imaginative works (in some cases classics) of Russian literature from a new perspective that focuses on moral issues without ignoring historical and formal qualities.

A thread running through the chosen texts is the theme of moral apostasy. Those writers or fictional characters who challenge conventional values, and whose religious or social views differ from those of their society, stand apart from the group by their thoughts and actions. Having abandoned society's ruling dogmas, they become moral apostates. It is their vision that will be explored here, for it is their vision that determines the moral significance of the texts.

However, the texts studied here were chosen according to a pattern and unifying objective only partially specified by the theme of moral apostasy. Spanning almost a century and a half, and written at intervals of twenty to thirty years, these works represent a variety of genres; furthermore, they are works which have stimulated, and continue to stimulate, strong critical interest and even controversy. Moreover, they all exemplify the many ways in which literature can engage our moral sensibilities, incorporate moral notions, and reflect moral attitudes.

The moral dimension of literature may be perceived in a variety of ways: literary works present visions of human activity that we normally describe with such conceptual terms as *justice, responsibility, obligation, right* and *wrong,* and *good* and *evil.* Literature reflects moral attitudes and ideas not only of the authors but also of the society in which the authors live. And when it is good, literature can also engage our moral sensibilities so that we look differently at our actions and our character. The difficult task of disentangling the dense thicket of theoretical relationships between the moral content of literature and the effect of literature on readers' behavior remains to be done. What I have attempted is more modest: to clear a space around each of the works I examine, to bring some measure of clarity to moral issues the texts raise. This is surely one of the best ways in which to progress in our efforts to understand the moral dimension of literature.

The relevance of ethics to literature is obvious: literary works abound in examples of human conduct and morally problematic situations. The issues considered here have been raised vividly and engagingly by some of Russia's most brilliant writers. Elucidating and defining the problems fictional characters or poets' personae deal with are goals worth pursuing, for by so doing we may come to a better understanding not only of the works but of the issues themselves. Moral perspectives, and moral frames of reference, have of course been applied to Russian literature before, and in particular to some of the works I examine here. Too often in the past, however, moral categories have brought little illumination; for not only is our moral language notoriously imprecise and problematic but also, when moral frames are applied to literature, the works examined are sometimes isolated from their historical, social, and literary contexts. In offering new readings, I have tried to avoid these pitfalls. While the interpretations are given in the spirit of democratic pluralism, they demonstrate a clear preference for the readings that function best now, in our age. All of them aspire to a freshness and clarity that I hope will enhance understanding and lead to new ways of seeing and appreciating these enduring texts from some of Russia's greatest writers.

ACKNOWLEDGMENTS

I HAVE BENEFITTED enormously in this long-term project from the advice and support of numerous people in my field. In this regard, I am indebted to J. Thomas Shaw, Gary Jahn, Victor Terras, Gerald Mikkelson, Herman Ermolaev, and Paul Debreczeny, who have read or heard earlier versions of several of the chapters and have offered valuable suggestions. To this list I must add the names of those who have stimulated my thinking about literature and have generously given advice on a number of different topics. In particular, I have learned a great deal from discussions with Edward Wasiolek, Lauren Leighton, John Schillinger, and my colleague in Russian literature at Northern Illinois University, Gavriel Shapiro; I have a special debt of gratitude to my colleague in history here, W. Bruce Lincoln, for his warm encouragement and friendly advice on a wide variety of matters. In addition, I am grateful to my former teachers—J. Thomas Shaw, Xenia Gąsiorowska, Victor Terras, and James Bailey—for imparting, through their teaching and their professional example, values that helped to shape my views of literature and literary scholarship.

The administration at my university has been extremely helpful in supporting my work. I have benefited from several grants from the Graduate School, which has had two very supportive deans, Dean Jaros and Jerrold Zar. I am also grateful for the support I have received from James D. Norris, the dean of my own college. At the Northern Illinois University Press I have had the good fortune to have been assisted by a friendly and professional staff; those who deserve particular mention are Kelli Harmon, Jo Aerne, Stephen Franklin, and especially Wanda Giles, an exacting editor who strove to ensure that my text meet the highest standards. I am of course grateful to the director of the press, Mary Lincoln, for her skill and good will in supervising the conversion of manuscript into book.

Finally, I owe thanks to my family—especially my wife, Lorraine

Gutsche, whose perceptive criticism of the emerging work was combined with gentle prodding and encouragement when other commitments began to threaten the book's progress.

I am grateful to Walter Arndt for allowing me to use his linear translation of *The Bronze Horseman* in chapter 2. Chapter 4 is a revised version of "The Role of the 'One' in Gor'kii's Twenty-Six and One," which originally appeared in the collection, *Studies in Honor of Xenia Gąsiorowska* (Columbus, Ohio: Slavica, 1983); Chapter 6 is a substantially revised version of "Sound and Significance in Pasternak's 'Leto,'" which originally appeared in the *Slavic and East European Journal* 25 (1983), 83–93. I am grateful to the editor of SEEJ for permission to reprint part of the original article here.

MORAL APOSTASY IN
RUSSIAN LITERATURE

C H A P T E R 1

MORAL ISSUES IN A LITERARY CONTEXT

> . . . *a work of art is a moral example.*
> John Gardner
> *On Moral Fiction*

RUSSIAN LITERATURE has always been an attractive subject for criticism from a moral perspective; fiction and poetry have been and continue to be important outlets for the expression of moral concern in Russia, even though the obstacles to such expression frequently have been formidable.[1] Elucidating this concern of Russian writers to readers in different times with different traditions is certainly one valuable task that criticism can fulfill: it can explain the ways in which obstacles have been overcome, and it can mediate between moral discourses of different ages and settings.

Moral criticism, especially in its more common forms, has had very clear, but often unforeseen, results. Critics often helped to bestow upon certain writers (Boris Pasternak and Alexander Solzhenitsyn are good examples) a larger-than-life status as moral exemplars. Again, the obstacles that had to be overcome played a role in this bestowal. Tsarist and Soviet censors have exercised restrictions of varying severity over the years, pressuring Russian writers to conform with official standards and to adapt their works and even their attitudes about what they can and should write to meet these standards. Those who have had the courage to circumvent or confront the powers of the state have achieved in this repressive milieu a moral authority unparalleled by writers in the West. And this moral authority has benefits: it carries with it a special power that appears to rival that of the state. One of Solzhenitsyn's characters says that writers are another government—and Solzhenitsyn himself appropriated just such a role both there and here in his Western exile, where he continues to speak, in his distinctively apocalyptic moral vocabulary, of the evils of communism and of the spiritual impoverishment and cowardice of the West.

Even before Stalinism, which promoted exclusively and narrowly an already existing sociological and ideological view of art, Russian writers were perceived as potential rivals to the throne, offering visions of the world different from those prescribed by political leaders. The editor Aleksei Suvorin noted at the beginning of the century that Russia had two tsars, one—Nicholas II—in St. Petersburg and the other—Lev Tolstoi—in Iasnaia Poliana. Indeed, recently Michael Holquist convincingly argued that the works defining the entire Russian literary tradition were essentially works of dissidence.[2]

Of course not all major Russian writers are discussed here: notable in their absence, though equally deserving of consideration from a moral perspective, are Nikolai Gogol', Fedor Dostoevskii, and Anton Chekhov from the nineteenth century and numerous rebels of the twentieth. All of these writers have contributed to that tradition which has given Russian literature its distinctive moral character. But those works I have chosen give ample illustration of the strength, variety, and vitality of Russian moral fiction and poetry. The works exemplify the ways in which controversial ideas can be raised in a literary context that has been historically dominated by the prescriptions of Tsar and Party. Though their works are my primary concern, these writers themselves had, to one degree or another, their problems with the state; and the aura of moral strength they project is derived from their works and from the confrontations connected with these problems.

There is something paradoxically positive about being victimized by the state; not only is there the potential for achieving a new moral stature for bravely confronting authority, but there is also the possibility of gaining insights into the nature of one's courage and values. Solzhenitsyn saw the benefits of state "justice" and often admitted that suffering through the Soviet camp experience significantly altered his perception of what was truly important in life. Moral vision and strength are unfortunately a partial product of conflict *in extremis*; and as the works discussed here will illustrate, such conflict helps, through the testing of former assumptions about life, to create new values. Though it is easy to exaggerate the effects of state oppression, especially in accounting for the quality of the art produced by Russian writers, it would be folly to dismiss entirely the moral and psychological implications of state policies.[3]

The courage to challenge authorities and endure the consequences of such a challenge is not the only source of Russian literature's moral prestige and the critical interest it generates. Russian writers have taken on a broad range of ethical concerns, from lofty quests for the meaning of life to more prosaic, but no less trying, problems relating to personal happiness and responsibility. Confronting death and its meanings, relating to others, being truthful, and maintaining integrity in the face of pressures to betray one's personal values are all deeply human matters that have less to do with the state than with society's reigning values (which may very well uphold the power of the state) and individual psychology. Our awareness of the tradition of the Russian radical critics and their sociological emphases should not obscure our vision so that we are unable to recognize that the moral dilemmas depicted by Russian writers can pertain to issues beyond state oppression and class exploitation.

The studies that follow do not focus on writers' problems with the state, the effects of state oppression, the ways in which moral stature can be conferred, or the distinguishing features of Russian literature's moral prestige. Rather, they center on imaginative visions of moral dilemmas particular Russian writers have offered in their creative works. Although the ways in which a writer's moral views are reflected in the written work are obviously relevant to a discussion of literature and morality, my concern is not so much the views themselves, as the manner in which the text utilizes them. My focus is primarily on the works; I consider the moral quality of the authors' lives only to the extent to which it is affected by the moral dimension of their writings. Judgments on personal morality are controversial, and even painful, because many readers are unwilling to admit that their favorite writers do not always live up to the high values articulated by their fictional heroes. Again Tolstoi and Solzhenitsyn stand out—the former because his message of love and nonagression was not reflected in the apparent cruelty he visited upon his family; and Solzhenitsyn, whose public posturing as a prophet and spiritual leader is somehow out of harmony with the sincere moral questioning and tolerance for human diversity manifested by his major characters. It is an unfortunate truism (reinforced by the recent attention given to Dostoevskii's anti-Semitism) that moral vision in art can hide the crudest barbarities and egocentrism.

For the critic, talking about moral dilemmas or literature in general from a moral perspective can be a dangerously complex and controversial enterprise. It is art's particular virtue that it can make abstract hypothetical problems vividly real, and in fleshing out these problems and their resolutions it can make us aware of causes and consequences of particular events and behavior. But the critical language we choose to describe the art that expresses these issues brings with it a conceptual baggage, an ideology, a set of assumptions about the world. The complex implications of hidden assumptions in the way we describe the world have become the focus of recent literary theory. Thus the critic's choice of a descriptive apparatus to capture insights about art is no longer seen as a simple matter of adopting an intrinsic or extrinsic approach. Roland Barthes, Michel Foucault, Jacques Derrida, and others representing a wide range of disciplines have brought into currency a suspicion of systems that purport to be all-embracing, to have a special way of getting at the truth. And this recent (and renewed) skepticism about privileged accesses to the truth has brought back into favor or thrown new light on past figures, philosophical forbears of the current scene such as Iurii Tynianov, Mikhail Bakhtin, John Dewey, William James, and Kenneth Burke.[4]

The quandary for the critic now, especially one interested in approaches that New Criticism and Russian Formalism tried to expel, is obvious: in an age that questions the existence of an anchor for all descriptions, the assumptions underlying all points of view, the privileged access point, how can one proceed in an investigation of the ways in which morality and art interrelate? With the once-universal (or nearly so) foundation pulled from under ethics as well as epistemology, where can one begin?[5] Such questions seem especially appropriate in the case of Russia, where pragmatism has never enjoyed a wide following in literature, literary criticism, and philosophy.

Ethical theory in Russia is well grounded in forms of the Absolute, whether religious or secular, whether Kantian, utilitarian, positivist, Hegelian, Marxist, or Orthodox; and these assumptions about platonic and Kantian atemporal essences are embedded implicitly and explicitly in the views of most Russian writers. Russia's most prominent literary critics and critical schools—the critics Vissarion Belinskii, Nikolai Chernyshevskii, Nikolai Dobroliubov, Fedor Dostoevskii, Konstantin Leont'ev, Nikolai Mikhailovskii, Nikolai Berdiaev, and the movements of Russian Formalism and Socialist Realism—display a wide variety of concerns and interests; yet all, to one degree or another, have based their critical efforts in a soil of certainty, an ultimate reality that lies at the bottom of everything. A perspective on literature that is pragmatic and not committed to the position that there is just one right way of understanding reality, morality, or literature may seem perverse at first; but I think it is a perspective that has a great deal of versatility: it can freely incorporate and use for its own purposes many of the valuable insights of other interpretive frames without concern for the broad theoretical claims these frames make.

I have taken a contextual approach to the study of the moral dimension of literature. It focuses on the literary presentation and uses whatever critical tools seem appropriate to illuminate this presentation in all of its immediacy. Too often moral talk is divorced from the text and the context in which the text has been produced; too often morality is perceived in terms of abstract principles in search of transcendental moorings or vague generalities garbed in theological rhetoric. The human dilemmas depicted in literature are more than hypothetical and abstract exemplifications of moral life, and the pain and passion that inform these dilemmas call for much more than the clarifying coolness of conventional moral discourse (as well as excessively formalist and structuralist discourses). Works that really move readers are not served well by isolation and abstraction.

My approach is pragmatic as well as contextual, in the sense that it does not speak to issues of ontology. It gives attention to such matters as which particular critical tools and perspectives can be useful in a particular context, under particular circumstances. Yet it frees these critical tools from service to well-worn and firmly entrenched moral categories and abstractions, while allowing access to different, more rewarding perspectives on the way right and wrong and good and bad are worked out in literature. It uses the instruments and strategies of philological positivism and documentary historicism without committing itself to the assumptions of these approaches. And it tries to balance microscopism with an awareness of the whole. If the recent developments in literary theory have taught us anything, it is that no critical language has a privileged status, that there was, after all, something reasonable about the "strategies" and "multiple perspectives" Kenneth Burke talked about.[6] There is no single preexistent meaning of a text for which one and only one critical language is designed— all critical languages are relevant and contingent in what they have to offer.

Two novels, two short stories, a narrative poem, and a lyric serve as the objects of analysis in this book. Central moral issues of each are explored from perspectives that are intended to bring out the richness and complex suggestiveness of the texts. In each case, the readings diverge from previous interpretations, emphasizing insufficiently appreciated moral issues and implications of the text. Although the ultimate goal of much moral criticism of the past has been to reach an improved understanding of human conduct in literature so that people might be changed for the better, hopes of reaching such a goal seem unduly optimistic (perhaps somewhat arrogant, even) in this age. Probably the most we can feel hopeful about, as critics and readers, is attaining the more modest goal of understanding something of the way our moral language and moral categories work in literature.

Literary works sometimes suggest modes of conduct that may be easily generalizable, offering explicit rules of behavior one should heed to lead a moral life; and overt didacticism is one way in which moral issues can be manifested and made to function in literature. But the moral statement of literature is not always so obvious. Literary characters in problematic situations often serve not just to exemplify behavior and character but also to illustrate how complex our moral lives are and how difficult it is to categorize actions and character in terms such as right or wrong, good or evil. The intertwining of psychology with ethics in good art is complex; and once one is sensitive to the various relationships between psychology and ethics, moral judgments become all the more difficult to make and defend. But this is not the only problem morally suggestive literature poses for the critic.

One task of criticism is to explicate the rich and complex implications of ideas found in literature; but such a task becomes difficult when ideas are purposely, for prudential or aesthetic reasons, embedded in ambiguity or expressed indirectly. Pasternak could not hope to survive an explicit attack on Stalinism in 1930, nor could Alexander Pushkin explicitly suggest that Nicholas I used his power in questionable ways. But prudence is not the only reason that moral ideas may not be expressed openly: direct expression is too often simply moralizing, and moralizing always makes for poor art.

Pushkin and Tolstoi had radically different conceptions of ethics and the function of art, yet each left works of fiction that were far from moral neutrality. Pushkin opposed the moralizing of art, and after 1880, Tolstoi could not envisage good art without a moral emphasis; but both Pushkin's and Tolstoi's art could achieve moral power. Tolstoi, unlike Pushkin, was always a teacher; and if we assume it was his intention, in his late fiction, to teach readers about the right and wrong way to live, surely his first task would have been to break down his readers' erroneous preconceived ideas. Such a task demanded all the subtleties of art, not explicit moralizing. Tolstoi knew that ideas would have little effect on readers and limited lasting power if the literature were not compelling; I argue later that Tolstoi by design embedded his moral ideas in an artistic work so that they would affect readers not by their logical force but by their emotional power, contextual power. The differences between his nonfictional and fictional expression of the same moral ideas vividly illustrate the complex relationship between ethics and art. Each discipline calls for its own strategies, and each may be effective in its own ways.

The Russian Formalist Iurii Tynianov offered an ingenious theoretical structure for dealing with the very question of the relationship between literature and other "orders" or areas of human endeavor.[7] In particular he was concerned to show how different realms of experience, different disciplines and perspectives, come to be incorporated in literary works. What makes Tynianov's theories so modern is his rejection of the notion that literature has an essence, that a literary genre has a fixed center, that the "literary fact" can be "statically" defined. All the centers are fluid, he maintained; and there are no fixed points from which we can perceive the text once and for all. Each generation finds its own "truth" in the literary text, interprets it from a different perspective that has no monopoly on a core of reality. Tynianov's dynamic literary system in many ways anticipates the modern "textualisms" represented in the writings of Barthes, Foucault, and Derrida; it also gives an indication, which was recently elaborated by Edward Wasiolek, of how intrinsic and extrinsic approaches to literature (such as the moral approach) can be constructively united. Following Tynianov's lead and employing Barthes's ideas of a semiological criticism, Wasiolek offers a criticism that opens up new perspectives:

> Barthes can invite the "extrinsic" disciplines into the critical task and at the same time pursue formal and structural ends because his interest in extrinsic disciplines is in their structural character and not in their truth value. They represent different semiological systems, or in less technical language, different ways of reasoning. He is not interested in the "truth" content in the doctrine of Freudianism, but in the structural relations of the system and how one reasons from premise to conclusion. He is not interested in whether or not the literary work has an oedipal complex or whether or not *Pere Goriot* shows the dominance of a particular economic class or the class character of the

author, but he is interested in the way Marx reasons about how productive relations determine emotions and ideas. To those who would
retort that there is only one way to reason about reality, because the
operations of human reason are universal, Barthes would retort that
our so-called universal reason is a prejudice, a deliberate choice of a
particular kind of reasoning masquerading as universal reasoning.[8]

The shift in attention from the relation between language and the world
to language as it creates the world and the attack on "universal reasoning"
point up connections between textualism and pragmatism. What is important for our purposes is that in pragmatic terms, language is a form of human
behavior, a way of coping with our environment, that does not offer any
extrahistorical archimedean point from which to view the world. Literature
has a cognitive dimension in the sense that it can help us cope: it can present
aspects of the world which are of moral import and which can be reward-
ingly defined and elaborated within the same ethical discourse we might
ourselves use, outside literature. Ethical discourse can be thus seen as both
an instrument for helping us get what we want from the text and a semiological system that has something to say about the relations of moral concepts
to emotions and ideas in the text.

In a fine comprehensive study of Pushkin's *The Bronze Horseman* published some thirty years ago, the eminent scholar Waclaw Lednicki noted
the variety of perspectives that had been brought to bear on Pushkin's narrative poem.[9] It was Lednicki's thesis that each generation brought to the
poem its own interests and theoretical frames: "And indeed, they err who
suppose that there exist in literary criticism and in the history of literature
definitely settled problems to which scholars might have no reason to return." Fully aware of the changing arsenal of critical approaches, though
overly sanguine about the firm basis of documentary historicism, Lednicki
singled out artistic works for their "richness and vitality": "These works
bloom for each generation with new flowers of truth and charm. And it is
possible to say that each new generation seeks in a work of art that which the
preceding generation was unable to find in it. Hence the ephemeral nature
of the work of a critic or historian."
Lednicki showed a strong sense of criticism's contingency as well as a sensitivity to the virtues of a variety of critical approaches and critical languages. His remarks, though in an older idiom, are not far removed from
Steven Marcus': "Living works of literature are always richer than the original interpretations or analyses that accompany them. We return to them, as
future generations will, to find the language we seek and the story we need
to be told."[10] To a large extent the studies collected here depend on a broad
awareness of critical perspectives. I am concerned to show how various
literary texts present challenges to moral commonplaces and to conven-

tional views of people's behavior. In a variety of ways the works insinuate or overtly propose alternative visions of the moral world, and to investigate these ways an approach will be required which can assess, appreciate, and incorporate what other special perspectives, from philological to structuralist, have offered.

Lednicki's discussion of the poem sought to illuminate it from all angles and in its numerous dimensions: its relation to Pushkin's biography within the context of his views of the state and his contemporaries; its relation to his other works as well as to texts by other writers; its devices, its characterizations, its tensions, and its ambiguities. Along the way Lednicki made use of the observations of a variety of other critics and writers representing diverse critical schools and approaches. From Vissarion Belinskii to Valerii Briusov, Andrei Belyi, and Dmitrii Blagoi, Lednicki extracted what he needed to weave an interpretive pattern for his generation. Determining the direction of his exploration was an effort to resolve what has been perceived by generations as the central conflict of the poem, a conflict that seemed to demand resolution if we were ever to be warranted in speaking of the poem's artistic unity.

A central problem of this poem ostensibly concerning Peter the Great (the "Bronze Horseman" of the title) is how to harmonize two quite different tones the poem produces. On the one hand, the poem is a hymn of praise to Peter and, on a more abstract level, to progress, historical destiny, and power. On the other hand, the central character is a quite ordinary man victimized by natural disaster, a great flood in St. Petersburg in 1824. The natural disaster does not seem quite so "natural," however, if one considers the fact that Peter chose to build his city in an area subject to flooding. Thus from one moral perspective, culpability can be assigned to Peter for the death and suffering that resulted from his decision. By extension, and further abstraction, not only Peter but subsequent tsars can be marked with disapprobation for arbitrary and cruel treatment of their subjects. Thus the conflict becomes the individual's right to happiness and security versus the interests of the state or the sovereign. Although critics have achieved virtual unanimity in their characterizations of the conflict, no such claim can be made for assessments of how the conflict is resolved. Views vary on the moral judgments the poem or the poet may or may not be making and depend for their support on a complicated fabric of historical, biographical, and textual relations.

One view shows Pushkin undermining a cliché by illustrating the implications and results of authority wielded in the name of "destiny." He is challenging received opinion, 'doxa', with what opposes it, *para-doxa*, carrying out, as art does so well, the implications of a particular view, the common rationale for autocracy.[11] This is not to say that Pushkin is unsympathetic to nationalistic aspirations but rather to affirm that the poem exposes the dark side of arbitrary power, the human implications of destiny, and the culpability of individuals, no matter what their status. The poem deflates stereotypes of nationalistic rhetoric by pointing up their all-too-human source. It shows how one vision, and one vocabulary, can be incongruent with and thereby question the assumptions of another.

Turgenev uses undermining visions of behavior to suggest the complexity of moral attributes and to question our correctness in applying them. The preoccupation of critics with social and political dynamics of Turgenev's novella *(povest')* *On the Eve* has virtually obscured the moral and psychological dimensions of the work. Written several decades later than Pushkin's, Turgenev's story may seem superficially to deal with an issue of concern to the generation of the 1850s, the possibility of heroic action in Russia. A young Russian woman falls in love with a Bulgarian revolutionary, a young man preparing to return to his homeland to fight for its independence. Answering demands of the age to present people who are heroic and dedicated in personal as well as public life, Turgenev appeared to offer examples of personal courage and altruistic dedication. But his offering contained something at odds with these ideals, something which challenged stereotypes and received opinions. What could be construed as efforts to make his characters full and psychologically true served to undermine their idealism and point up the primacy of psychological factors in the development of their moral codes. And these factors served to deprive heroism of its meaning and to cast a pall over the text's optimistic language of moral idealism. Once again, *doxa* met *para-doxa*, not to form a synthesis at a higher level of explanation but to suggest the complexity and mystery that underlie conventional conceptions of the heroic and altruistic.

Tolstoi too waged battle against the conventional, undermining several discourses with his own. On the surface, his story "The Death of Ivan Il'ich" (1886) attacks the hypocrisy of those who live by society's rules and values, doing all they can to avoid thoughts of their own mortality and the meaning of their lives. But society's evasions are not the only received opinions undercut in the story: there is an elaborately developed subtext of allusions to another reading of life's meaning, a reading based on conventional understandings of the story of Christ. And this "understanding" of the meaning of life and death is modified and undermined as surely, though not as obviously, as society's. More explicitly and confidently than all the other writers discussed, Tolstoi presented the foundation on which our moral lives are to be based, a new understanding built from the old. But even here, Tolstoi's fixed views, which he held in all certitude, show a vulnerability he himself may not have seen.

Art's power and immediacy time and again point up the contingency of accepted truths, whether philosophical, religious, or social. Gor'kii's famous story "Twenty-six and One" (1899) depicts the reverential and highly idealized love a group of bakery workers develops for a sixteen-year-old maid who works in the building adjoining their basement factory. Her mere appearance at the window of their workshop brightens their otherwise dreary days. But when she becomes sexually involved with someone outside their group, their near-idolatry turns to hatred. The story explores the nature of exploitation, idealism, and relations between men and women—but the real focus is idealism, which Gor'kii emphasizes and subtextually expands in significance before exposing its psychological underpinnings, limitations, and implications.

Between the physically oppressive milieu of a pre-1917 basement factory and the open expanse of the Ukrainian countryside there would appear to be an enormous chasm; but the oppressive atmosphere of the factory in Gor'kii's story has much in common with the spiritually repressive air of the Stalinist state in 1930. Pasternak's lyric "Summer" renders a moment of that time and a glimpse at its texture. The poem embodies the moral dilemma of the sensitive and open-hearted poet in a society that forbids honesty and openness. Society's reigning values here are not pleasure and avoidance of the unpleasant but conformity and obedience to authorities, with one's security and life hanging in the balance. The subtexts of Pasternak's poem are used to undermine values of the Stalinist age—they recall, and in this way historically reaffirm, values that have sustained and given courage to others in similar situations in the past. They come in the form of a revelation to the poet, and they support him in his rejection of contemporary values.

The last work considered in this book, Solzhenitsyn's *Cancer Ward*, also deals with Soviet society, this time after Stalin's death. And with the change in leadership comes an uncertainty about the values that the state has taught and imposed for a quarter of a century. Solzhenitsyn explores competing systems of values and examines a number of attitudes toward the Stalin years. A variety of characters are introduced in this exploration, but two in particular will be considered closely: the hero, Kostoglotov, and a fellow patient, Shulubin. While the hero is on a quest to find the meaning of life amidst a confusing array of ways of living, Shulubin is obsessed with moral issues relating to Stalinism. Not only is he concerned with assessing complicity and culpability, but he is also interested in explaining what it is in human beings that allows them to participate in evil. The state morality is again posed against moralities of previous ages and historical vocabularies that have been replaced. Like Tolstoi, Solzhenitsyn depicts the search for a foundation for the moral structure. But such a foundation, the novel makes plain, is very difficult to find. It is only hinted at by the characters' revelations and some very suggestive philosophical and literary texts.

In all of these studies I have offered correctives to critical views that have missed the mark and failed to do justice to issues that constitute the moral dimension. Pushkin's narrative of a common man's clash with a sovereign, a clerk driven into madness by the vengeful statue of Peter the Great, has provoked a wide variety of readings but has eluded satisfactory interpretation that gives appropriate scope to the work's moral implications. Pasternak's lyric poem has a profound moral message, but its stylistic qualities have attracted critical attention. Emphasis on the sociopolitical implications of Turgenev's novella and Gor'kii's short story has tended to obscure what the works suggest about the psychological foundations of our moral categories. And though the centrality of moral issues in "The Death of Ivan Il'ich" and *Cancer Ward* has rarely been doubted, previous accounts have failed to provide an adequate conception of the complexity of the moral issues worked out in these texts. In dealing with each of these texts, I have used the theme of moral apostasy as my starting point. From here, the specificities of each work generate the questions that I pursue—and often these questions involve consideration of formal matters, biography, thematics, and psychology. The wide-ranging scope of the analysis is justified only insofar as it illuminates fundamental moral issues of the text.

When Solzhenitsyn referred to the positive side of his experience in the GULag, he was indicating how a context of mortal danger can engender moral revelations, how a new understanding of values can emerge from life-threatening situations. Virtually all of the works considered here involve death and the fear of dying. In Pushkin's poem the protagonist, Evgenii, dies, succumbing to the ravages of madness brought on in large part by the loss of his fiancée, Parasha, and her mother in the flood. Turgenev's novel takes its Bulgarian hero to a premature death and traces the consequences of both the awareness of impending death and death itself in the consciousness of the heroine Elena. Death here forces a reconsideration of values, both those she rejected in joining her revolutionary husband and those she adopted in her new life with him. Death is of clear significance in Tolstoi's story, forcing Ivan to recognize the falseness of his past way of life and leading him to consciousness of a better alternative. Gor'kii's story concerns not so much literal as figurative death. The values the author counterposes to conventional values are intimately connected with what it means to be truly alive: a teenage girl's proud independent spirit, willingness to take chances, and openness to new experiences are contrasted with the narrow and rigid values of the workers, values which ultimately lead them to a spiritual death.

The intimate link between love and death, so often elaborated in art (as well as in psychology), can be seen not only in Gor'kii's story of an idealized and ultimately betrayed love but also in Pasternak's lyric, where danger and the threat of death enhance the life-giving values of love and friendship. In Solzhenitsyn's novel, Shulubin is so constantly under the threat of death that he is forced to confront directly his own moral cowardice in the face of social pressures that have compromised his integrity. Death here and in most of the works studied in this book is viewed as a constructive force, compelling fundamental reevaluations; and in each case one view of death is replaced by another.

There is a deconstructive dimension to all of these works as well, as if the authors were exposing the unacknowledged assumptions that support conventional views and values. Death is used to charge the fictional situation with meaning, to force open the cover of comforting conventionality so that new values, in new language, can come forth with the force of discovered truth. Again and again new values are linked with other texts, with beliefs and values whose origins lie in other stories, other forms of narration. The basic impulse of the art discussed here is not metafictional, but the metafictional plays a key role. When the veils are ripped aside, it is not really important whether the truth or merely another description in another vocabulary is discovered: what is important is that what emerges affects us, that it works, that it makes us see in a different way, and that it helps us make sense of our own moral lives by linking the discourses and insights of art with what is outside art.

John Gardner wrote simply and profoundly about the role of morality in art:

> In great fiction, the dream engages us heart and soul; we not only respond to imaginary things—sights, sounds, smells—as though they were real, we respond to fictional problems as though they were real: We sympathize, think, and judge. We act out, vicariously, the trials of the characters and learn from the failures and the successes of particular modes of action, particular attitudes, opinions, assertions, and beliefs exactly as we learn from life. Thus the value of great fiction, we begin to suspect, is not just that it broadens our knowledge of people and places, but also that it helps us to know what we believe, reinforces those qualities that are noblest in us, leads us to feel uneasy about our faults and limitations.[12]

These comments about the referential and instructional possibilities of art seem to run counter to interests of contemporary theorists who are fascinated with point of view in fiction, alternate but simultaneously valid viewpoints, the relativity of all judgments, the impossibility of objectivity, and the observational and evaluative biases of all writers. Insofar as the comments reflect adherence to one particular version of truth, a platonic eternal anchor for statements about what obtains in the world, an incompatibility certainly exists. But we need not be overly concerned with Gardner's commitment to a particular view of truth as representation; we may take his remarks pragmatically, as claims about what fiction can do, how it can help us with its examples of moral dilemmas described and resolved to meet our needs, interests, and desires.

Fiction in its very immediacy and vividness urges the resolution of moral conflict in contextual ways; it does not work according to abstract rules, competing rights, and notions of fairness. These contextual ways involve more than anything an emphasis on the complexity and multifaceted nature of character, characters in interaction, and situation. Indeed, literature seems especially attuned to moral discourses that emphasize interpersonal behavior with expressions such as caring, love, and compassion. The works of Russian literature examined here reemphasize the interdependence of self and other, and the sustaining value of love and concern for others.[13]

The works studied here provide vivid examples of people dealing with the moral complexities of life; the problems encountered are far-reaching, as important to us as to those living in the nineteenth century: responsibilities of leaders, individual rights in conflict with the common good, maintaining integrity under pressure. Time and again conclusions of a moral nature turn out to depend on how we construe the words within our own schemes. But within these schemes we can come upon revelations, new meanings that can help us recognize and deal with the complexity of our own moral lives, whether the issues are social or personal.

PUSHKIN'S *THE BRONZE HORSEMAN*

Fearfully clear became his thoughts.

I
F THE MARK of a great work of art is its amenability to various and divergent interpretations in different ages, then Pushkin's *The Bronze Horseman* (1833) easily qualifies. The reading offered here is in some ways related to and dependent on earlier interpretations. It extends and deepens these readings, however, by giving more attention to the poem's center of emotion. Furthermore, it proceeds from assumptions about how meaning is created in the poem that differ from those that have been used in the past: these assumptions, relating to literature's potential for rendering emotional events in a concrete and vivid way, direct attention to emotional high points and to the factors at play in constituting these high points. And scenes of high emotional tension in turn provide a basis for the elucidation of the work's moral complexities.

In the abundance of interpretations of the poem that keep appearing year after year the same concerns are apparent. The readings center on the poem's vision of the individual and the state and the place and scope of each with respect to the natural world, fate, and historical destiny. Interpretations differ not only in how much prominence they give to individual, state, and nature but also in the manner they resolve the tensions between them. Overlapping and intimately entwined with these more abstract readings are interpretations that treat the poem as a literary polemic or as a veiled reference to people and events of Pushkin's time. There are many designs in the intricate fabric, and most carry moral implications. The reading offered here, by focusing on two scenes and what they imply, shows new possibilities within the moral dimension. The poem displaces the conventional, undermines the commonly accepted, and challenges overly simple characterizations of the moral world that place some people beyond morality and that replace human feeling and sensitivity with destructive abstractions.

Conventional views of Peter I and his city, his great project on the marshy banks of the Neva, were positive in the early nineteenth century, if we can judge by the poetry of Pushkin's predecessors and contemporaries. St. Petersburg represented a tremendous human achievement even though the price exacted in its construction was the death of thousands of conscript workers. The source of the city's mysterious beauty is not easy to identify: its geometrical design and stately architecture mark it as a tribute to human ingenuity, will, and effort; but the city somehow gives an impression that is more ambiguous and complex. This impression may be partially connected with its history. Its very birth was morally tainted by the anonymous graves of its builders, and its actual existence has been threatened periodically by the water that surrounds its various islands. Indeed, as if underlining the city's ambiguous and fragile foundation, the Neva seems poised to take vengeance on its human inhabitants whose leaders arrogantly thought they could control nature's forces. Moreover, there is a fantastic quality to the city's artificial design and its "unnatural" white nights. St. Petersburg—as a city of beauty and eerie malevolence, a product of rational planning and somehow the focus of irrational forces—became one of Russian culture's most productive myths for writers in the nineteenth and twentieth centuries. Pushkin's poem *The Bronze Horseman*, set in this city, was the first expression of the myth.[1] Giving voice to the city's sinister, even diabolical, dimension represented in itself an undermining of conventional perspectives, which tended to see the city only as a remarkable human achievement and a victory of human will over environment.

Though completed by Pushkin in 1833, the poem was never published in its entirety during his lifetime. Nicholas I allowed only its introduction (with some omissions) to be printed in 1834 under the title "Petersburg: Fragment from a Poem."[2] That the poem presented problems to Nicholas in its original form suggests something about the sensitivity of the issues raised in it. With Nicholas serving as his personal censor, Pushkin faced obvious risks in saying anything unconventional or provocative.

Pushkin had been in trouble with the authorities on previous occasions. The main problem was the political outspokenness in his writing, an outspokenness exemplified in his youth by the widely circulated ode to freedom ("Vol'nost'"), his poems "The Village" ("Derevnia") and "The Dagger" ("Kinzhal"), and later his poetic tribute to the French poet, André Chénier.[3] Pushkin's violations of convention extended beyond political taboos into religion as well; his extremely impious parody of the Annunciation, "The Gavriiliada" (1820), for example, caused problems for him when a copy later came to the attention of the authorities. In a letter he wrote while in exile in the south of the Empire, he expressed his attitudes on religion. The letter was intercepted by the police, and for his skepticism about the deity he was dismissed from government service. But his most dangerous encounter with authority was not over his youthful eloquence on the limits of autocracy and the desirability of freedom, his imprudent behavior, and his so-called atheism (agnosticism would perhaps be more appropriate) but over his connections with the ill-fated Decembrist revolt of 1825.

On the very square where Falconet's statue of Peter on horseback stands, some three thousand soldiers and officers gathered on 14 December 1825. Under instructions from the leadership of several underground organizations, they were to use the confusing circumstances of interregnum following the sudden death of Alexander I as an occasion for protesting autocratic rule. The new tsar, Alexander's brother Nicholas, put down the revolt that same day and in the next few months arrested, tried, and punished, either by exile or by hanging, leaders and participants. Pushkin was not in St. Petersburg at the time of the revolt, but there is reason to think that had he been there, he would have been seriously implicated. As it was, he was called to Moscow in 1826 and questioned by Nicholas himself, presumably regarding his relationship with the Decembrists. It was following this personal interview that Nicholas became Pushkin's censor, thus assuming a direct involvement in the poet's literary career.[4]

It is doubtful that Pushkin's poem was kept from publication because of its relationship to the Decembrist revolt, for the possibility of so relating the poem involves a literary sophistication probably beyond that of Nicholas or his advisers. It is, however, a possibility that has occurred to numerous critics. Nicholas and the Decembrists represent a story that is surely a subtext of the poem, another layer of meaning to the depiction of the confrontation between tsar and subject.[5] But this particular historical reading is not the only one with connections to the moral dimension. The poem, with its confrontation, is not limited to historical events of Pushkin's time.

Criticism of *The Bronze Horseman* has amply demonstrated that the poem is amenable to a wide variety of systems of meaning. The title itself suggests that the issue of signification will be crucial: a statue of Peter on his horse is to be the focus of attention, perhaps even the hero.[6] Indeed, a semiotic frame can easily be applied to the poem: the statue is a sign pointing someplace else, referring to something other than itself; it is an announcement that what follows will require attention to signifying and what is signified. But there is no one-to-one relationship between signifiers and signified, no exclusionary set of meanings established by convention or context. The poem always escapes single systems; it in fact utilizes, even capitalizes on, the multivalency of its signifiers, for their very ambiguity is a source of richness.[7] The first step, if we are to gain access to these potentials, is through the so-called literal meaning: the story of Evgenii, the statue of Peter, and the St. Petersburg flood of 1824.

Pushkin subtitled his poem a "Peterburgskaia povest'" or "St. Petersburg Tale." But the tale does not begin immediately: first there is an introduction of almost 100 iambic tetrameter lines (approximately one-fifth of the entire work, which is 481 lines), in which Peter is praised, in a fashion reminiscent of the ode, for building a city in such a forlorn place. The poet views him here as the emperor who envisioned the military potential of the city, the man who invoked nature's imprimatur for an important cultural step (one laden, it might be mentioned, with implications to be exploited subsequently in controversies between Slavophiles and Westernizers), "to hack a window through to Europe":

> I dumal on:
> Otsel' grozit' my budem shvedu.
> Zdes' budet gorod zalozhen
> Nazlo nadmennomu sosedu.
> Prirodoi zdes' nam suzhdeno
> V Evropu prorubit' okno, . . .   (ll. 12–16)

> (And he thought:
> From here we shall threaten the Swede,
> Here shall a city be founded
> To spite the puffed-up neighbor.
> By nature we are destined here
> To hack a window through to Europe, . . .)

Turning then to the city itself, the poet himself, in lines which have since become inextricably bound with the myth of St. Petersburg, underlines his strong feelings for the capital:[8]

> Liubliu tebia, Petra tvoren'e,
> Liubliu tvoi strogii, stroinyi vid. . . .   (ll. 43–44)

> (I love you, Peter's creation, ·
> I love your austere, comely look. . . .)

The poem shifts from this expression of fondness for the city (in lines that are far too personal to be stylistically characteristic of the panegyric ode) to praise for the city's martial spectacles. An eloquent apostrophe in which the poet bids it to stand "unshakable, like Russia" is then followed by a strangely ominous expression of hope that the elements not "disturb" Peter's "slumber." Ironically, the narrative will show that water, the "conquered element" (which turns out to be unconquered), will not wake Peter, but the "spite" of rebellion will.[9]

> Krasuisia, grad Petrov, i stoi
> Nekolebimo, kak Rossiia,
> Da umiritsia zhe s toboi
> I pobezhdennaia stikhiia;
> Vrazhdu i plen starinnyi svoi
> Pust' volny finskie zabudut
> I tshchetnoi zloboiu ne budut
> Trevozhit' vechnyi son Petra!   (ll. 84–91)

(Flaunt your beauty, Peter's city, and stand
Unshakable, like Russia,
And may even the conquered element
Make its peace with you;
Would that the Finnish seas forget their enmity
and ancient bondage
And trouble not with empty spite,
Peter's eternal slumber.)

The poem abruptly changes its tone in the last verse paragraph of the introduction, moving now into the narrative with a portentous forewarning:[10]

Byla uzhasnaia pora,
Ob nei svezho vospominan'e . . .
Ob nei, druz'ia moi, dlia vas
Nachnu svoe povestvovan'e.
Pechalen budet moi rasskaz.   (ll. 92–96)

(There was a dreadful time,
Fresh is the memory of it . . . Of it,
my friends, for you
I will begin my narrative.
Sorrowful will be my tale.)

The narrative, which constitutes most of the poem, is in two parts, telling the story of the clerk, Evgenii, who becomes crazed with grief after his fiancée and her mother are killed in the great St. Petersburg flood of 1824. He defiantly expresses his rage and frustration at the statue of Peter on Senate Square, and is, or imagines he is, chased through the streets by the statue. Later he is found dead, washed up by the waves onto an island. The poem traces the rising waters of the flood, Evgenii's fears, his futile search to find his Parasha on the following day when the flood has subsided, the city's return to normal, Evgenii's mental deterioration, his outburst in front of the statue, and finally his death.

The poem is resonant with ambiguities, suggesting numerous lines of interpretation. It is a work that tempts one to look for a unified central meaning, or at least a main emphasis that gets at the poem's essence. The approach to literature outlined in the previous chapter is not directed at finding a meaning that will do once and for all, that will encompass all others. Rather, it is one that seeks readings that satisfy definite purposes; in this case moral issues are primary, and a perspective that highlights the moral dimension is obviously required. In the case of a work as evocative as this one is, the application of one frame can sometimes shed light on others, on ways of seeing not only new meanings but also the interplay of mean-

ings. A moral approach is particularly good at showing how the poem un-
masks conventional meanings and responses—ways of looking at the world
that have become "naturalized."[11]

Most interpretations of *The Bronze Horseman* have identified the statue not
just as Peter, or even Russia, but as the state in general; with levels of
abstraction so easily accessible, such identifications have a certain validity.
The story of Evgenii and the statue is seen as a clash between the rights of
the individual to happiness and security and the rights of the state to fulfill
its destiny. From a contemporary perspective, the poem shows the tension
between the claims of the state (national interest) and the claims of its citizens, at whose expense the state was created. Much of the critical controversy surrounding the poem has to do with attempts to determine who
comes out best or what is emphasized: Evgenii (the individual) and his
plight or the state and its right to make policies that serve higher purposes.
A third element of the poem, a third player in the plot, is nature, sometimes
loosely associated with fate or destiny, always elemental and unpredictable,
not so much indifferent to human efforts and emotions as malevolent. Interpretations bounce from point to point, with methodologies that strain for
the interpretation that accommodates and reconciles the poem's di-
chotomies and tensions.[12]

Usually mentioned in general accounts of the poem, but rarely com-
mented on extensively, are questions of culpability—responsibility for
wrong actions.[13] Ethical issues are not ignored in most accounts of the
poem, but they are usually approached peripherally, and on an abstract
level. Here, priority will be given to examples of behavior to which moral
terminology, especially the language of responsibility, is normally applied.
A nest of moral questions can be perceived in two crucial scenes involving
the statue and Evgenii. The following sections define the context of these
scenes and explore their implications.

Much of the controversy surrounding the poem has centered on the ambiguous picture of Peter: does the poem come down for or against him and
his accomplishments? Through analyses of tone, style, and meaning,
within a variety of critical frameworks, judgments have been made on the
status of the emperor. It is not surprising that critics, who have exhaustively
analyzed almost every nuance of the poem, have found evidence of Peter's
less-than-heroic stature.[14] In contrast to the basically positive characterization of Peter in the introduction (he stood "filled with lofty musings"; he
confidently built a city of beauty for military reasons, to "spite a proud
neighbor" and to fulfill Russia's destiny), the epithets applied to his statue in
the "tale" are ambiguous, suggestive in ways that tarnish his moral image.
Thus Lednicki sees the Giant pursuing Evgenii as a "crack in the smooth
surface of panegyrism."[15] Nor does Peter escape from the introduction
without blemish; one can argue that his picture there is morally com-

promised by mere proximity to the sad tale of Evgenii. Furthermore, the poet's expressed wish near the end of the introduction that the elements make peace with the city Peter has built (lines 84–91) suggests that not everything is subject to Peter's will and that the rhetoric of praise may be only rhetoric in the end.[16]

As commentators have noted, the narrative in particular subtly undermines the exalted view in the introduction. In part 2, when Evgenii has returned to the place near the statue where he had waited out the flood, the poet's reference to Peter is different in tone from earlier references:

> Evgenii vzdrognul. Proiasnilis'
> V nem strashno mysli. On uznal
> I mesto, gde potop igral,
> Gde volny khishchnye tolpilis'
> Buntuia zlobno vkrug nego,
> I l'vov, i ploshchad', i togo,
> Kto nepodvizhno vozvyshalsia
> Vo mrake mednoiu glavoi,
> Togo, ch'ei volei rokovoi
> Pod morem gorod osnovalsia . . .   (ll. 404–13)

> (Eugene shuddered. Fearfully clear
> Became his thoughts. He recognized
> The place where the flood had sported,
> Where the preying waves had crowded,
> Rioting viciously about him,
> And the lions, and the square, and him,
> Who motionlessly loomed,
> His brazen head in the dusk,
> Him by whose fateful will
> The city by the sea was founded. . . .")

Here Peter is seen as the ruler whose "fateful will" founded a city "by the sea" (with "under," as well as "by," suggested by the word *pod*)[17]: what is hinted at is Peter's complicity in all the violence surrounding him, his cold indifference to it, and his culpability in exposing people to uncontrollable natural forces. Furthermore, the poet suggests that though Evgenii has gone mad, his thoughts at this moment have become "clear"; it is as though his misfortune has given him a special vision, unique insight into what has happened. What is only hinted at—the monarch's lack of empathy and withholding of commiseration for the misfortunes of the subjects of the Empire—will be underscored in other ways in other parts of the poem.

Recent scholarship,[18] pushing for a link between introduction and narrative parts of the poem, indirectly supports the moral connection between Peter's project and Evgenii's fate. Rhyme, contiguity of lines, thematic echoes (such as Peter's dreams and Evgenii's nightmares), and verbal parallels (forms of the word for *horrible* and *horror*), tie beginning more closely together with middle and end; and all that brings Evgenii and Peter closer together tightens the net of culpability around Peter.

Peter and Evgenii have two dramatic scenes together; the second, which was referred to above, will be discussed shortly. The first is in part 1: Evgenii sits on the statue of a lion, surveying in horror the Neva's awesome power and fearing for the safety of his beloved:

> Togda, na ploshchadi Petrovoi,
> Gde dom v uglu voznessia novyi,
> Gde nad vozvyshennym kryl'tsom
> S pod"iatoi lapoi, kak zhivye,
> Stoiat dva l'va storozhevye,
> Na zvere mramornom verkhom,
> Bez shliapy, ruki szhav krestom,
> Sidel nedvizhnyi, strashno blednyi
> Evgenii. On strashilsia, bednyi,
> Ne za sebia. . . .   (ll. 220–29)

> (It was then that on Peter's square,
> Where in a corner a new house had risen tall,
> Where over its lofty porch,
> Paws upraised like live creatures,
> Stand two guardian lions, astride on the beast
>   of marble,
> Hatless, arms crossed,
> Sat motionless, terribly pale,
> Eugene. He was in terror, poor soul,
> Not for himself. . . .)

Unlike Peter, who presumably was concerned with matters of Russia's destiny and perhaps his own personal glory, Evgenii is worried over his fiancée and his personal happiness; he sits in marked contrast to the statue of Peter, whose very pose indicates a lack of concern for his immediate surroundings.

> Ego otchaiannye vzory
> Na krai odin navedeny
> Nedvizhno byli. Slovno gory,
> Iz vozmushchennoi glubiny
> Vstavali volny tam i zlilis',
> Tam buria vyla, tam nosilis'
> Oblomki . . . Bozhe, bozhe! tam—
> Uvy! blizekhon'ko k volnam,

Pochti u samogo zaliva—
Zabor nekrashenyi da iva
I vetkhii domik: tam one,
Vdova i doch', ego Parasha,
Ego mechta . . . Ili vo sne
On eto vidit? il' vsia nasha
I zhizn' nichto, kak son pustoi,
Nasmeshka neba nad zemlei?   (ll. 235–50)

(His despairing gaze
Upon one distant range
Was fixed unmovingly. Like mountains,
From the stirred-up deeps
Rose up the billows there and raged,
There howled the storm, there drifted
Wreckage . . . God, God! there—
Alas, close, very close to the waves, almost right on the gulf—
Is an unpainted fence, and a willow, and
A frail little house: there are they,
The widow and her daughter, his Parasha,
His daydream . . . or is it in a dream
He sees this? Or is all our
Very life nothing but an idle dream,
A mockery of heaven at earth?)

Wondering if the devastation of the flood and the threat to his happiness are a dream (the line between dream and reality is repeatedly blurred), Evgenii is as if transfixed to the lion, "bewitched," while the "Idol" Peter, *with his back to Evgenii*, stands with an outstretched hand over the raging Neva:

I on, kak budto okoldovan,
Kak budto k mramoru prikovan,
Soiti ne mozhet! Vkrug nego
Voda i bol'she nichego!
I obrashchen k nemu spinoiu,
V nekolebimoi vyshine,
Nad vozmushchennoiu Nevoiu
Stoit s prostertoiu rukoiu
Kumir na bronzovom kone.   (ll. 251–59)

(And he, as though bewitched,
As though onto the marble riveted,
Cannot get down! About him
Is water and nothing more!
And with his back turned to him,

In unshakable eminence, over the tumultuous Neva
Stands with outstretched hand
The Idol on his bronze steed.)

With malevolent elements threatening on all sides, the two figures, Peter
and Evgenii, are depicted mounted and hatless, one with arm pointed out to
sea, and the other with arms crossed; we know what concerns Evgenii, but
Peter's thoughts are opaque, and with his back to Evgenii it is clear that he
is not concerned with mortals and their problems. Even the position of the
arms signifies a difference in orientation: Christian compassion and empathy versus commitment to a personal goal or idea, no matter what the
human cost. Underlying these issues is the notion that one's goals and concerns may only be gestures in the end, that there may be no difference between "standing unshakable" and being "bewitched" and "riveted" to one's
place. If this reading is valid, then one can conclude that the poem is challenging exalted notions of human capability: Evgenii assumes a pose similar
to that of Peter (the symbol of pride and confidence); but in fact he is anything but confident, for he fears losing his Parasha and his chance for happiness. If in assuming such a pose Evgenii had hoped to emulate the proud and
confident Peter, the poem proves his efforts futile. Evgenii, despite his elevated position, is hardly a superman; and that he is not carries the suggestion that Peter may not be as well. Pushkin used such a theme before; in
his miniature tragedies, a would-be superman tries to put himself above
others, only to be unmasked as a pretender.[19] The question is whether
Peter, or the one represented by the statue, is to be unmasked within the
poem by forces he cannot control.

The second encounter between statue and human is far more dramatic,
with strong emotions expressed by both figures. It takes place about a year
later. After his loss, Evgenii has gone mad, wandering homelessly in rags,
alienated from society, tormented by "some dream" and the sounds of the
storm:

> On oglushen
> Byl shumom vnutrennei trevogi.
> I tak on svoi neschastnyi vek
> Vlachil, ni zver' ni chelovek,
> Ni to ni se, ni zhitel' sveta
> Ni prizrak mertvyi. . . .   (ll. 373–78)

> (He was deafened
> By the rushing noise of anxious inner
>   turmoil.
> And so his miserable span of life,
> He dragged on, neither beast nor man,
> Neither this nor that, neither dweller

of the earth
Nor specter of the dead. . . .)

One night, sleeping by the Neva, he awakens, "vividly" *(zhivo)* remember-
ing the horror of his experiences:

> Vskochil Evgenii; vspomnil zhivo
> On proshlyi uzhas; toroplivo
> On vstal; poshel brodit', i vdrug
> Ostanovilsia, i vokrug
> Tikhon'ko stal vodit' ochami
> S boiazn'iu dikoi na litse.   (ll. 390–96)

> (Eugene jumped up; he vividly recalled
> The former horror; hastily
> He rose, went off to roam, and of a sudden
> Came to a halt—and round about
> He gingerly allowed his eyes to wander,
> Wild apprehension on his face.)

Drawn from his lethargy, Evgenii is brought to life by sounds and a memory of the former "horror"—he now stands in marked contrast to his previous self (a being then neither dead nor alive). The suggestion is that the
strong emotions he now feels (the "wild apprehension" or "fear") are a sign
of life, expressions of the force of life that have brought him from the limbo
in which he had been living. He suddenly finds himself *(ochutilsia,* related to
ochuvstvovalsia, suggests coming out of an unconscious and unfeeling condition) in a familiar place, by the lions (which are as if alive) and the statue of
the horseman (the inanimate Idol):

> On ochutilsia pod stolbami
> Bol'shogo doma. Na kryl'tse
> S pod"iatoi lapoi, kak zhivye,
> Stoiali l'vy storozhevye,
> I priamo v temnoi vyshine
> Nad ograzhdennoiu skaloiu
> Kumir s prostertoiu rukoiu
> Sidel na bronzovom kone.   (ll. 396–403)

> (He found himself beneath the pillars
> Of a great house. Upon the portico
> With upraised paw, as though alive,
> Stood lions sentinel,
> And straight, in his dark eminence,
> Above the railed-in crag,
> The Idol with his arm stretched forth

Was seated on his steed of bronze.)

The stage is set for the dramatic moment. Evgenii circles the pedestal crazed with anger; seized by a "black force," he hurls a reproach at the the statue of the one of "fateful will":

Krugom podnozhiia kumira
Bezumets bednyi oboshel
I vzory dikie navel
Na lik derzhavtsa polumira.
Stesnilas' grud' ego. Chelo
K reshetke khladnoi prileglo,
Glaza podernylis' tumanom,
Po serdtsu plamen' probezhal,
Vskipela krov'. On mrachen stal
Pred gordelivym istukanom
I, zuby stisnuv, pal'tsy szhav,
Kak obuiannyi siloi chernoi,
"Dobro, stroitel' chudotvornyi!"—
Shepnul on, zlobno zadrozhav,—
"Uzho tebe! . ." I vdrug stremglav
Bezhat' pustilsia. Pokazalos'
Emu, chto groznogo tsaria,
Mgnovenno gnevom vozgoria,
Litso tikhon'ko obrashchalos' . . .   (ll. 424–42)

(Round about the Idol's pedestal
The poor deranged man walked
And cast fierce glances
Upon the countenance of the ruler of half the world.
His chest tightened. His brow
Was pressed against the chilly railing,
His eyes filmed over with dimness,
Flame ran over his heart,
His blood seethed. Scowling he stood
Before the prideful statue
And, teeth clenched, fingers tightened into fists,
As though possessed by some black power,
"All right then, wonder-working builder!"
He whispered with a shudder of spite,
"I'll show you . . .!" And suddenly full tilt
He set off running. It seemed
To him that the dread Tsar's face,
Instantly aflame with wrath,
Was slowly turning . . .)

The moonlit scene ends with the "wrathful" statue in pursuit, bearing down on the hapless Evgenii through the night; and subsequently, whenever the poor man would pass the square again, he would show confusion, press his hand ("as if soothing its agony"), take off his hat, and keep his "abashed eyes" lowered as he avoided a confrontation. At some indefinite later time, he is found dead, his body washed up onto an offshore island at the threshold of a house (Parasha's) that has also been washed ashore. The confrontation between the statue and Evgenii is clearly the emotional center of the poem; it is from here that the poem's moral implications derive their power.

Evgenii is largely propelled into the situation by outside forces. He has already been driven mad, and now some strange power has dragged him to the place where he was during the flood. The origin of the compulsion is not easily explained: no conscious motivation has moved him to the square, no conscious plan for his protest. His anger at the statue is spontaneous, but one can conjecture that he was provoked both by the sorrow of his loss and by the sudden perception, in a moment of lucidity, of Peter's complicity.[20] This perception of complicity, of course, suggests that Peter's culpability extends far beyond Evgenii's personal loss to include all victims in his own and future generations.

But in what does this complicity lie, and how is it shown? From one perspective, it is in remaining so impassive, so lacking in feeling for Evgenii's suffering and loss. The image of an awe-inspiring, all-powerful ruler of the elements is tainted by suggestions of insensitivity and indifference. In the following passage, everything depends on how Peter's immense power is seen: is it awesome or threatening? It is more threatening than comforting if there are questions about how he uses it:

> Uzhasen on v okrestnoi mgle!
> Kakaia duma na chele!
> Kakaia sila v nem sokryta!
> A v sem kone kakoi ogon'!
> Kuda ty skachesh', gordyi kon',
> I gde opustish' ty kopyta?
> O moshchnyi vlastelin sud'by!
> Ne tak li ty nad samoi bezdnoi,
> Na vysote, uzdoi zheleznoi
> Rossiiu podnial na dyby? (ll. 414–23)

> (Awesome is he in the surrounding gloom!
> What thought upon his brow!
> What power within him hidden!
> And in that steed, what fire!

Whither do you gallop, haughty steed,
And where will you plant your hooves?
Oh, mighty potentate of fate!
Was it not thus, aloft hard by the abyss,
That with curb of iron
You reared up Russia?)

The passage is ambiguous, dependent for its meaning on the context given to it. In a context that is not so favorably disposed toward Peter, the questions about Russia's destiny and the "curb of iron" cast a shadow of doubt over the nature of the "thought," "power," and "fire" of the horseman and his steed. Moreover, Evgenii's rage helps cast this shadow: it is beyond what might be expected from the mere perception of Peter's culpability. It is extreme in its intensity: his eyes are dimmed over, his blood is seething, his chest and fist are tightened, a flame runs over his heart, he throws fierce glances, and he is filled with spite. This is the kind of deep, all-pervading anger that defies easy explanations. This anger borne of frustration, impotence, and anxiety has found a target in the "proud" statue of Peter, the "Idol" who raised up Russia too close to the "abyss." Evgenii's feelings are engendered by his return to Peter, and this return to the square also marks Evgenii's return to life. He has found something to which he can attach his feelings of rage and frustration: the statue, representing the founder of the city, is a locus of the malevolent forces of "fateful will" and destiny that deprived him of happiness.

Depending on frame of reference, one can go in several directions from here. One can look for an overall philosophy of the poem, a theory that places the poem's many facets (panegyric, conflict, tragedy) in a satisfying and unified picture. One such picture offered in the past is the deep sense of fatalism that appears here, as elsewhere in Pushkin's works. Pushkin the man was fascinated with insanity, death, and the "seductive nature of dark, elemental, anarchic passions."[21] Thus Evgenii's anger can be seen as a reflection of these forces within; a bottled-up rage, a dangerous and ill-considered leap into another world of mysterious and ominous forces. The world of emotions depicted here is one over which humans can have no control. Emotions originate from the same source as the elemental forces that destroy Peter's city. A feeling of spite unites Peter's project (to "spite" the Swedes he built his city), Evgenii's rebellion, and the statue's response; elemental forces orchestrate the destruction of Peter's city and Evgenii's happiness; they force him into madness, tempt him into a confrontation with the state, and lead him to death. All humans are subject to these forces, and the poem illustrates the tragic implications of this view of reality.[22] Whatever its implications on an abstract level (such a view deprives notions of choice and responsibility of meaning), this kind of fatalism brings sovereign and subject to the same level: they are both subjects of a higher power. Taking a different perspective—one that focuses on Evgenii—can bring out psychological features of the second encounter.

Through a psychoanalytic window, Evgenii's reactions to his loss follow a pattern of identification, loss, and melancholia. Even before he realizes his loss, he identifies himself with the statue, or the one the statue represented. Identification is a defense mechanism used to relieve anxiety about inner conflicts: about to be married and to start a new life, Evgenii assumes the confident exterior of someone who seems free of anxiety. But identification has a dark side: it can be a defense against the anxiety of socially impermissible hostility toward an authority figure who is both resented and feared. Evgenii's "madness" in the end will allow him to express this hostility. Striking the pose of Peter in the beginning, he sits on his own mount surveying the violence around him. Evgenii, however, sits motionless because of fear, not confidence; and he cannot imperiously (and statue-like) hold out his hand and control inner and external forces. He cannot face the elements in the manner of the one whose stance he has imitated, for he experiences normal human feelings, anxiety about the fate of his beloved and the possible destruction of his dream. When he realizes this dream (the house, the widow, the daughter, his hopes) has been destroyed, he experiences a reaction that goes far beyond normal grief: he totally withdraws from the outside world, no longer acts, has no self-esteem, and has what Freud has described as a "delusional expectation of punishment."[23]

A Freudian scheme might go a long way toward accounting for Evgenii's return to the square, his provoking the statue, and his subsequent punishment; for the statue can be easily seen as a form of conscience.[24] And this kind of interpretation could pursue then the ambivalent feelings projected in the poem concerning Peter and the complex mixture of hostility, identification, displacement, guilt, and loss.

While unifying theories and psychological approaches offer rich interpretive possibilities, a different sort of discourse is appropriate for dealing with the moral implications of the second encounter. We have seen already how Peter can be culpable, his impassivity reflecting his (and the state's) lack of concern for his subjects in building his city and empire. But there is another moral issue, one that derives from the situation in which the statue leaves its pedestal and begins to chase the clerk. The statue's reaction to Evgenii's rebellious gesture is unexpected; it is also laden with moral implications. It is pointless to say that the living statue is probably a hallucination and thus can never be appropriately designated with moral terminology, for what is relevant from a moral perspective is *how a particular figure is portrayed—in behavior and character*, not whether or not the figure is the product of a dream. Both dreams and madness can be used to express deeply held convictions otherwise inhibited by social constraints.

One might expect that a ruler larger than life, one with superhuman qualities, would remain motionless and indifferent to Evgenii's angry demonstration. No response at all to Evgenii would reflect the separate worlds of the two figures, with their separate scales of values. But instead, the horseman responds with vengeful ire to the little man's audacity and drives him to submission and ultimately death. Evgenii's initial outburst and all-too-sudden humbling provide an instructive moral for those who would seek to rebel against the state in any way. But such a moral can be conveyed only with a cost. An image of a notably flawed ruler emerges. The "wonder-working builder," as Evgenii sarcastically calls him, remains implacable and victorious against the elements that destroy his city but unfeeling in the face of his subjects' suffering and vengeful and persistent in his desire to pursue and punish a civil servant for daring to raise his voice; he is not an example of moral courage or heroism, nor does he represent the exalted nature of the state. The moral qualities he exhibits are vindictiveness and tyranny—the use of excessive force against a defenseless opponent. The poem is hardly neutral in its implied judgment here, if we mean by neutrality the refusal to take sides and to judge behavior. Tsars and subjects live in the same world and are subject to the same forces; the image of the ruler as a divinely sanctioned superman is undercut by the words and actions of Peter's descendent, Alexander I:[25]

> Na balkon
> Pechalen, smuten, vyshel on
> I molvil: "S bozhiei stikhiei
> Tsariam ne sovladet'." On sel
> I v dume skorbnymi ochami
> Na zloe bedstvie gliadel. (ll. 204–9)

> (Onto the balcony,
> Sorrowful, troubled, he came out,
> And spoke: "Against God's element,
> There is no prevailing for tsars." He
> sat down
> And thoughtfully, with stricken eyes
> Gazed at the grim calamity.)

The impotence of mortals, whether sovereigns or lowly citizens, in the face of the elements is one of the major themes of the poem, suggested largely by its emphasis on loneliness and vulnerability. Even Alexander I seems forlorn and alone: during the flood, he is sad-eyed, and his palace is like a sad island. The entire poem is framed by solitary figures.[26] The solitude, isolation, and vulnerability of the individual are all relevant components of the picture the poem presents. Human will is contingent, and pride is self-deception; both Peter and Evgenii are subject to superior forces; by implication both figures are part of the same moral realm. The poem links the Peter of the introduction with the "sad and horrible story" of Evgenii; it also portrays Peter leaving his pedestal, descending to an earthly plane, experiencing emotions of a low nature, and persecuting an insane clerk. The poem clearly undermines conventional exalted and even mythic notions of Peter, or any tsar; but it expresses another dangerous idea: that moral attributes are not limited to citizens of the state. The idea that tsars can be criticized on moral grounds is garbed in the protective clothing of madness, dreams, living statues, and martial glory. But nonetheless it is there.

The nightmarish image of the statue chasing Evgenii has several important implications. Even if only an hallucination or dream, the issue of persecution of the powerless is unquestionably raised. There is more here than Peter's culpability for building a city in an area susceptible to frequent flooding. Even if he were responsible for the suffering and death associated with the building of St. Petersburg or for the victims of subsequent generations in this inhospitable area, what might limit his culpability is a view of history and human action that pictures behavior as determined, impersonally executed by human agents: in such a context, Peter merely fulfills Russia's historical destiny, playing an assigned role as an actor in the theater of history. Such a view has obvious relevance to descriptions of the poem's moral dimension. It also is at the basis of interpretations that speak to the poem's tragic conflict, its unresolvable confrontations of the rights of the state and the rights of the individual. Accordingly, the poem promotes neither individual nor state but merely illustrates the tragic lot we all share, our powerlessness in a world of forces beyond our control.

Interpretations that rest on the unresolvability of the confrontation—a variation of the fatalistic interpretation outlined above—represent one way of dealing with the poem's apparent disharmony between a positive portrait of Peter (in the introduction) and a sympathetic depiction of Evgenii and his fate. The shift in tone from the patriotic rhetoric and celebration of Peter and his city in the first verse paragraphs to something quite different in the story of Evgenii is thus encompassed in a unifying explanation, an account that brings the poem's various tones into an all-embracing harmony. Achieving such a perspective has costs, however; for this way of looking at the poem does not do justice to the dramatic clash between the statue and Evgenii. If the sovereign is indeed fulfilling the destiny of the state and standing above mortals because of his special social and historical role, then there is no point in ascribing culpability. The sovereign is necessarily above and beyond moral categories; and with no possibility of choice the moral significance of his actions is diminished. The sense of overall unity gained in emphasizing the unresolvable nature of the conflict between citizen and state does not adequately account for the intensity of emotions displayed by both sides in the second scene at Senate Square. What is sacrificed is the meaning interpersonal relations have in particular contexts; such a view takes the emphasis off events and their consequences, emotions with their causes and effects, and places it on more abstract considerations. Theoretical satisfaction is gained at the expense of appreciation of the interplay of emotions and values, the concrete and pragmatic texture of behavior in its emotional intensity and fullness.

One of the most eloquent and convincing statements of the "tragic unresolvability" thesis is that of Victor Erlich, who offers the view that the claims of Peter and the claims of Evgenii are ultimately irreconcilable and incommensurate, that the conflict at the poem's heart is tragic and, as such, unresolved.[27] His view, like that of D. S. Mirsky,[28] emphasizes the conflict itself as the meaning of the poem: a dramatic presentation of two "equally valid" but competing truths. The grandeur and harmony of Peter's city cannot be said to justify the destruction of an individual's dreams and life, for it is on a different plane of discourse. In advocating, in effect, Pushkin's "moral neutrality," Erlich sees the poem on the one hand challenging a cliché, indicating the costs of a venture, and on the other promoting the idea that conventional views of reality are often unreliable, that martial glory and great achievements in culture and warfare are not the entirety of truth. Pushkin is, in this account, "toying with clichés," taking a "set of images embodying a moral commonplace—a relatively simple and readily available proposition or preconception" as a thesis to be tested and modified, if not rejected.

Elegantly stated; Erlich's thesis about Pushkin's moral "realism," a realism derived from the poet's "recognition of the ineradicable and often tragic complexity of the human conflict, a distrust of simple and cheery answers" (p. 167), points out how the given is undercut, the conventional shown to be a comforting simplification badly in need of qualification. But it is possible to go beyond identifying the "essential thrust and structure of Pushkin's moral vision" as a tragic and unresolvable central conflict, especially if we consider the emotional power of the second encounter between Evgenii and the statue; there is more to the poem's moral vision than modification, or even rejection, of moral stereotypes in favor of a vision of conflicts somehow immune to moral judgment.

Testing, modifying, and repudiating carry with them assumptions about the way life is, and counter-examples are ways of describing that, if they are to have any force at all, must be part of the same discourse as moral commonplaces. If moral discourse is applicable to the statue (Peter, sovereign, state), there is no reason to think that it is in a different realm than Evgenii's. As if to underline their identical moral footing, the poem shows Evgenii sitting, like Peter, atop a stone mount during the flood, and Peter descending from his pedestal to Evgenii's level (although with the power of his steed under him) in their second meeting. Nature itself reinforces the likenesses in their status: both are above the flood, and both are subject to human nature's powerful emotional forces. Evgenii's angry explosion is not ignored by the statue; it prompts an equally explosive emotional reaction. Peter does not persecute Evgenii out of a sense of duty, according to principle, or by some kind of higher logic privy to leaders of the state;[29] he responds in kind, and comes down to the same moral level as the "clerk." It is not just external manifestations of nature that challenge the control of tsars but also forces within.

The horseman's pursuit and persecution of Evgenii in the second part of the poem represent not merely an abstract conflict between rights of state and citizen. They mark a vivid and nightmarish aftermath to a clash of strong emotions. We should not lose sight of the drama of this clash as we move further toward abstraction. Some issues surrounding the central scene, though peripheral, provide a context that gives it added significance; we shall explore these issues as they are raised in distinctly sociopolitical readings before making some concluding remarks about the duel between Peter and Evgenii.

Understood from a social perspective, Evgenii is a representative of clerks in general, the nobility in hard times, and individuals with modest desires for happiness and security. Their misfortunes may be attributed to the indifference and arbitrariness of their rulers, as well as to the atmosphere of indifference the state breeds. Thus the poem shows that the awesome threat to life the flood represented has not diverted people from their materialistic values.[30] The tsar maintains control and authority, enforcing and supporting a status quo in which the populace goes unfeelingly about its business, as if nothing has happened:

> Utra luch
> Iz-za ustalykh, blednyx tuch
> Blesnul nad tikhoiu stolitsei
> I ne nashel uzhe sledov
> Bedy vcherashnei; bagrianitsei
> Uzhe prikryto bylo zlo.
> V poriadok prezhnii vse voshlo.
> Uzhe po ulitsam svobodnym
> S svoim beschuvstviem kholodnym
> Khodil narod. Chinovnyi liud,
> Pokinuv svoi nochnoi priiut,
> Na sluzhbu shel. Torgash otvazhnyi,
> Ne unyvaia, otkryval
> Nevoi ograblennyi podval,
> Sbiraias' svoi ubytok vazhnyi
> Na blizhnem vymestit'.   (ll. 328–43)

> (The ray of morning
> From behind tired, pale clouds

Glinted over the silent capital
And found no more traces of yesterday's calamity; with purple
  cape
Already covered was the mischief.
Everything settled back into the former order.
Already along clear streets with their cool indifference[31]
  people were walking. Officialdom,
Having left the night's shelter,
Was off to work. The plucky tradesman,
Undaunted, was opening up
The cellar looted by Neva,
Preparing to recoup his grave loss at his neighbor's cost.)

There is no period of mourning for the loss of life occasioned by the flood. At least one thing suggested by the "purple cape" is that the state wants people to forget what has happened and return to their customary, orderly, cold, and insensitive pursuit of profit at their neighbors' expense. The evil (another meaning of *zlo*, "mischief") covered by imperial color is not just the flood's damage but a way of life that is insensitive to human needs and higher values. Picturing this way of life in juxtaposition with the depiction of Evgenii's loss severely questions its validity. The lives and losses of numerous Evgeniis are buried in a policy that refuses to acknowledge the consequences of nature's assault and covers its evasion by pretending nothing has happened.

Extending the social frame into the historical and political as well, we can view Evgenii's rebellion as the Decembrist revolt, or the Polish revolt of 1830–1831, or any social revolt. Similarly, the poem's implications about Peter and his city can be considered as part of Pushkin's polemic with the Polish poet Adam Mickiewicz.[32] The poem's numerous levels of reference present critics with numerous paradoxes: thus, combining personal, social, and artistic themes, Andrei Belyi suggested that Pushkin and Evgenii could be identified, while Andrei Siniavskii more recently has suggested that Pushkin and Peter are doubles.[33] Of the abundance of possible references to the poet's life and times, some are more satisfying than others. What is of interest here is a reading that captures the emotional and moral power of the confrontation between the statue and Evgenii.

It has already been demonstrated that Evgenii and Peter are presented on the same moral plane, that they both may be appropriately described in the languages of morality and emotion. Thus questions about behavior are legitimized—questions relating to nobility, mercy, and the responsible use of power. If these questions are there, it is not difficult to understand why they are not *obviously* there. Pushkin, like Evgenii, could easily have been deprived of his chance for happiness: his fate was held precariously in the balance by the whim of Nicholas. The history of his relation to Nicholas is

a story of tension, revolt, and compromise.[34] Pushkin's problem in accepta-
bly presenting a clash between tsar and subject is thus obvious. There could
be no question about the outcome of such a conflict: Evgenii could hardly be
expected to claim victory with even a symbol of the autocracy. The risk was
considerable, calling for the careful use of removes: Pushkin cast the action
in the past and began the poem with praise for Peter and his city. But in the
end the past is shown to be relevant to the present, and the praise for Peter
is called into question.

The two sovereigns literally in the poem are Peter and Alexander I. Images of both are tainted: Peter's as was shown above and Nicholas's brother
Alexander's because he is shown to be less than ideal (especially when his
passive behavior during the flood is contrasted with the confidence and
dynamism of Peter in the introduction). Anything negative has to be implied; it cannot be stated directly: there are no practical options for portraying Russian monarchs in any but conventional ways. Criticism of behavior
had to be contextual, a subtle pattern in the general pattern, discernible
only by readers who know what to look for, how to understand the disorienting language of statues and dreams, and how to appreciate the incongruity between the story of Evgenii and patriotic words of the introduction.
The disorientation of the conventional and the customary helped Pushkin
to deal with a complex and dangerous theme. Through its descriptions of
the flood that suggest a living, rapacious force (for example, the flooding
waters of the Neva are compared to thieves), the poem makes fluid the
boundaries between the animate and the inanimate—and by doing so lays
the groundwork for the use of moral phrases in unusual contexts.

Moreover, contributing to this distortion of conventional perspectives is
the very placing of a "sad" tale in the context of a panegyric to Peter, the
mixing of genres—the formal ode with something quite different—so that
what resulted was not ode nor elegy but a "tale" *(povest')*. In the disoriented
world of the poem, it would not be unusual to ascribe human qualities to inanimate objects. Though his form may be inhuman, the statue is linked
with Peter. In this context even the quality of being "statue-like" can be understood morally. The machine of state is not beyond moral judgment because it is like a machine.

The confrontation of Evgenii and the statue is a moment of strong emotions: the rage of hatred and frustration is met by Peter's injured pride and
desire for revenge. Our window to the emotions so vividly depicted is
Evgenii and his perception: the ways in which he perceives the situation,
feels it, and reacts to it constitute the scene's emotional impact and immediacy. From an emotional standpoint, when Evgenii feels he is being followed
by the horseman, whether or not he is dreaming is irrelevant.

The themes of conflict with authority, persecution by authority, and loss
caused by authority are suggestive of other narratives, historical and biographical. These other perspectives combine the moral with the historical

and represent potentials for seeing the poem as an even more dangerous act of the poet. They also serve to bring together clusters of secondary themes and images into coherent wholes: the poem says something about unequal relations between tsar and subject, about the ignoble use of power, about isolation and madness. And tantalizing images of death and burial beg for a context that can give them significance.

One such context is the Decembrist revolt. This historical subtext depends on the acceptability of analogy for its cogency. If Evgenii is understood as analogous to the Decembrists, we can understand the revolt, like Evgenii's, as the futile and even insane action, an unplanned and spontaneous expression of impotent fury directed at and punished by the symbolic cause of the revolt. This is a meaningful reading, though perhaps unsatisfying to those who wish to see the revolt and its participants in an aura of moral heroism. Also unsettling, then, is the speed with which, following his encounter, Evgenii is brought to toe the line. Though there is no question that the poem is designed to evoke our sympathy for him and his plight (the narrator frequently uses the epithet "poor" in reference to him, and, as Briusov has noted, stylistic details point to his elevation to heroic status when he challenges the statue),[35] the analogy raises questions about the rationality and motivation of leaders and participants of the revolt.

If the statue's "behavior" is the focus, the analogy becomes revealing in a different way. Pushkin's personal belief that justice should be tempered by mercy was not well served by Nicholas's treatment of those implicated in the revolt. In reference to events in late 1825, Peter's raised hand is more menacing than protecting, and what his horse is crushing is not superstition but opposition.[36] Those implicated in the revolt were, like Evgenii (if Peter is considered to be alive), guilty of treason, of acting against the state. Pushkin could very well have felt how indiscriminate, unjust, and vengeful Nicholas was in the judicial proceedings and in the verdict. His excessive, and in some cases capricious, punishments (all under the guise of duty and responsibility)[37] provide clear examples of the irresponsible, or at least unfeeling, use of unlimited power. Moreover, Pushkin was acquainted with some of those Nicholas cajoled, tricked, or personally broke in interrogations. And possibly Pushkin was aware of the impression Nicholas gave to foreign diplomats: the French ambassador, for example, was so impressed with Nicholas's handling of the revolt that he called him a new Peter![38] The protest of Evgenii and the immoderate response of the horseman seem designed to suggest the unjustifiable and excessive reaction of a monarch who comes down from his lofty status to persecute and drive into submission his own subjects. There are even personal parallels: Pushkin, like Evgenii, was not swept away in the revolt on Senate Square, although he was subsequently called to an accounting by Nicholas; and there is no question he sincerely grieved over the fate of his comrades in the aftermath of the revolt. Whether he felt guilty for not being there and whether he was too outspoken with Nicholas or too meek are matters of conjecture; the point is that biographical parallels enhance the moral import of Evgenii's rebellion.

Perceived through a Decembrist grid, some of the details take on added significance. For example, the poem refers eerily and ominously to coffins floating down St. Petersburg streets during the flood:

> Osada! pristup! zlye volny,
> Kak vory, lezut v okna. Chelny
> S razbega stekla b'iut kormoi.
> Lotki pod mokroi pelenoi,
> Oblomki khizhin, brevny, krovli,
> Tovar zapaslivoi torgovli,
> Pozhitki blednoi nishchety,
> Grozoi snesennye mosty,
> Groba s razmytogo kladbishcha
> Plyvut po ulitsam!
>   Narod
> Zrit bozhii gnev i kazni zhdet.
> Uvy! vse gibnet: krov i pishcha!
> Gde budet vziat'?   (ll. 190–202)

> (Beleaguerment! Assault! The angry waves,
> Like thieves, climb through the windows. Boats
> Swooping, smash panes with their sterns.
> Pedlar's trays under sodden cover,
> Fragments of huts, beams, roofs,
> The merchandise of thrifty trading,
> The chattels of pale beggary,
> Bridges carried away by the storm,
> Coffins from the flooded cemetery
> Float down the streets!
>   The people
> Gaze on the wrath of God and bide their doom.
> Woe! all is perishing: Shelter and food!
> Where turn for them?)

Anonymous corpses can be associatively linked with the builders of St. Petersburg, Evgenii's fiancée and her mother (missing victims of the flood), and Evgenii himself, whose body is washed up onto the island where it will eventually be buried:

> Navodnen'e
> Tuda, igraia, zaneslo
> Domishko vetkhii. Nad vodoiu
> Ostalsia on, kak chernyi kust.

Ego proshedsheiu vesnoiu
Svezli na barke. Byl on pust
I ves' razrushen. U poroga
Nashli bezumtsa moego,
I tut zhe khladnyi trup ego
Pokhoronili radi boga.   (ll. 472–81)

(The inundation
Thither in its play had swept
A frail little house. At the waterline
It had been left like a black bush;
The foregoing spring
They hauled it off on a barge. It was empty
And all in ruin. At the threshold
They came upon my madman,
And on that spot his chill corpse
They buried for the love of God.)

Evgenii, like the corpses in the street and the bodies of Parasha and her mother, is buried "homeless," in the wrong place, not where one would expect, and not where he had hoped to be buried. Just as fear of madness links the poem with Pushkin's own views,[39] so does concern for burial rites: there is evidence that Pushkin was disturbed by the fact that Nicholas did not allow a proper burial for the five Decembrists who were hanged in 1826 and whose bodies were buried without ceremony, anonymously in unmarked graves.[40] Pushkin apparently sought earnestly, almost obsessively, the location of the burial site in St. Petersburg. There is another connection: bodies of some Decembrists, thrown into the Neva by the authorities during and after the revolt on Senate Square, were frequently found washed ashore in spring of 1826.[41]

Pushkin's strong feelings about the need for appropriate burial were reflected in Evgenii's monologue, in which he articulated his modest goals and values; among his wishes, he hoped to be together with his wife until the grave, and to be buried by his grandchildren:

"Zhenit'sia? Mne? zachem zhe net?
Ono i tiazhelo, konechno;
No chto zhe, ia molod i zdorov,
Trudit'sia den' i noch' gotov;
Uzh koe-kak sebe ustroiu
Priiut smirennyi i prostoi
I v nem Parashu uspokoiu.
Proidet, byt' mozhet, god-drugoi—
Mestechko poluchu, Parashe

Preporuchu khoziaistvo nashe
I vospitanie rebiat . . .
I stanem zhit', i tak do groba
Ruka s rukoi doidem my oba,
I vnuki nas pokhoroniat. . . ."   (ll. 145–58)

("Get married? I? Well, why not?
It would be hard going, certainly;
But what of it, I am young and healthy,
Ready to labor day and night;
Somehow I'll surely manage for myself
A humble and simple refuge,
And in it I'll settle Parasha
to a peaceful life.
A year or two perhaps will pass,
And I'll receive a modest position;
To Parasha I'll entrust the family
And the upbringing of the children. . .
And we shall begin our life, and so to the grave
The two of us will go hand in hand,
And our grandchildren will bury us. . . .")

By evoking respect for the dead, the poem calls attention not only to the Decembrists but also to values that should supersede those the state represents and promotes. It also suggests a literary predecessor, Sophocles' *Antigone*. Antigone was doomed when, in the face of the state's denial of her brother's proper burial—which rites represented moral law, which was of greater importance than the right of the state to punish him—she herself buried Polyneices.[42] Pushkin's suggestion that state and sovereign are accountable to higher principles amounted to criticism of the conventional images of glory, authority, and just government which the state promoted as its own self-image. Such criticism could only be conveyed obliquely, in a disguised form. And what helped to disguise this subversion of conventional attitudes was the atmosphere of disorientation described above. The world projected is dream-like, as if between life and death, neither one nor the other; Evgenii himself after the flood seems to belong to neither world.[43] As Roman Jakobson pointed out, static and dynamic images, like life and death states, interchange with each other, replace each other, and overlap; the same is true for oppositions such as madness and sanity, victory and defeat.[44] But disorientation functions in another way as well, and it points to yet another dimension of meaning.

Isolation, fragility, and vulnerability seem very prominent as features of the human condition in a world offering no point of orientation. Pushkin himself undoubtedly felt a sense of isolation and vulnerability in 1833. Having just started a family, he was in a sensitive and precarious position with respect to Nicholas. Necessarily dependent on the tsar's beneficence, he had also to be wary of the tsar's power. Jakobson notes how Pushkin in the late 1820s was being pressured into capitulation to the authorities, and how he gradually changed his opinions about the possibility of gaining more freedom. In his desperation, even madness represented a kind of freedom, a chance to express what could not be expressed in "sane" society. He felt a sense of weariness and disappointment over conditions in the aftermath of December 1825. It would be virtual madness to do battle with the government then. Thus he seemed critical of the eighteenth-century writer Alexander Radishchev who incurred Catherine's wrath through his writing;[45] and after the Decembrist revolt he admitted to his friend, the older poet Vasilii Zhukovskii: "Whatever may have been my political and religious way of thinking, I am keeping it to myself, and I have no intention of insanely opposing the generally accepted order of things, and necessity."[46] Although the letter was intended to be shown to the tsar (an expectation that suggests that the words were carefully chosen), it demonstrates, even in this strained context, an awareness of the connection between opposition to the state and madness. It also suggests the kind of humbling represented by Evgenii's doffing his hat, holding his hand (which he had "raised" against the state), and averting his eyes.

To say that Pushkin in the poem was essentially experimenting with literary material and testing political and moral commonplaces is to suggest a somewhat misleading and overly narrow perspective. It is as unwarranted as pretending that the theme of the possession of one man's beloved by another man—the theme around which Pushkin's narrative poem *Angelo* (written in the same period) revolves—was not as important to the poet in 1834 as toying with literary models. As Walter Vickery has demonstrated, Pushkin was attracted by some literary models (such as Shakespeare's *Measure for Measure*) rather than others because the issues they contained were significant in his personal life. For *Angelo* he found in Shakespeare the problem of an individual's vulnerability with respect to someone else's unlimited power.[47] Pushkin's feelings of vulnerability, especially relating to his wife and Nicholas, are well documented in his letters and his diary. And as Belyi has noted, there is a lot of Pushkin in Evgenii—especially the sense of injustice and persecution he felt at the thought of being robbed of his "Parasha" and his sense of impotence and isolation in St. Petersburg high society.[48] Like *Angelo*, *The Bronze Horseman* can be read as a story about Nicholas and the real or potential loss of a loved one. It may easily be seen as a reflection of Pushkin's concern over madness and punishment as well. Whether they had to do with his relationship with the Decembrists or his concerns about his family and his sanity, all of the personal issues are covered here, as elsewhere in Pushkin's works, in a "mantle of objectivity and impersonality."[49]

Focusing on the clash of state and citizen, Peter and Evgenii, opens the door to social and personal meanings. *The Bronze Horseman* is a poem about a strongly felt sense of vulnerability and frustration, about the way power is wielded and the effects it has, about rage and revenge. On a moral plane it is a poem that offers a damning judgment about the unrestrained use of power. In its rich psychological complexity, it undermines simplistic notions of morality and subverts conventional views of state power; what is offered instead is a view of human nature that implies a common moral code for all people, regardless of their status. The poem expresses deeply felt feelings in such a way as to draw attention to social issues involving insensitivity and irresponsibility; it emphasizes the consequences and implications of actions as others feel them and contrasts concern for others with indifference and righteous moral anger with personal and vindictive rage.

The poem offers modern generations a powerful expression of the impotence and pain felt by the victim of state indifference and abuse. And by implication, it reaffims subtly and indirectly mercy, understanding, and responsibility.

TURGENEV'S *ON THE EVE*

I have been led to the edge of the abyss and must fall.

TURGENEV'S third major novel, *On the Eve* (1859), follows *Rudin* and *A Nest of Gentlefolk* and precedes his masterpiece, *Fathers and Sons*. Like its two predecessors, it focused on problems facing the Russian intelligentsia on the eve of Alexander II's reforms. Published in 1861, shortly before the emancipation of the serfs, the novel has little to do with the particular question of liberating Russian peasants from bondage, though liberation as a general idea and sympathy for the oppressed are certainly part of its moral fabric. Turgenev's work that dealt with the lower classes, the highly successful collection of stories, *Notes of a Hunter* (1852), had become controversial because of its treatment of peasants, its sympathetic depiction of them as real people with their own culture and spiritual values. The stories in the collection played a role in promoting the movement to abolish serfdom and in securing for Turgenev the moral authority of a spokesman for liberal causes. In his subsequent fiction he continued to be preoccupied with contemporary social and political issues, especially as they related to the Russian intelligentsia, but the social and political never occupied center stage: within the worlds Turgenev created, these issues seem secondary, mere reflections of deeper currents and mysterious forces that not only control human behavior but also determine the outcome of events.

There was in *On the Eve*, as well as *Fathers and Sons* and later novels, a view of human nature that seemed to imply, by its emphasis on psychology, that political and social behavior was but a surface product of something more fundamental and that the springs of human behavior flowed from sources beyond human knowledge and control. Social conditions did not determine psychology in Turgenev's world, but rather psychology, in league with these deeper currents, determined how people responded to the sociopolitical reality.[1]

Among the topical issues *On the Eve* dealt with were the increased activity of women in politics, debates between liberals and radicals about reform and revolution, and discussions of the need for action and for models of heroic action.[2] But connected with the treatment of these issues were matters of a more general philosophical and psychological character: the nature of social idealism, the nature of self-sacrifice, and the problem of reconciling one's personal needs and desires with an ideology that had no room for personal needs and desires. Though *On the Eve* is not regarded as Turgenev's best novel, it has undeniable and often overlooked or unappreciated virtues, particularly in characterization, that make it suitable for our purposes. The attention it draws to the psychological bases of human behavior, and the fatalistic worldview that it implies, have important consequences for ordinary conceptions of morality. In presenting conventionally praiseworthy impulses for self-sacrifice, altruism, heroism, and philanthropy in a new light, the novel forces us to see them differently, perhaps more critically. What is undermined by Turgenev's vision is the confidence that conventionally accompanies the ascription of some of the most positive moral attributes.

The twenty-year-old heroine of the novel, Elena Stakhova, was the focus for many of the social and psychological issues the novel raised. Like most of Turgenev's fictional women, she commanded attention for her strong will, her decisiveness, and her willingness to flout conventions in pursuit of her goals.[3] Her traits were vividly illustrated in her relationship with the Bulgarian idealist Dmitrii Insarov, a relationship that required Elena to break with her parents and society and to dedicate her life to humanitarian service in a foreign land.[4] Against a background of sociopolitical issues and controversies stand psychologically complex characters who are portrayed in such a way as to counter overly simple representations of the nature of moral idealism and heroism.[5] The remarkable depth of the heroine, as revealed in her actions, her internal monologues, and her biography, serves to undermine the notion that the moral stances people take are simple matters of free choice, that so-called moral modes of behavior are consciously chosen on the basis of moral considerations.

This novel contains a tangled web of interconnected ideals, motives, and actions, all in a context complicated by mysterious relationships between experiences of childhood and character traits of the adult. Without her awareness of them, Elena's early experiences set the pattern for her adult behavior, especially in her relationship with Insarov. Though past affects present in ways that are far from clear, it is nonetheless possible to find in her past hints of explanations for Elena's enigmatic thoughts, feelings, and behavior, particularly in later sections of the novel.

The complexity of Turgenev's applied psychological theory has implications for the moral dimension of his work. Elevated notions—self-sacrifice for a worthy cause, freedom for one's country, solidarity with one's compatriots regardless of class, and total loss of the self in philanthropy—are represented by characters in the novel, but when they are set in practice by these characters, they turn out to be somewhat different from what might have been expected, tainted and perhaps even psychologically determined by their connections with less than noble emotions. For our purposes, the sources of Turgenev's views on human psychology are not important (Schopenhauer's theories of instinctual behavior are probably the most relevant psychophilosophical source).[6] Rather, our focus in on the way in which the novel presents moral idealism, especially in its complex and mysterious psychological origins and connections with feelings such as guilt and revenge.

Turgenev may have set out to satisfy his desire to portray new types and new heroes required on the sociopolitical scene, but his skill was manifested above all in the psychological portraits of his leading personages; and in the end psychology overshadows political issues.[7] Here, as in all of the works we examine in this book, love and death are crucial elements of the moral design, the principal forces that give vitality and human significance to abstract issues. In picturing the development of love between hero and heroine, Insarov's eventual death, and Elena's pledge to continue to serve her husband's ideals, Turgenev involves readers in a world of emotional subtleties with powerful implications: death and dying set a context for the most positive moments of the novel and also bring into focus a fascinating interplay of psychological and moral issues.

On the Eve is a novel about a Russian woman who falls in love with a Bulgarian nationalist. Only temporarily in Russia as a student, Insarov soon plans to return to his homeland to fight for its independence from Turkey. Elena, who is unsatisfied with the Russian men courting her, finds something strangely attractive in this foreigner, who appears wholly dedicated to political and nationalistic ideals. Their growing love for each other is described with a subtlety only rarely appreciated by critics, if one can judge by the brief, and usually unsatisfying, discussions of their relationship found in critical literature devoted to this novel.

Mutual declarations of love lead to a daring and unconventional marriage, which is followed by a belated blessing from Elena's parents and the couple's departure from Russia. Insarov, who had fallen ill while still in Russia, never fully regains his health and ultimately dies from consumption in Venice, with Elena nursing him in his final days. After his death she does not wish to return to Russia but plans to go on to the Balkans as a nurse, tending to the needs of Slavs fighting against the Turks.

There is no question that Elena is the central character in the novel, for it is primarily her moral sensitivities and sensibility that command narrative attention. On the surface, she seems an ideal subject of positive moral epithets: empathetic, sensitive to the sufferings and feelings of people, indignant at injustice, and longing to do good in the world. On this level, it is not difficult to account for her interest in a Bulgarian national who is dedicated to the noble idea of liberating his country. Her altruistic impulses and Insarov's selfless dedication to a cause give them a spiritual kinship. By uniting her life with his and supporting him in his cause, Elena can satisfy, in ways impossible in her life in Russia, her need to perform good deeds for others; at the same time it is apparent that Elena can satisfy other emotional needs, needs related to vague and troubling anxieties she sometimes suffers and which are at least partly sexual. Before Insarov's arrival on the scene, these needs found expression in her attention to two secondary characters: Bersenev, the philosophy student, and Shubin, the sculptor.

But all this is on the surface, offering only the outline of the novel's psychological pattern, which on closer inspection reveals a richly suggestive texture and design. Through its sympathetic portrayal of characters (such as Insarov, Elena, and also Bersenev) who embrace high ideals, the novel appears to promote such values as fidelity, support for the underdog, empathy for suffering, and tireless effort in behalf of others. But other values which are innocent enough on the surface—duty and obligation—nonetheless come to play a more sinister role as the novel progresses: they carry with them a punishing force derived from an unspecified but clearly present guilt in the heroine. Her guilt is somewhat at odds with her positive altruism and idealism, qualities that of themselves are supposed to offer sufficient motivation. Serving high-minded ideals as a form of penance for past sins may be morally commendable, but it is surely not as commendable, in conventional terms, as serving freely and spontaneously out of a pure and simple love for others. The evocation of taint within the motivation of praiseworthy human behavior casts a somber light over the whole novel and forces a sober, evaluative attitude toward the high moral idealism of the central characters.

And there is yet another sobering factor: the novel expresses a strong current of fatalism, a sense that there is really no such thing as free choice, that the foundations of human behavior are impenetrable, and human events are determined by suprahuman forces. This fatalistic current has the potential to carry away with it the whole moral framework. By emphasizing self-delusion, human frailty, and the all-too-human propensity for rationalization, the novel shows the central characters as tragically deluded victims of their own rationalizations, as mere players of roles given them in their childhood by society or by biology in a game that develops according to preset patterns.

Turgenev's heroines, illustrating the author's fondness for patterning and proportion in plots, generally fall into similar situations: as if waiting for something or someone, gripped by indefinable expectations, they stand ready to meet male protagonists who generally come from the world outside their immediate society.[8] After meeting, they fall in love; and the author applies his powers of psychological analysis, describing the manner in which hero and heroine form their bond. In *On the Eve* Turgenev shapes this bond by combining several different narrative perspectives. Elena is characterized by others; she is shown interacting with others; she is shown through her recorded thoughts in her diary; and she is shown through thoughts, feelings, and dreams recorded by the narrator, who also gives a succinct biography of her.

Elena's first romantic interest in the novel is not Insarov but Bersenev, a twenty-three-year-old Russian studying history and philosophy. What is shown in this relationship is Elena's receptiveness to men of sincerity who are seriously committed to a goal. Both Bersenev and his friend Shubin, an artist with a keen perception of character and a very practical turn of mind, are in love with Elena. Shubin observes her predisposition toward "remarkable" people and soon comes to the realizations that despite his talent he is not "remarkable" enough and that she will never love him. Even Bersenev, a suitor of greater promise, soon senses that he will also fail to be her choice. Neither character can excite her; clearly, both lack the qualities—whether physical or moral—she is seeking. In the very first chapters, Bersenev and Shubin not only state the major themes of the novel, but they also establish the contours of the heroine's character and set the stage for the appearance of the novel's hero.[9]

Although the relationship between Bersenev and Elena appears to have potential, it turns out to have nothing to grow on: in a scene alone before her window one night Elena admits to herself that he is not the one she is waiting for. (Bersenev too comes to recognize this, although he avoids thinking about it; his tendency is to seal himself off from emotions relating to personal love by burying himself in his books.) The window scene in chapter 5 represents the first sustained analysis, from within her consciousness, of Elena's thoughts and feelings. Assuming such a position, in front of the window looking out on the world as if from a cage is, we learn, a habit of hers. We also learn that she is intolerant of dishonesty, moral weakness, and stupidity and that she has on occasion been reproachful in her prayers—all of which suggests a strong sense of injustice and a judgmental nature. The narrator also underlines her longing for activity (reading was not enough): to satisfy this longing she helped beggars, the hungry, the sick, and the oppressed. Alone and independent of parental authority, she at times would become depressed, questioning the meaning of life; at other times she would experience deep anxieties alternating with moments of tranquility. She felt a need for love but saw no one to love.

Elena's predisposition for helping the weak and the injured, her vague longing for someone to love, her strong moral convictions, and her rejection of parental authority all serve in direct ways to prepare the way for her future relationship with Insarov. Especially significant is the inner agitation and excitement we are told she feels when helping the oppressed. Her inclinations toward self-reflection and self-doubt, together with her strange shifts in mood, show a different, less confident side of her nature.

Insarov's presence is announced by Bersenev at the end of the first third of the novel (chapter 10); he is characterized in terms of his "ruling idea," the liberation of his homeland from Turkish domination, but also in terms more conventional: he is stubborn, sincere, able to concentrate, and strong-willed; moreover there is an air of secrecy about his behavior. The sound of the words "to liberate his country" has a powerful effect on Elena. In the following chapter we hear of more fine features—intense patriotism, decisiveness, and a firm commitment to promises given—and earlier ones are reinforced. Having moved in with Bersenev, who does not live far from the Stakhov family, Insarov is in an excellent position to carry on a courtship with Elena.

The first meeting of Elena and Insarov disappoints her expectations (she has expected something more "fatal" in him, rather as if she were expecting a romantic hero),[10] though she finds his directness appealing. Shubin provides a new perspective: he admits the Bulgarian's capacity for work, his strength of character, and his political eloquence; but he also notes his limitations in artistic matters and his aridity. (Later he will produce a sculpture of Insarov, showing him unflatteringly as a ram.) Shubin concludes, ironically, that such a man cannot be attractive to a woman. The interplay of perspectives on human character in the novel is an important device, for in pointing to the contingency of character and the relativity of judgment, what Turgenev suggests is that life and people are not as simple as they seem and that idealism too may show different faces through different perspectives. The novel clearly establishes a tension between the strong and definite ideals articulated by the protagonists and the contingency of the real world, where preoccupation with a single goal can be interpreted as stubborn blindness as well as exemplary dedication.

As the novel progresses, Elena's fascination with Insarov grows, fed in subtle ways by her own predispositions and hopes. His words and expression fascinate her, especially his eloquence on nationalism, the public (versus the private) interest, and his complete dedication to his cause. He in turn is affected by her reactions. There is something paradoxical in the very personal responses ("strange" feelings) evoked in Elena by Insarov's eloquent promotion of public and abstract ideals. The opposition of the personal and the public will become important to the protagonists, for people who view personal and public loyalties as opposing forces will necessarily associate feelings of personal love with conflict.

Two events hasten the development of their relationship. Insarov disappears for several days, and Elena assigns a mysterious significance to his absence. This profound effect is not lessened by the mundane explanation that is eventually provided, simply that he had gone off to settle a dispute between some of his fellow countrymen living not far from Moscow.

The second event is far more dramatic: on a group outing at Tsaritsino Insarov throws into the water an enormous drunken German who had insulted the women in the group. Elena and the others are stunned by the incident; she in particular experiences "peculiar" feelings when she notices something unpleasant, dangerous, and malicious in Insarov's face. His actions here, and her reactions, are important components of Turgenev's psychological portrait, a portrait drawn by the narrator and by Elena herself in her internal monologues and diary entries.

Her thoughts and feelings, including her eventual realization that she has fallen in love, are recorded in her diary (chapter 16). Filtered through her consciousness, her experiences and impressions are played off against her recollections, dreams, and desires: she makes explicit her strong interest in coming to know new people and in doing good, and she reiterates her need for someone. The roots of her fascination extend deeply and complexly into her past. Critics have tried to explain why Elena finds Insarov so attractive, why she falls in love with him. Some believe the source of Insarov's appeal is his ideological conviction, and they are partly right. Where they are wrong is in suggesting that this is the whole picture.

Turgenev offers many hints that what is on the surface plays but a minor role in human relationships. Elena is only partly aware of what is happening. Undoubtedly Insarov answers needs Elena has, but her needs are not always so clearly defined. She has a need to help people, and, feeling at the outset that she is as if in a cage, she desires the freedom of a bird; but she also longs for the security of a nest (8:82) and less figuratively, the life of a servant (8:81). Although her love for Insarov is obvious to readers long before Elena understands it, her own ambivalent feelings preclude easy explanations of why she is so attracted to him.

Critical efforts that go beyond the simple appeal of his noble goal have suggested that Insarov is the one best able to realize Elena's ideals for her;[11] that Insarov, who has a moral superiority to her, has successfully integrated personal and social values;[12] that he was necessary to her so that she could act out her "private fancies and inclinations, to raise her freeing of flies from spiders and care of stray kittens to something more heroic";[13] and that she fell in love with the "principle, the strength," and not the man. Some of Turgenev's contemporaries (Nikolai Nekrasov and Vasilii Botkin) failed to see adequate motivation for her love in the text.[14] Virtually all have ignored a very obvious fact that, though it has no specific relationship to Insarov's political or social views, can serve as a partial explanation: she finds him sexually attractive. Related to and perhaps underlying this attraction are personal qualities he possesses, qualities that are expressed in his physical features, his mannerisms, his voice, and his energy. Elena's diary has prepared for us a picture of someone who is yearning for someone to love. When Insarov enters this picture, much more than the content of his views is given: all kinds of details about his manner and his effects on Elena are presented.

Though not handsome, he exudes, we are told, a sensuality and vitality, especially when he grows excited, as when he talks of his country and of killing Turks. Though part of his appeal may be ascribed to his views, their specific content may not be as important as what they represent. His selfless dedication in a heroic quest, his thirst for conflict, and his propensity for violence pervade his demeanor and, undoubtedly, all contribute to his sexuality.

Insarov's recognition that he has fallen in love threatens their relationship, for in yielding to the personal he believes he is betraying his cause and his duty. His decision to leave Russia without delay—and possibly even without a farewell to Elena because of the "threat" to his ideals she represents—forces her to act, to take the bold and unconventional step of going to him. In a scene whose intensity is dramatically heightened by a storm, Elena sets out to find Insarov but is forced to seek shelter in a roadside chapel. Here she finds an old beggarwoman to whom she gives a handkerchief as alms. The old woman promises to take away Elena's sorrow with the present, and she also gives advice: "When a good man has turned up, not a silly one, you hold on to him, hold on stronger than death. If it is to be, then it will be; but if it isn't, then it must not be pleasing to God." (8:91)

The scene with the old woman abounds in ironies: her words have a yet-to-be-realized significance. Death will come, for "it" is not to be; and Elena will hold on stronger than death by continuing Insarov's mission to Bulgaria without him. Removing Elena's sorrow, however, proves to be beyond the powers of the old woman. The themes of mendicancy and death run into the following scene: Elena finds Insarov, and they declare their love for each other. Both are caught up in emotion, achieving a joy beside which other aspects of their life pale. For her there is a sense of harmony and fulfillment:

> "He is here, he loves . . . and what else is there?" The stillness of bliss, the stillness of an imperturbable refuge, of a goal achieved, that heavenly stillness which confers both sense and beauty even on death itself, filled her completely with its divine wave. She did not wish anything because she possessed everything. (8:93–94)

And for Insarov, there is initiation into a world of emotions he had never known before, feelings that temporarily displace his cherished ideals from their primacy:

> And he stood motionless, encircling with his strong embrace this young life which was surrendering itself to him; he felt on his chest this new, infinitely precious burden; a feeling of tenderness, a feeling of inexplicable gratitude, shattered his stern soul into dust, and tears he had never known before came to his eyes. (8:94)

Their blissful oblivion is short-lived (a quarter of an hour), and they soon shift attention to the hardships their relationship will entail. Insarov tells her that he is almost a beggar and that she will have to leave her family for another world—one of danger and humiliations. Their love, in fact, is not destined to offer much of the bliss that these first moments have promised.[15] The hints of death offered by the old beggarwoman and the narrator will prove to be well founded, and the "burden" Insarov feels while embracing Elena foreshadows the weight of duty and guilt that will ultimately crush all hopes for lasting happiness.

As if to underscore the deceptiveness of appearances, the calm after the storm that accompanies their declaration of love fails to bring equilibrium. Elena's emotional life becomes even more complicated after this scene with its obvious signs of death and predetermination. Their pledge of love is followed by a period of separation, and guilt toward her parents replaces the inner peace she had initially felt. Guilt will become increasingly more prominent. It is obviously externalized when she imagines that the birds and animals which she cared for and protected since childhood are no longer friendly toward her. This self-punishment is abetted by pangs of conscience and the return of former anxieties.

After several weeks of separation from Insarov, her calm is restored. She begins a secret correspondence with him when he has returned to Moscow to make final preparations for their departure. Once reunited with her, he again reminds her of his homelessness and solitary position. There is something paradoxical about this reminder, something reminiscent of romantic individualism that is at odds with his avowed solidarity with the common cause and the shared ideals of his country and its people.[16] Moreover, his statement is at odds with actual circumstances mentioned in the novel: Insarov, we are told, is admired by his people, is called upon to settle disputes, and is anxiously awaited in his homeland. All this belies his repeated insistence that he is alone; what it suggests—and this will be taken up later—is that his own goals may be much more private than he is willing to admit.

Elena too emphasizes how isolated their position will be, although in her case, separated from her country and friends, such emphasis seems more appropriate. She reinforces a previous image of her position, comparing herself to a runaway maid she remembered from her childhood. Though she is firm in her commitment, her confidence that their youth and vitality can overcome all obstacles will prove to be misplaced, for Insarov becomes ill while trying to obtain an illegal passport for Elena and he never fully recovers. Caring for him while he is ill, she develops a keen and very personalized sense of mortality; it is not just that death can come to anyone at any time, but that death is selective, choosing those who are deserving of punishment. Though early in his illness she has insisted that she had done nothing wrong and that her conscience was silent, her obsession now with guilt and responsibility indicates otherwise.

Elena's relationship with her parents deteriorates, especially after they discover that she and Insarov have married and, despite his illness, are planning to leave. Ultimately parents and daughter are reconciled, but their reconciliation does not dispel her remorse for what she perceives as wrongful behavior toward them. When the couple leaves for Venice, the atmosphere of doom is clearly borne along with them.

Venice, however, turns out to be an interlude that actually provides the couple with some of their most fulfilling shared experiences.[17] Though Elena and Insarov have given no indication of a refined artistic sensibility, they nonetheless find themselves entranced by Venice's cultural beauties.[18] With all its artistic treasures, the city serves as a backdrop for the tragic finale of the novel, giving the couple's final trip together a quality of beauty on a base of ephemerality. It was this quality, together with the intensified meaning the proximity of death gave to their experiences, that so impressed the nineteenth-century critic Apollon Grigor'ev:

> The general poetic aim [of the novel]: an effort to portray two passionate existences which have collided in a fateful and tragic way— and which in the exceptional setting of Venice are slipping over the abyss and destruction—and the thirst for life and intoxication with it on the edge of death and destruction, amidst the wonders of a poetic and obsolete world; this is the aim which has been brilliantly fulfilled and which has created in the novel a kind of feverish Byronic episode, a magnificent and fascinating poem.[19]

The excitement of the struggle with death brings a heightened awareness of life. It also serves to intensify their spiritual longings, which, along with Venice, turn their attention toward art. In this setting the couple is attracted by and feels a kinship with artistic models of idealism, expiation, and martyrdom. They admire Titian's *Ascension* and marvel at the strength of the Madonna aspiring to God's bosom (p. 135); the painting is an obvious suggestion of their own strivings, their own idealism, and perhaps the idealism that will sustain Elena in her future role. They attend a performance of *La Traviata* and find particular meaning in lines about youthful death. They walk near St. George's Cathedral, which is dedicated to a martyr, and the church of the Redentore—the Expiator—which is described as being "dressed like a bride"; Elena will labor after the death of her husband (as a widowed bride) in expiation for her own perceived sins. Their chosen way of life is reflected here in the beauty and power of art, and the experiences relating to this art and their circumstances in Venice mark a high point in their relationship. The aestheticism of the Venetian chapters cannot help but carry implications for the novel's moral import. Clearly art confers meaning on self-sacrifice, but it also gives heightened significance to the final days of hero and heroine: both selflessness and mutual love are glorified as values beside which sociopolitical aims seem pale and inessential.

Later, with Insarov asleep and feverish, Elena sits gazing out the window contemplating the cold and silent reality around her; she thinks of loneliness, miracles, and death. Feeling guilty for the happiness they had, she once again conceives of death as a form of punishment and once again insists that her conscience is clear. But thoughts of conscience lead again to thoughts of her mother and the guilt she feels as, in her view, the cause of her mother's grief. On the night of Insarov's death, she falls asleep while sitting at the window only to awaken from her dream to his last words. She cannot pray after his death, for she feels that God has punished her beyond the measure of her guilt—a guilt which she cannot fully understand. Guilt, as the narrator interposes, is shared by all who are alive, and neither good deeds nor motives can give one the right to live (8:164). Elena, however, will continue to be dominated by another model of life, one built on the concepts of personalized punishment, reward, and retribution.

We have returned to the themes of the conversation of Bersenev and Shubin in the first chapter of the novel: the interconnections of love, happiness, self-sacrifice, and death. Bersenev defended a view of love as self-sacrifice, as total loss of self (and he demonstrated his dedication to this ideal in his selfless care of Insarov in the early days of his illness), while Shubin promoted the notion that love was ultimately directed at self-gratification: "the thirst for love, the thirst for happiness, and nothing more!" And love, as Shubin suggests at the end of their exchange, has mysterious links with death as well:

> "I don't quite agree with you," he [Bersenev] began; "not always does nature hint to us of—love." (He did not pronounce this word right away.) "She also threatens us: she reminds us of terrible—yes, of inaccessible secrets. Isn't it nature who must swallow us up, isn't she constantly swallowing us up? Both life and death are in her; and death in nature speaks just as loudly as life."
> "In love too there is life and death," Shubin interrupted. (8:13)

It is death, tied up closely with guilt, that preoccupies Elena in the end. Her final letter to her mother (which will be cited in the following section) gives expression to her guilt, a guilt which Turgenev intensified in succeeding editions of the novel published during his life. [20] Her guilt now, as she explains it in her letter, extends not only to her mother but to her responsibility for Insarov's death. Divine judgment, in her view, requires that guilt must be matched by punishment. Thus she envisages him coming back to take her with him into the abyss. She closes her letter with talk of death's power to reconcile all, and she makes a final request for forgiveness. The novel ends without telling us exactly what has happened to her, though there are stories of her service as a nurse (in Hercegovina) and of her death (by drowning at sea). What remains clear, however, is that her future life, though on the surface noble, will be joyless. The moral model her idealism offers is not very inspiring.

Just as in Pushkin's *The Bronze Horseman*, death and rebellion are linked in *On the Eve* not only to each other but also with intense experiences of life. Elena's rebellion against family and homeland is followed by the death of her beloved Insarov. She protests, but her protests are only vaguely focused, neither clearly at God nor at fate, although conventional religion is clearly of little importance in her life.[21] Her anger is directed principally at herself: it takes the form of powerful feelings of guilt. And this self-punishing guilt obviously plays a role in motivating her choice for a future life. She carries on in an apparently unfeeling way (the day after Insarov's death, she is like "stone"), presumably intent on burying all her emotions in service to others. Of course the possibility that her service represents some kind of expiation for past wrongs has a bearing on the moral quality of her actions. Charity may still be charity regardless of motives; but, as Tolstoi illustrated so well in his fictional characters, there is a difference between charity undertaken mechanically, because of a guilty conscience or by an abstract logic of compassion, and charity deriving from a more immediate and intuitive sense of compassion for the suffering and mistreated. Though Elena's early efforts as a child to protect and care for the helpless may come close to the latter definition, the motivation underlying her later dedication to charitable service is not quite so clear. There are hints that there is much that is unsettling beneath the surface, that her altruistic behavior may have parts that compromise its character.

What has been for the most part ignored in critical accounts of Elena's character—in particular with respect to her urge to serve others—are the patterns for her responses and emotions that Turgenev has provided for us in his descriptions of her childhood. Here can be found a wealth of suggestive material to support hypotheses about her love for Insarov, her decision to leave home and break with her parents, her fatalistic sensibility, and her guilt. Furthermore, her personal history is relevant to an assessment of the moral and political implications of her abandonment of home and country. Examination of this history may help to explain why critics have sensed beneath the surface of her idealism something alien to the spirit of altruism.[22]

From one perspective, Elena's interest in concrete ideals, her willingness to break social conventions, and her social concern may seem to give evidence of the author's desire to provide moral models for social action. But this is not the only perspective one can take: Robert Dessaix in a recent book has convincingly argued that Elena and Insarov are not realists, but "late-flowering romantics" with a strong strain of mysticism. Her love for Insarov is based on her "personal, romantic" need for "remarkable men," and what is important is not so much what he believes but *that* he believes.[23] Dessaix's interpretation rightly emphasizes the complexity of human motivation and the importance of considering Elena's personal, and not necessarily conscious, needs in understanding her behavior.

What Elena seeks in the present reflects what she sought in the past. If we examine Elena's childhood experiences as she and the narrator relate them, we see that there are numerous curious correlations between her past and her present, correlations that may affect the moral import of her actions. In her childhood, we are told, Elena developed a desire to do good things, a thirst for "active good." She even dreamed of the poor, the hungry, and the sick; they tormented her in her thoughts; she tended for them with an unusual seriousness and excitement (8:33). Just as her interests as a child turned from reading to doing, in her maturity her interests in men turned from the thinker Bersenev to the activist Insarov. In no way does Insarov teach Elena the virtues of deeds, the need to act in behalf of the good. His dedication strikes a responsive chord already deeply rooted in her psyche. No proselytizing is necessary—she was by predisposition attracted to those dedicated to social action and to doing what she could to serve those less fortunate than herself. She was predisposed as an adult to choose a man of action, or at least a man who talked of action, over a man of reflection like Bersenev. The novel, by its discussion of Elena's early interests, suggests that what gave her satisfaction in childhood could also be used to sooth those peculiar torments she suffers in her maturity. But as an adult—and a woman in Russia in the 1850s—her sphere of socially acceptable action was limited.[24] Her father made very clear his opposition to idealistic self-sacrifice. Marriage was virtually her only option, but she found the men around her, with the exception of Insarov, lacking.

Elena's thirst for doing good deeds and helping those who were oppressed is clearly in harmony with Insarov's professed goals. It is undeniable that she, lacking a sense of purpose in life, admires the fact that he has a goal; and her awareness of this fact represents part of his appeal to her. But there is something else, perhaps even more important, at the basis of his appeal. His bold treatment of the rude German, together with his demeanor before and after the feat, have a strong effect on her. The act itself, if marked off from its general significance (critics have pointed out with some justice that it was hardly an act of heroic stature) and Insarov's emotional intensity (an "unkind," "dangerous" something expressed in his face), had a strange importance to her. The immediacy and emotional authenticity of his actions, the tremendous emotional energy she perceives in his anger, make a deep and lasting impression.

Insarov's manner rivets her attention and suggests that the basis of his attractiveness may lie in something other than his dedication and idealism.

We are given access to the event from two perspectives:

[Narrator]: "Insarov seemed very threatening to them, and not without reason: something unkind *("nedobroe")*, something dangerous, revealed itself in his face." (8:77)

[Elena]: ". . . I shall not forget yesterday's trip for a long time. What strange, new, terrible impressions! I was not frightened when he suddenly grabbed that giant and threw him like a ball into the water, I wasn't frightened . . . but he frightened me. And then— what a sinister, almost cruel face! The way he said: 'He'll float up!' That upset me. So I have not understood him. And later, when everyone was laughing, when I was laughing, how hurt I felt for him! He was ashamed, I felt that, he was ashamed because of me. He told me that later, in the carriage, in the darkness when I tried to make out his face and was afraid of him. Yes, you cannot joke with him, and he knows how to stand up for himself. But why that malice, those trembling lips, that poison in his eyes? Or perhaps it cannot be otherwise? Isn't it possible to be a man, a warrior, and to remain meek and gentle? Life is a rough business he told me recently." (8:83)

Insarov's appeal has a dark side.[25] In the "poison" in his eyes and his "trembling" lips, there is a malicious anger, a rage that seems excessive. The dark potential expressed here remains vivid in her consciousness, though she is well aware of his other qualities. However, even these other qualities have a physical component. Along with more abstract features of his personality (he is just, reliable, and somehow more impressive than the other men she knows), how he looks at her, and even how he sounds are important. His voice is like "steel"; and when he talks of his country, his whole being is transformed. The physiological basis for his attractiveness goes beyond the ideological, and it matters little whether he is seen as a romantic idealist or a political activist. The personal factor is independent of the content of his ideas, though it is probably closely tied to the emotional intensity of his dedication and his willingness to sacrifice his personal life for the sake of his people.

Elena's fascination with Insarov is obviously not entirely at a rational and conscious level. She does not respond to Insarov immediately. Between their first meeting and their eventual declarations of love there is a period of inner turmoil and confusion for Elena. The puzzlement, tension, apprehension, inner agitation, and strange dreams she experiences do not make for a simple picture of nascent love. Once again, the patterns of the past have relevance to her emotional life: she is not isolated in time with traits and emotions we expect of a twenty-year-old. Though the foundation of her personality may not be clearly visible, its contours are suggested not only in several childhood scenes but also in her dreams and reveries and in the narrator's occasional remarks on her family. Her emotional responses to Insarov as a man of flesh and blood, a man capable of malice and violence, and a man who takes promises seriously, resonate distinctly, though distantly, with chords first sounded in her childhood.

At the age of ten Elena made friends with a beggar girl named Katia and went secretly to meet with her in the garden, took her sweets, and gave her kerchiefs and kopeks—Katia would not take toys. They sat down next to each other on the dry ground, in a remote spot, behind a clump of nettles; with a feeling of joyful humility she ate the beggar girl's stale bread and listened to her stories. Katia had an aunt, an evil old woman, who often beat her; Katia hated her and kept talking about how she would run away from her aunt, how she would live in *God's freedom*.

Elena listened with a secret respect and fear to these unknown new words, and looked fixedly at Katia; and then everything about her— her dark, swift, almost animal-like eyes, her sunburnt arms, her hollow little voice, even her tattered dress—seemed to Elena to be something special, almost holy. Elena would return home and then for a long time think about beggars, about God's freedom; she thought of how she would cut herself a stick from a nut tree and put on a pack and run away with Katia; how she would wander along the roads, wearing a chaplet of cornflowers; one time she saw Katia wearing such a chaplet. If any of her family entered the room while she was thinking about all this, she would avoid them and look unsociable. (8:33–34)

It is not difficult to see parallels in Elena's relationships with Katia and In-sarov. Katia too has a purpose grounded in hatred for an enemy; and she tells stories of her hatred and her hope for liberation—just as Insarov later will fascinate Elena with stories of his hatred for the Turks and his hopes of liberating his people. Both Katia and Insarov are exotic in appearance and in voice, dark in complexion with unusual ("guttural" *[gortanyi]* and "toneless" or "hollow" *[glukhoi]*) voices and striking eyes; Insarov is literally a foreigner, while Katia, with her beggar's clothes and status, is a foreigner in the Stakhovs' world. The words of both Katia and Insarov have an unusual effect on Elena: they are "unknown" and "new"; and both inspire in her humility and altruistic service to a cause: there is something almost "holy" about their struggles. The thrill she experiences in adopting a style of life far below that of her class, in "sharing" Katia's stale bread, and the dreams of flight from her home and family all attest to how carefully Turgenev has set the stage for Elena's attraction for Insarov. But the parallels do not stop here, for actual events in Elena's childhood are played out in modified form in her later life.

The effect of the incident with the German indicates how closely Elena attends to Insarov's physical being, his emotions as they have been reflected in his face and bodily movements. Similarly, she is fascinated by his animation when he speaks of his country. It is not just the strength of his convictions that affects Elena but his physical presence, his animal vitality. Regardless of their talk about duty, self-sacrifice, and noble idealism, Elena and Dmitrii are not content with a platonic relationship, a marriage of spirits; in her second visit to him during his illness they ignore his weakened state (which he uses as part of their rationalizations) and, at her initiative, have sex (8:131).

There are hints of the source of his appeal in the very personal relationship Elena had with Katia, one constituted by secrecy and a mysterious bond of affection. Elena more than once refers to Insarov as a "brother," recalling her "sisterly" relationship with Katia; and Elena also notices something "familiar" about Insarov—as if she recognizes an old friend. In the beginning Katia too was "new" in her physical appearance and firm in her dedication to a cause (escape into "God's freedom"). Moreover, Elena's relationship with Katia, like her later relationship with Insarov, caused friction with and even separated her from her parents:

> One day she ran to meet Katia in the rain and got her dress dirty; her father saw her and called her slovenly, a peasant girl. She flared up with her whole being—and in her heart she felt terrible and marvelous. Katia often sang some half-wild soldiers' song; Elena learned the song from her . . . . Her mother overheard her and became indignant.
>
> "Where did you learn that filth?" she asked her daughter.
>
> Elena only looked at her and did not say a word; she felt that she would sooner let herself be torn apart than betray her secret, and she again had a terrible and sweet feeling in her heart. Her acquaintance with Katia did not continue for long, however; the poor girl fell ill with a fever and died after several days. (8:34)

There are numerous parallels here: Elena's preadolescent rebellions involved a secret relationship and behavior that compromised conventional morality; undoubtedly the "filth" in the soldiers' song involved some sexual references. As might be expected, her behavior provoked outrage in her parents, who reprimanded her in strong terms. Furthermore, Elena's curiously ambivalent feelings consisting of the "terrible" (strashno) and the "marvelous" and "sweet" (chudno and sladko) offer a hint of the complex and contradictory emotions—the joy and the guilt—she will feel in her relationship with Insarov.

It is unreasonable to expect certainty in psychological conclusions based on such meager data; nonetheless, some hypotheses seem stronger than others. Undoubtedly the young Elena's challenge of parental authority was accompanied by a feeling of guilt—and pleasure in having the power to provoke such strong reactions even if, or possibly because, they led to punishment. The narrator makes it clear that she is willing to undergo torture—virtual martyrdom—rather than betray her friend; and this thought of suffering for her fidelity to her friend, not the rebuke from her mother, gave her the combination of opposite feelings, the horror and pleasure *(strashno and sladko)*.

The impulses and desires that ultimately lead Elena to Insarov and, later, to a guilt-ridden fatalism can thus be traced back to her childhood; and hints in the text of early patterns for the development of Elena's feelings can lead to other lines of speculation as well. We know that after being devoted to her father early in her childhood, she later turned cold to him; that her early closeness with her mother also went sour (though some "sympathy" always remained); that Elena was virtually free of supervision by the time she was sixteen; and that throughout her childhood her mother for the most part ignored her, although she told her (and anyone else who would listen) of Elena's father's infidelities. With an appropriate developmental theory, one could make connections between Elena's views of fidelity, her choice of Insarov as a mate (a man who boasts total fidelity to his cause), and her feelings for her father. For in her mature years, Elena, as if in reaction to her father's behavior, takes fidelity extremely seriously and chooses a man who views fidelity in the same way.

Psychoanalytic interpretations, which of course are not the only way to view Elena's life, might advance her choice of ideals as an unconscious anger against her father, a desire to avenge earlier betrayals. And Elena's early propensity for nurturing animals as well as her later socially acceptable role nurturing adults (Insarov and, presumably, wounded freedom-fighters in the Balkans) could be understood as efforts to be the "mother" she longed for but never had. In a discourse such as this Elena's motives for rebelling against her parents, for following the *lex talionis* not only in her choice of a childhood friend (Katia) but also in her choice of Insarov, become more understandable.[26]

But it is possible to pursue the enigmas in Elena's behavior along slightly different lines. For Elena, one of Insarov's most intriguing and exciting qualities is his unqualified commitment to his cause; nothing can get in the way of his dedication to his goal. And it is from this very ideal that Elena diverts Insarov, though she is fully aware of his belief that love for a woman could jeopardize the success of his task. She challenges his rigid idealism, which allows no room for the personal (belittling his earlier declaration that he had no need of a "Russian's love"), and with little difficulty leads him into the "infidelity" of betrayed ideals; he remains aware of the limits their love imposes on him (he refers to the "burden" and "chains" [8:128] it represents), yet he and Elena delude themselves into thinking they are truly free to fulfill his ideals. The initiative Elena takes in cementing their relationship entraps her in a web of guilt, for from this point on she must see herself as responsible for whatever happens. Her very aim of identifying with someone who is a paragon of fidelity to a high ideal paradoxically involves her in a situation where she abets his "betrayal" of the ideal. This perspective on her behavior gives us an explanation for the mordant guilt she feels at the end of the novel.[27]

Whatever psychological framework is applied to Elena and her life, there can be no denying that the parallels between her childhood and mature years have an aesthetic significance and power derived from our perception of design in the novel. Events of the present reverberate with the past, and what is given to us from her past cannot easily be ignored. If past events have psychological import as well (and it would be hard to believe that such an import was not intended by Turgenev), then, whatever the theory used to interpret them, they are suggestive of a psychological complexity whose mysteries undermine any simple assessment of human motivation.

Not only does the childhood relationship with Katia offer possible sources of Elena's attraction for Insarov, it also provides a partial explanation for her growing sense of fatalism as the novel draws to a close. The walk in the rain, the forbidden liaison, the vows of secrecy, and the illness and death of Katia all set a pattern of unconscious expectations in her mind, not only for moments of terrible and pleasant feelings but also for the eventual death of her beloved Insarov.

After Katia's death, the child Elena for several nights thinks she is being called from beyond the grave (8:34). She experiences the feeling of being called twice again in the novel, at two crucial points. The first comes when she deliberates whether to go to Insarov before he leaves Russia (8:89), the second in a dream late in the novel (8:161), while Insarov is dying.[28] Elena's sense of doom and resignation is certainly unsurprising, for the two people closest to her in her life have been suddenly and inexplicably taken away from her by death. Illness has preceded both deaths—and, perhaps more important, her parents' punitive displeasure. The connections between death and punishment in Elena's mind undoubtedly have a source here. Her resolution to continue her life according to an altruistic ideal clearly suggests an expiatory rite. But it also suggests a realization of her childhood dream to take to the roads with a sack on her back and a chaplet on her head in search of the land Katia sought, the land of "God's freedom." With her feelings of guilt and gloom, however, the nurse's cap she is to assume when she leaves Italy seems only a poor substitute for Katia's chaplet of flowers,[29] and service to Insarov's cause in a strange land only a pale reflection of the glorious quest for God's freedom.

Katia's reappearance at the end of the novel in Elena's dream underscores the little girl's importance and, again, the underlying importance of Elena's childhood impulses and feelings in her maturity. But there are other aspects of Elena's psychology—what she was like after Katia died and until Insarov appeared—that make simple conclusions about her character even more problematic.

We learn that years go by like "waters under snow" and that she lives constantly at the mercy of inner anxiety; she also lives a lonely life, estranged from parents and from other young people:

> Her soul both flamed up and died down alone, and it beat like a bird in a cage, but there was no cage: no one constrained her, no one restrained her, but she longed for something and languished; sometimes she could not understand herself, and was even afraid of herself. Everything around her seemed either senseless or incomprehensible. "How can one live without love? but there is no one to love!" — she thought, and she became horrified by these thoughts, by these sensations. (8:35)

She suffers a near-fatal illness when she is eighteen (which her father thinks had lasting effects on her temperament) and then becomes aware that she wants something unusual from life:

> Sometimes it occurred to her that she desired something that no one desired, that no one in all of Russia thought of. Then she grew calm, even laughed at herself, spent day after day without a care, but suddenly something strong and nameless which she was not able to control boiled up within her and begged to be let out. The storm passed and the tired, unused wings were folded; but these outbursts came at a price. No matter how hard she tried to keep from betraying what was happening in her, the longing of an agitated soul was expressed even in her outward tranquility, and her parents were often right in shrugging their shoulders, in being surprised at, and in not understanding her "peculiarities." (8:35)

The anxieties within her threaten to surface at any time; her moments of tranquility offer only temporary respite from these inner forces. During the entire course of her later relationship with Insarov, the inner forces struggle to come to the surface; in the end they find their way into her dreams: as Insarov is breathing his last, Elena falls asleep and experiences a dream that explicitly links earlier themes as well as Katia and Insarov:

> The dream she experienced was strange. It seemed to her that she was in a boat on the Tsaritsino lake with some people she did not know. They were silent and sat motionless, and no one was rowing; the boat moved on by itself. She was not terrified, but bored; she would have liked to have known who the people were and why she

was with them. She looked, and the lake widened, and the banks fell away—it was no longer a lake, but a restless sea: enormous, azure, silent waves majestically rocked the boat; something thundering, threatening, rose up from the bottom; her unknown fellow travelers suddenly jumped up, screamed, and waved their arms. . . . Elena recognized their faces; her father was among them. But a white whirlwind swooped down on the waves . . . everything began to whirl, to become confused. . . .

Elena looked around her: everything all around was white as before; but it was snow, snow, snow without end. And she was no longer in a boat, she was riding, as when she left Moscow, in a sleigh; she was not alone: next to her sat a little creature wrapped up in a very old coat. Elena looked closely: it was Katia, her poor little friend. Elena became terrified. "But didn't she die?" she thought.

"Katia, where is it we are going?"

Katia did not answer and wrapped herself in her little coat; she was shivering. Elena, too, felt cold. She looked down along the length of the road: a town was visible in the distance through the powdery snow. Tall white towers with silvery cupolas . . . Katia, Katia, is that Moscow? No, thought Elena, that is the Solovetskii Monastery: there are many, many small, narrow cells there, like a hive; it is stuffy and close there—Dmitrii is locked up there. I must free him. . . . Suddenly a gray, yawning abyss opened up in front of her. The sleigh fell, Katia laughed. Elena, Elena!—a voice was heard from the abyss." (8:161–62)

The dream resonates with previous themes. Now her father, Insarov, and Katia are linked, all three in the dream. The motif of Elena being called by Katia (this time from the abyss) is reintroduced. The dream gives expression to the emotional shifts Elena has always experienced: tranquility suddenly giving way to turmoil and confusion (the waters under the snow). On a more abstract level the dream expresses the precariousness and vulnerability of her position (and the human condition): a calm sea can quickly turn threatening, and a sleigh in the snow can easily fall into the abyss. But equally strong is the suggestion that one's plans and one's motives can be delusional: what looked like Moscow turned out to be stifling confinement, a monastery, the locus of asceticism and idealism but also a place of confinement and imprisonment; idealism may be more confining than liberating and may entail death and the abyss as its ultimate consequences.

If Insarov's idealism and the life dedicated to it are understood negatively, as the deprivation of freedom rather than the quest for it, then not only the dream but also much of the novel's imagery take on a new meaning. Throughout the novel Elena compares her life to that of a bird; at times she feels that she is in a cage that is not really a cage and that she longs to fly. The empty cage in Insarov's room is significant, a suggestion that not only was it with him that she could and would find a place but also that the freedom she wanted might be delusional, that in connecting her life with Insarov's she might merely be replacing an imaginary cage with one more substantial.[30] And though this notion may sound paradoxical at first, it has explanatory power. How else can we account for Elena's longing at times to be a servant, her desire to yield up all personal choice to an abstract sense of duty? Unconsciously she may be striving for the comforting limits, the sense of having found a place, that Insarov's patriotism and strong sense of duty would offer her.

The bird imagery frequently found in her thoughts connects with another dimension of Elena's life: her susceptibility to ominous portents. In a world where one's intimates can be suddenly and inexplicably taken away, all signs have meaningful potential. Earlier in the novel, she was driven by a voice (Katia's?) to take the initiative and to go to find Insarov; she came upon the old beggarwoman—whom she treated just as she treated Katia, offering her a gift and listening to her "story"—and this incident set a fatalistic tone in reaffirming Elena's decision to link her life with Insarov's. And at the end of the novel Elena is again looking for a sign, something to help her plan for the future. She sees a white gull circling above the water as if looking for a place to land; she thinks it will be a good sign if the bird flies toward her. Instead, it suddenly folds its wings and with a cry disappears behind a ship. The import of this sign rings true: Elena will drop from sight, like the bird, after the death of her husband.

The portentous quality of these incidents underlines the heavy presence of fate and the limitations of human will in deciding the course of events. Of course the powerlessness of humans to determine their own happiness is shown by more than portents: Elena's willing submission to a life of dutiful service, her resignation, her pessimism, and her overriding sense of guilt all contribute to make a convincing case against free and rational choice. The guilt she feels and the sense she has that she is being punished for some undefined sins (a punishment that she thinks is incommensurate with the sins) are issues that call for some final comments.

Like Russia's other great novelists, Turgenev shared an interest in and preoccupation with the concepts of freedom and necessity. Tolstoi and Dostoevskii spoke with enthusiasm of the virtues of total submission to "ineluctable and incomprehensible" forces and illustrated in their works the destructive power of the unconstrained will.[31] Turgenev, too, in a more qualified way, paid homage to these same polarities. Elena longs for both the freedom of a bird and the enclosed world in which all sense of self is obliterated in submission to an external goal; her imagery of birds reflects her awareness of the two poles of freedom and submission, and her words and actions betray her ambivalence. Her love for Insarov has moments of personal gratification and sexual excitement.[32] But there are also times when abstractions reign supreme, when their love is conceptualized as duty, self-sacrifice, and responsibility—and at these times yielding to the demands of the personal is viewed as somehow sinful, a sign of impermissible weakness. In their world, only submission to such elevated notions as duty and service to the cause has moral validity. Tilting toward submission at the end of the novel, Elena turns from personal mourning to a morality of abstraction, an altruism devoid of passion. Her new role as a nurse in foreign lands goes hand in hand with a deep pessimism. It is clear in her final letter to her mother that the submission Turgenev pictures represents neither heaven nor hell:

> I do not know what will happpen to me, but even after D.'s death I shall remain faithful to his memory, to the task of his whole life. I learned Bulgarian and Serbian. Probably I shall not survive all this— so much the better. I have been led to the edge of the abyss and must fall. Not without reason did fate unite us: who knows, perhaps I killed him; now it is his turn to carry me along after him. I have sought happiness—and I shall find, perhaps, death. Evidently that was to be expected; evidently there was guilt. . . . But death covers and reconciles all—is that not so?
>
> Forgive me all the grief I have caused you: it was not in my power to act otherwise. But to return to Russia—for what reason? What is to be done in Russia?
>
> Accept my last kisses and blessings and do not condemn me.
>
> E.   (8:165)

Her fidelity remains, along with a total submission to an external power, another's ideals, and resignation to death. She has paradoxically taken her ideals from the very forces oppressing her: she has taken submission as a goal, while all that brought her happiness and fulfillment—the moments following the couple's recognition of their love for each other and the days in Venice—was of a personal nature.

What picture of life could she have had that would have organized her choices in such a way? There is undoubtedly another axis here, not just submission versus self-willed freedom. Dominating Elena's view of life are abstractions like duty and responsibility and a harsh eye-for-an-eye and tooth-for-a-tooth logic. When Elena thinks, and the narrator affirms, that guilt is entailed merely by living, that one person's happiness entails the misfortune of others,[33] what is conjured is a picture of life in which guilt and punishment are to be weighed and balanced with rewards and happiness. The scale is rigid and allows no exceptions; the negative end harshly exacts its toll. And the axis itself determines the distinctness of Turgenev's worldview, for what is positive in life is seen always to come with a price:

there are no rewards without punishment, there is no happiness without guilt. To escape the oppressive logic that governs personal life, one can only yield to impersonal abstractions. Duty as envisaged in Turgenev's world has little to do with personal sharing and caring; it is cold and faceless, somehow at odds with personal fulfillment. The moments of happiness experienced by Elena and Dmitrii showed what life could offer. But these experiences, and what they represented, were overshadowed by an oppressive moral theory dominated by impersonal abstractions, a theory that in its obsession with duty, responsibility, and an avenging fate, left no room for personal fulfillment and personal happiness.

Elena's final letter, as we might expect, is characteristically colored with *lex talionis*—it is his turn to take her with him (for she "caused" his death); her half-hearted admission of personal guilt is consistent with her new worldview: if death reconciles all there is no point in dwelling on guilt.[34] In any case, the grief she caused her parents would be beyond her power to avert.

The axis of self-willed freedom and submission here is the same as Tolstoi's and Dostoevskii's, but the moral qualities of the poles are not as categorical, not merely or clearly representative of evil and good. There is no paradise to be gained by submitting to impersonal and incomprehensible forces beyond her control; nor is there anything obviously evil about her brief quest for personal happiness. What her fate illustrates is that idealism can be built out of self-delusion[35] and pride, and that duty, when connected with personal misfortune and a fatalistic worldview, loses much of its glamour and authenticity. Moral categories in this world Turgenev has created seem strangely out of place, abstractions that have only a remote relationship to interpersonal relations, futile efforts to rationalize modes of behavior that are determined by unseen and incomprehensible forces. Readings that point to the pessimism and even nihilism of this novel have a solid basis.[36]

Early in their relationship, Elena expresses her feelings about the ideal way of life. Here is one of the clearest statements in the novel relating to her conscious motives for admiring Insarov:

> "It seems to me that D. (I will call him D., I like this name: Dimitrii) has such clarity within him because he has given himself entirely to his cause, his dream. What should he be worried about? Whoever has given himself entirely . . . entirely . . . entirely . . . has little sorrow and is not responsible for anything. It is not *I* want, but *it* wants."
>
> (8:83)

Obedience to an impersonal directive has the obvious benefits of enabling her to expel from consciousness what she does not want to think about and to lose all consciousness of self in submission to the cause. Perhaps surrendering will help her to repress painful and unresolved feelings that may go back to her childhood and to evade self-doubts and pangs of conscience of whose nature we become even more aware after Insarov's death. Significantly, both attempts to link up her life with beings who are, as she has imagined them, above such pain and responsibility have been identifications ending in the death of their subjects; Katia and Insarov die, reinforcing Elena's feelings that she was being pursued by a malevolent fate that punished her for pleasures she derived from these relationships. This same fate burdened her with a feeling of responsibility for some unspecified wrong. Surrendering herself entirely to an ideal or a cause proves in the end to be futile, for the inner anxieties she experienced earlier in her life have merely been replaced by more pain and guilt. What is different in the end is that she no longer has hope.

It was Turgenev's characterization of Elena that determined the nature of the novel's moral dimension. She does not share Dmitrii's moral "clarity," and this lack gives her story a tragic dimension. The fascination we have for her character and seemingly impenetrable motivation clearly derives from the suggestive details the author has left in the text, particularly details that indicate how mysterious and complex her relationship with Insarov is in its origins. These details suggest that her fascination with Insarov and her later emotional problems could very well derive from pleasurable and painful experiences of childhood that led her later through idealism to fatalism, experiences that put her under the power of a rigid logic which demanded that personal pleasure be paid for with guilt.

The disorienting perspective Turgenev gives to Elena's idealism is also applied to Insarov's. His noble idealism also has connections with childhood. As a boy, he suffers the rape and murder of his mother (her throat was cut) by a Turkish officer and the execution of his father in an attempt at revenge. If one does not accept his selfless idealism at its face value, Insarov's socially commendable goal of national liberation can easily be seen to conceal an unquenched thirst for revenge. The incident with the German gives a hint that there is something deeper, below the surface, at work when Insarov "avenges" the "foreigner's" insult: the malice of his action seems incommensurate with the German's "crime," suggesting that this rage toward the German (or, later, toward an arrogant Austrian officer in Venice) might be connected with earlier feelings of anger and revenge toward the foreigner who had harmed his parents. The roots of his feelings are even evident in his denials. When asked by Elena whether he ever met the man responsible for his parents' deaths, he responds by diminishing the importance of private revenge:

"Elena Nikolaevna," he began at last, and his voice was more quiet than usual, which almost frightened her. "I understand which man you referred to now. No, I did not meet him, thank God! I did not look for him. It was not because I did not consider myself justified in killing him that I did not look for him—I would have very calmly killed him—but because there is no place for private revenge when the matter is one of national, general vengeance—or no, that word is not suitable—when the matter is one of national liberation. The one would interfere with the other. In its own time the other will not escape either . . . . It will not escape either,"—he repeated and shook his head. (8:67)

And shortly afterward, he tells Elena:

"I am sure you will love us: you love everything that is oppressed. If only you knew how rich our land is! But meanwhile it is trampled on, torn to pieces," he picked up the thought with an involuntary movement of his hand, and his face darkened, "they have taken everything from us, everything: our churches, our laws, our lands; the foul Turks drive us like a herd, slaughter us——" (8:67–68)

Insarov's words and looks here have an effect on Elena: we are told that this conversation marks a turning point in their relationship. As we indicated above, the physical component of his appeal is extremely important; and part of its significance surely is related to the passion and anger that inform his entire physical being when he speaks of revenge, vengeance, and liberation. In view of her own punishing anxieties, she must surely envy his ability to shift his rage from the personal to the impersonal. But whatever the source of his attraction, Insarov's impassioned explanations point to the close relationship between his idealistic feelings and his feelings of personal anger. The personal basis of his anger toward the Turks is transparent: they have taken his parents from him, slaughtered his mother (he used the revealing term *rezhut*—signifying "slaughter with a knife"—in describing how the Turks kill his people) and executed his father. The way in which he handles his rage is illustrated by his slip of the tongue, first replacing "revenge" with "vengeance" and then with "liberation." The biographical details we have been given and the very language Insarov and Elena use with each other throw into doubt the purity of their idealism.[37]

It will not quite do to say simply that it was Insarov as a man of strength and of principle that attracted Elena, for such an explanation leaves too much unexplained. His faith in an all-consuming ideal, much as Katia's in her "God's freedom," is attractive to her—as well as his physical being, his personal tastes (they both like the same flowers), his aura of strangeness (something that no one in Russia has), and the impression he gives of being beyond the ambivalence and anxiety Elena herself suffers from. Dessaix rightly argues that Elena needs Insarov "in order to act out her private fancies and inclinations, to raise her freeing of flies from spiders and care of stray kittens to something more heroic."[38] Elena surely has a need for active good, for doing things for others; and it is not unreasonable to suppose that she has longed to elevate this personal need into an impersonal and "heroic" dedication to a cause. But the psychological details Turgenev adds to the characterization of Elena and her parents—her ambivalent wishes, her strange moods, her recurrent feelings of guilt and responsibility, her mother's indifference toward her and emotional abandonment of her as a child, as well as her father's relatively open infidelity—are the crucial factors that undermine simplistic readings that refer to love based on idealism, idealism broken by fate, and happiness as a vain delusion.

Dessaix is undoubtedly right in arguing that "egotistic impulses" rend the novel's idealistic fabric in the end, though the concept he uses for it—"egocentric romantic idealism"—should be broadened to include consideration of impulses underlying any kind of idealism. Indeed the novel expresses a cynicism about social activity, especially heroic activity in behalf of a cause. Underscoring the futility of heroism as conventionally conceived is the novel's strain of "superstitious pessimism," which points to mysterious suprahuman forces and laws that doom human actions and goals.[39] But surely one of the most prominent forces underlying the streak of pessimism and romantic idealism is psychological: the overwhelming sense of guilt Elena feels forces her into a way of life that can enable her to quell the bad feelings, to lose herself and her personal anxieties in service to others.

Dominating her consciousness, and Dmitrii's as well, is a peculiar logic—the logic of the second axis referred to above—which links the desire for personal fulfillment with guilt and punishment; shortly after he falls ill, Insarov and Elena explicitly refer to this logic:

[Insarov]: "Tell me, has it occurred to you that this illness was sent to us as a punishment?"
Elena looked at him seriously.
[Elena]: "This idea did occur to me, Dmitrii. But then I thought: for what shall I be punished? What duty have I failed to honor? Against what have I sinned? Perhaps my conscience is not like that of others, for it is silent; or, perhaps, my guilt is toward you? I will hamper you, I will stop you."
[Insarov]: "You will not stop me, Elena, we will go together."
[Elena]: "Yes Dmitrii, we will go together, I will go after you. . . . That is my duty. I love you . . . . I do not know another duty." (8:128)

Elena has hoped that her dedication to Insarov and his ideals would free her from these feelings of guilt and punishment, but they persist in her thinking: she cannot help conceiving of adversity as personally directed at her, as a form of punishment for her sins. The categories of sin and punishment help shape her reactions to what happens and determine Elena's final course.

On the moral plane, the novel provides models of self-sacrifice. It shows a person whose basic impulses are to help the poor and oppressed, it depicts models of dedication to high ideals, and it shows people who attach great value to fidelity and truthfulness. The characters representing these moral models gain in vividness and verity as we learn more about them, their past and their thoughts. But past action and behavior illuminate the present in a light that is not always flattering, one that sometimes exposes a less noble side to even the highest of motives. Gains in verity come at a cost: the very factors enhancing the reality of the characters undercut the novel's moral idealism by suggesting that all is not what it seems, that the most praiseworthy of character traits have complex and mysterious origins that may compromise the high value we give to them. One can always choose to adopt a pragmatic course and focus on results of charitable and self-sacrificing behavior rather than motivation or psychological origins. And such a choice may correspond with Turgenev's intentions, for we know how positively he valued what he generally found extremely difficult for himself: total loss of self in dedication to an external ideal (which to him fell into the categories of nation, art, love and knowledge).[40]

What is important may not be whether a particular psychological theory explains the behavior of the two protagonists but simply that Turgenev has given, in details frequently overlooked, unusual depth and suggestiveness to his characterization. The patterns of childhood and adult experiences in the novel diminish the importance conventionally ascribed to consciously articulated ideals and motivations of adults. The complex world given here does not have simple solutions, and clear visions of the moral life seem hopelessly delusional.

Moments of emotional intensity have a value in Turgenev's world, but they stand apart, offering no direct guidance in the moral sphere. If anything, they underscore the indifference of the universe to human experience, for in the context of a lifetime these moments prove to be only tantalizing promises of something better, hints whose unreliability is tragically demonstrated in subsequent events. Elena's longing to find a place where she can "fit" may appear to have been satisfied in the end, and indeed she may be in harmony with the moral order as she and Turgenev conceive it, even though she feels no joy nor relief from feelings of guilt. But if her final position is unsatisfying to us, it is surely because we have another moral theory, one that gives more prominence to the joy of personal relationships and to personal fulfillment and much less to abstract conceptions of duty and responsibility which, when fully realized, amount to annihilation of the self.

TOLSTOI'S "THE DEATH OF IVAN IL'ICH"

"So that's it!" he suddenly pronounced aloud. "What joy!"

TOLSTOI is a towering figure in Russian literature and culture. Much of his prominence derives from the moral passion and earnestness of his search for the right way to live and from his efforts to bring the news to others when he had found it. It is hard to discuss any of his writings without referring to moral issues, for his constant grappling with problems of right and wrong was reflected in everything he wrote. Not all readers find his obsessive concern with morality and his uncompromising directness in treating moral problems palatable.[1] Nor has the worldview he constructed, promoted, and embedded in his fiction achieved any kind of lasting appeal and influence on the world of ideas. People have come to view Tolstoi the moralist with a combination of mild praise for his strong position against violence and bemused indifference toward his vegetarianism, cult of simplicity, and prohibitions against sex.

Tolstoi's moral presence, though often felt in his pre-1880 short stories and novelistic masterpieces, *War and Peace* and *Anna Karenina*, was felt even more sharply in writings after his spiritual crisis of the late 1870s. Largely as a result of this crisis and his perception that most art was morally tainted, he devoted most of his energy in the years following *Anna Karenina* to nonfiction, to study of the world's major religions, to exegesis and translation of the Gospels, and to the exposition of his religious and moral views. Fiction, presumably revalued for its moral potential, returned to his arsenal to play an important role in the mid-1880s; from this time until his death in 1910 he wrote numerous enduring works, which include short stories, plays, and one more large novel, *Resurrection*.

His religious views in later years were controversial, offensive not just to official Russian Orthodoxy but also to those who believed in virtually any conventional Christian doctrines. It cannot be, and was not then, easy for Christians to appreciate the seriousness and intensity of Tolstoi's moral

convictions and at the same time maintain equanimity in the face of his vitriolic attack on conventional Christian doctrine and those who spoke in its behalf. Religion (which Tolstoi defined in a particular way) represented in its usual forms a pernicious threat to the purity of childhood and the integrity of conscience:

> From a very early age—when children are most susceptible to suggestion, when those who bring up children cannot be sufficiently careful about what they communicate to them—children are hypnotized with the absurd, immoral dogmas of the so-called Christian religion, incompatible with our reason and knowledge. Children are taught the dogma of the Trinity, which a healthy reason cannot hold; the coming of one of these three Gods to earth for the redemption of the human race, and his resurrection and ascent into heaven; they are taught to expect a second coming, and punishment with eternal torments for disbelief in these dogmas; and they are taught to pray for their needs; and many other things.[2]

He follows this list of Christian doctrines and practices with a strong accusation: the Trinity, the Resurrection, and hell as a punishment for those who do not believe what the Church teaches are corrupting impositions on susceptible children who will grow up spiritually distorted, no longer believing in their own conscience, having yielded it to the authority of the Church. If people only would learn to trust their own reason and conscience, Tolstoi argues, they could distinguish right from wrong and truth from lies. The established church perverts the spiritual life, robbing people of the ability to make moral choices on their own:

> And when all these notions, which are incompatible with reason, contemporary knowledge, and human conscience are indelibly stamped on the impressionable minds of children, they are left to themselves to find their way as best they can in the contradictions which flow from these dogmas they have accepted and assimilated as the unquestionable truth. No one tells them how they can and should reconcile these contradictions. If, however, theologians try to reconcile these contradictions, their attempts confuse the matter even more. So, little by little, people become accustomed to not trusting their reason (the theologians strongly support this distrust of reason), and therefore to the notion that anything is possible in the world, that people do not have within them anything by means of which they can themselves distinguish good from evil, or falsehood from truth; and that in what is most important for them—their actions—they should be guided not by their reason but by what others tell them. It is understandable what a horrible perversion of a person's spiritual world

must be produced by such an education reinforced in adult life as well by all the means of hypnotization which, by the aid of the clergy, are continually exercised upon the people. (35:188)

It is no wonder Russian religious philosophers have reacted so strongly in condemning this religion that does not have the customary trappings of mystery, sensing behind it an anarchism and distortion of holy writ and ridiculing Tolstoi's mundane obsession with rules of behavior.[3] Although it is quite true that rules against violence, anger, lust, and taking oaths are important components of Tolstoyism, his religious views consist of more than rules. Underlying his views is a belief in the power of reason to direct one's moral life and, more important, a belief that all people have within them a moral sense that can easily be distorted by conventional religious education. And in addition to these beliefs, there is throughout his late writings a deep concern for the right relationship between behavior and attitudes, for actions in harmony with reason and conscience, and for behavior that is engendered spontaneously by the proper attitudes toward life.

To Tolstoi, striving for goodness, truth, and universal brotherhood has no moral validity unless such striving is deeply rooted, unreflective, and untainted by self-consciousness and abstractness.[4] What is important is being oneself, finding the God within, understanding within oneself the meaning of life. "Repentance" (in a quite particular sense, "realizing the right way to live") is possible through self-understanding; brotherhood is a natural result of serving oneself and the God within.

By living truly for oneself, one will be naturally in the right relation to others. In the story "The Death of Ivan Il'ich," the central figure's realization of this truth comes suddenly, and he does not subject it to deep analysis. He simply becomes compassionate; for compassion, a self-sacrificing love for one's neighbor, is what Tolstoi believes people will discover as the meaning of life if they use their conscience as a guide. Ivan's compassion is not a product of abstract reasoning or of judging that one code of conduct or set of rules is more reasonable than another. Because it is not abstract and mechanical, the altruism that flows from this compassion has the right psychological basis: it is firmly rooted within him.

Much of what has been written about Tolstoi is flawed in two ways: first, by a failure to appreciate how important it was for actions to have their source in a morality that was "natural" to a person, not imposed from the outside; and second, by a failure to appreciate how critical Tolstoi was of Christian dogma. It is curious but true that many of the readings of "The Death of Ivan Il'ich" rely on concepts Tolstoi explicitly rejects in his nonfiction and, it will be argued, implicity rejects in the story as well.[5] There is, however, something in this fiction that attracts explications that utilize a conventional Christian perspective, applied with appropriate concepts and terminology.

The purpose of beginning this chapter, which is devoted to the story, with some of Tolstoi's typical pronouncements on Christianity is to establish a context for our discussion of so-called Christian interpretations and to give the basis for a new reading designed to cohere with Tolstoi's views on religion as expressed in his other works. In what follows an effort will also be made to account for the story's perplexing capacity to attract a wide variety of readings. "The Death of Ivan Il'ich" will be shown to illustrate very clearly the genesis of a quintessentially moral—but hardly Christian, except in an extended sense—vision: the hero's experience of dying leads to disorienting experiences culminating in a final vision. And this vision "on the edge" offers a new way of understanding life and an unconventional way of attaining immortality.

"The Death of Ivan Il'ich" (1886) was the first major fictional work by Tolstoi in his post-1880 period. Long regarded as a classic of short fiction, it has stimulated numerous and varied readings. The moral dimension of the story is readily apparent: Tolstoi indicts society's reigning values, personal pleasure and propriety, and advocates compassion and love as the best foundation for living. However, the moral and religious context in which the simple message of compassion and moral authenticity is expressed may not be so apparent to readers. Although it is easy to see that Tolstoi advances compassion as one of the highest of human virtues, the moral framework in which we are to see this conventional Christian virtue is, on close reading, far from clear. Tolstoi is usually accused of being heavy-handed in his manipulation of his readers[6]—and heavy-handedness is usually associated with the unequivocal expression of moral imperatives. But, paradoxically, this work has occasioned a variety of interpretations, suggesting that it is not possible to derive a simple, universally and univocally appreciated and understood moral.

As his first major fictional work in ten years, the story represents Tolstoi's recognition of and return to art as a means for illustrating his moral and religious views. On the basis of the rigorous demands Tolstoi made on his art after 1880, those features he ascribed to true art in his later treatise *What Is Art?* (1898), one might well expect in such a story a simple thesis that would lend itself to virtually uniform readings. In his treatise on art, he would argue for an art accessible to and understandable by everyone, an art with universal situations and a clearly moral function, which was to persuade people that they are all brothers and sisters, that they all have within them manifestations of the same spirit (his notion of "God").

One value clearly offered in "The Death of Ivan Il'ich" is compassion, and there is no doubt that the moral advocacy of compassion for the suffering of others exemplified in this story is what Tolstoi later urged in his essay. The fact remains, however, that the advocacy of compassion is part of a very complex context that is susceptible to readings of a diverse and even contradictory character. These readings concern, in the end, the origins, place, and implications of the compassion Ivan, in his last moments, identifies as the meaning of life. The language and the settings surrounding Ivan's discovery suggest the Resurrection. Tolstoi is hardly paying his respects to conventional Christian dogma here. It can be argued, however, that the Christian suggestiveness is designed both to demonstrate Tolstoi's understanding of Christianity and to give solemnity and significance to the deathbed realizations of an ordinary man. Thus traditional Christianity becomes part of a strategy serving a higher purpose: the advancement of Tolstoi's own, radically revised Christianity. It is important to understand how this revised Christianity differs from other forms.

Tolstoi did not hide his skepticism about prevailing views of salvation and redemption. He was painfully blunt in numerous works: *Harmonization and Translation of the Four Gospels* (1880–1881), "What I Believe" ("*V chem moia vera?*", 1882–1884), "On Life" (1886–1887), "Investigation of Dogmatic Theology" (1881–1882), and "The Kingdom of God Is within You" (1890–1893). In the latter, for example, he condemned the "idolatry" of Russian Orthodoxy, its veneration of icons, and its reliance on church rites, on salvation, on redemption, and on prayer:

> The Sermon on the Mount or the creed: it is impossible to believe in both. And church people have chosen the latter: the creed is taught and read like a prayer in churches, and the Sermon on the Mount is even excluded from gospel readings in churches, so that churchgoers will never hear it, except on days when all of the Gospels are read. And it could not be otherwise: people who believe in a cruel and unreasonable God who has damned the human race and condemned his son as a sacrifice and part of mankind to eternal torment—cannot believe in a God of love. A person who believes in Christ as a God who is coming in his glory to judge and punish the living and the dead cannot believe in a Christ who commands us to turn the other cheek to the offender, to refuse to sit in judgment, and to forgive and love our enemies. [Here follows an attack on the Old Testament, which Tolstoi describes as "filled with abominations ."] A person believing in the teachings and sermons of the church about the compatibility of Christianity with executions and wars no longer can believe in the brotherhood of all people.
>
> But the main thing is that a person who believes in the salvation of people by belief in redemption or in the sacraments can no longer try with all his might to fulfill in life the moral teachings of Christ.
>
> A person who has been taught by the Church the blasphemous doctrine that a person cannot be saved by his own powers but that there is another means, will invariably run to these means, and not to his own powers on which, he is assured, it is a sin to rely. Church doctrine of

any sort, with its redemption and sacrament and even worse, Orthodox doctrine, with its idolatry, excludes the doctrine of Christ.

(28:60–61)

This strong rejection of the authority of official representatives of religion and morality—and repeated insistence on the validity of the individual's unmediated sense of religious and moral truth—is combined with a carefully elaborated alternative religious doctrine. Tolstoi is usually seen as a moralist with rules of behavior, as a religious thinker deriving his philosophy from Matthew and the Sermon on the Mount (and the above quotation supports this view) rather than from the Book of John, with its revelatory concept of being born again that so impressed Dostoevskii. This distinction is acceptable so long as one realizes that Tolstoi views rules as living parts of a person: they inhere in demeanor and are reflected in behavior that is moral not because it is consciously in accordance with rules but because it derives from the proper attitude toward the world—one characterized by love for others. Behavior is then manifested naturally, in harmony with rules. As Tolstoi's many religious writings demonstrate, it was more than recognition of universal brotherhood and sisterhood that he wanted. His religion was a religion of actions in this world, together with the proper attitudes and feelings; he promoted love and compassion, and, especially, avoidance of any kind of violence, whether the coercive activities of the state, of the church, or of other individuals. Compassion was not compassion, however, unless it was sincere and deeply rooted in the distinctive relationship an individual had with the world. This relationship was, Tolstoi insisted, attainable by all who would use their own reason and conscience.

The notion of morality as something instinctive and spontaneous, a guide to action that is accessible to all people without external guidance, finds a suitable niche in Tolstoi's aesthetics as well. Tolstoi believed art should strive "to make that feeling of brotherhood and love of one's neighbor, now attained only by the best members of society, the customary feeling and the instinct of all men. By evoking under imaginary conditions the feeling of brotherhood and love, religious art will train men to experience those same feelings under similar circumstances in actual life; it will lay in the souls of men the rails along which the actions of those whom art thus educates will naturally pass."[7]

Art as moral training "in the realm of feeling," as "laying the rails" for the proper feelings that serve as the basis for the proper actions in life, is what "The Death of Ivan Il'ich" should exemplify if it is to live up to Tolstoi's demanding criteria. And these feelings should help to establish that relationship between people and the world which Tolstoi labeled "religion."

A proper balance between artistic verity and moral explicitness is an obvious desideratum of moral fiction. Ivan is not a superficial vehicle for moral truth, a sacrifice to moral clarity. Nonetheless, there is a strong aura of the ordinary about Ivan that comes dangerously close to depriving him of the fullness we expect in a fictional character. He is given a particularized but unexceptional life as a child, youth, and adult; he is by design to be perceived as a very ordinary person; he is an obvious consequence of Tolstoi's effort to generalize and to represent a way of life familiar to everyone—and a death everyone will some day face. Only as he comes to grips with death does he become truly individualized; and as he yields to the impersonal force he finds within, he becomes even more individualized.

After a conventional childhood and schooling, Ivan makes a career choice, law, that is also unremarkable. Climbing the professional ladder, Ivan became a judge whose work involves condemning or absolving others from guilt and deciding legal right and wrong. Appropriately respectful of his elders and social betters, he makes no waves and observes all of society's conventions, living "comme il faut," developing "stability" when it is expected of him, and acquiring a wife and family at the appropriate junctures. He masters and internalizes the appropriate responses, so that he knows exactly the kind of a wife appropriate for him and the kind of living quarters that would suit his status. Maintaining propriety and avoiding unpleasantness are the ruling principles of his life and those of the people around him.

Living by the law of society, expressed in the twin terms "pleasantness" and "properness" ("priiatnost'" and "prilichie"),[8] leads him progressively to higher and more prestigious positions; it also channels him (because in a Tolstoyan world doing what society desires takes one further and further from meaningful life) into increasingly formalized relations with his family and his colleagues. He reaches the very top of the metaphorical ladder: a judgeship and new living quarters. And in these very quarters, at the pinnacle of his career, at the height of his success, he accidentally tumbles from a real ladder, injures his side, and slowly dies. What seemed to be a simple bruise turns out to be far more serious. In its trivial origin and profound consequences, the accident has much in common with Insarov's catching a cold while securing Elena's passport. But the insights that come to Ivan are radically different.

Having judged and condemned the behavior of others, Ivan is suddenly condemned himself and must now ponder the rightness of his life. This abrupt and ironic turnabout from health to disease is the first in a series of disorienting experiences for Ivan: he will fall from success to failure, experience hope and despair during the course of his illness, deteriorate while imagining he is getting better (chapter 9), change his values (between chapters 6 and 7),[9] and in the end, find his suffering replaced by joy. During his decline, suffering physically and morally, he is himself "formalized" as something unpleasant by former friends, his doctors, his daughter, and his wife; and he is pitied only by his son, Vasia, and his peasant servant, Gerasim.

After intense suffering, Ivan finally comes to understand the falseness of his past life and the nature of real life, and feeling pain and death have been vanquished, he dies. A veritable paradigm in its vivid illustration of the genesis of moral revelation "on the edge of the abyss," the story dramatizes a mythic conversion.[10] Failing in his flight from the ultimate horror, Ivan must confront it; and confrontion leads to moral clarity and victory over the fear of death.

Critics have explored the sophisticated structural patterns Tolstoi employed to undercut the values by which Ivan lived before his illness[11] with particular attention on the first of the twelve chapters, Ivan's funeral—chronologically the end of the story. Here we are given an intimate view of the hypocrisy of Ivan's society, the falseness of conventional relations between people, and the various ways in which they avoid thinking about what is truly important. Tolstoi's moral strategy is transparent: he first presents the values Ivan himself lived by most of his life—and these are the values his society continues to live by after his death—and later shows through Ivan's example those values are inadequate, indeed base. Readers who share the narrator's scorn for the hypocrisy exhibited by most of the people at the funeral are presumably then sympathetically disposed toward Ivan's final revelations. Throughout most of the narrative, while Ivan struggles to discover what went wrong with his life, Tolstoi sustains a critical tone. When Ivan dies, no one except possibly his son shows any awareness that the kind of life promoted by society is based on delusions designed to protect people from unpleasant realities. No one seriously thinks about the most unpleasant of these realities, death; but the story, from the title to the end, keeps this unpleasant reality always in close view.

Earlier drafts indicate that originally Tolstoi had a different strategy. Ivan himself and a friend, not an omniscient narrator, told the story; in the final version the friend, Peter Ivanovich, receives Ivan's diary from his widow, reads it, and then articulates the main message for all to hear:

> "It is impossible, impossible, impossible to live as I have lived and as we all have been living." This is what Ivan Il'ich's death and his notes disclosed to me. I shall describe how I regarded life and death before this event; and I shall relate his notes as they have come to me, supplementing them only with those details I learned from his domestics.[12]

Tolstoi's decision not to illustrate, through Peter Ivanovich, the desired effect of Ivan's story (renunciation of one's previous way of life) but to imply it through Ivan's example alone marked a clear gain in the story's persuasive power. Although the presence of a converted friend of Ivan would be consonant with Tolstoi's didactic aim—it might underscore the thesis that ordinary human life is false and immoral—it would also tend to blunt the effect of the ending, the manner in which Ivan comes to realize that ordinary life is immoral. The newly converted friend is too explicitly moralistic and too easily converted into a critic of society. Moreover, there is a problem of balance: the friend's critique gives too much weight to the negative thesis and not enough to the right way to live, which Ivan discovered only at the end. With the diary narrative, rendering Ivan's last inner thoughts and revelations would present difficulties.

In the early version, the negative moral—the shallowness of conventional life—is succinctly summarized and the persuasive model laid bare: the story of Ivan's life has had a strong effect on his friend, the one we may assume Tolstoi wished us to feel as well. The story is designed to make us question the way in which we have been living and, ultimately, to renounce it. But in the end Tolstoi elected not to model the effect of Ivan's personal story in the verbal response of another character. He chose instead to present the story through the eyes of a narrator who was separate from the events but who had access to thoughts and feelings of all of the characters. Tolstoi also fashioned the events so that only Ivan undergoes a radical change in perspective.

The result is a clearer focus on Ivan and the model of "right" living he becomes in the end, a model unobscured by demonstrating the effects of the example on others. Such blurring in focus and its attendant possible violation of verity could very well have undermined the evocation of feelings Tolstoi strove for. Replication of the appropriate response is too strong a requirement to place on moral art if it is to differ from homily. Laying the rails is part of a program of education and training that can hardly be expected to obtain immediate results.

When Tolstoi recast the story in the third person, Peter Ivanovich was given a different role. We learn that neither he, one of Ivan's best friends, nor Praskov'ia Fedorovna, Ivan's wife, is ultimately converted or affected by Ivan's example, a fact that considerably reduces the optimism engendered by Ivan's joyful revelations. Tolstoi was only too aware of the power of his society's modes of living and thinking, and of course he harbored few illusions about the human capacity for self-delusion.[13] People in Ivan's world are dedicated to the pursuit of pleasure and comfort and to the avoidance of what is discomforting: they cannot imagine their own deaths.

Nevertheless the narrator shows considerable interest in portraying Peter's thoughts and discomfort at the funeral. Three times in the first chapter Peter is given a chance to comprehend the significance of Ivan's death, and thus the meaning of life. In the old days they had been close, they had gone to school together, and in maturity they played cards together. And Peter, more sensitive than other friends of Ivan, had recognized early that Ivan was dying (26:62). The first chance Peter has to step out of society's perspective, which conceals what is really important, is when, looking at the corpse of his friend, he sees that Ivan's face seems more handsome and significant in death than in life. And his expression indicates that "what had to be done was done, and done right." This sense of "fitness" reflects Ivan's achievement of what he had been striving all through his illness to discover, the "right" way of life. "Right" here and throughout the story (Ivan several times will say that his life was "ne to," "the wrong thing"; he lived it "the wrong way") is not necessarily a moral category but an assessment of aptness or congruence with some standard or set of standards. Also within Ivan's expression was a "reproach" or "reminder to the living." Something in what he saw was unpleasant to Peter; so he crosses himself, turns, and leaves, in the kind of pain one feels upon recognizing a truth one is conditioned to avoid.

The second moment causing Peter discomfort occurs when he hears from Praskov'ia how much Ivan suffered in his final days (26:66)—it "horrified" him, and he feels "fearful" because Ivan has lived an ordinary life: one would not expect it to end with extraordinary suffering. His reference to the unfairness of suffering underlines an important issue in the story: why does such an ordinary man have to suffer so much? Is there an explanation for the extreme pain the author gives him? One answer relates to Tolstoi's strategy: Ivan's suffering has a shock value;[14] Peter is disoriented enough to begin to think death and suffering could happen to him (26:67). "It is horrible"—"strashno"—is repeated. What restores his calm is the socially conditioned reflex. "The customary thought came" ("prishla obychnaiia mysl'") that it happened to Ivan, not him, and he believes that it could not happen to him. This, of course, mirrors Ivan's reaction in the early stages of his illness, when he would become concerned about his recovery and resist thinking that he too could die. Like Ivan, Peter evaded thoughts of his own death.

But there is another possible explanation for the incongruity between Ivan's suffering and the quality of his life. One part of the "picture" of life that Tolstoi attacks is the notion that there is a link between sin and suffering. Though Ivan has lived superficially and falsely, he was no monster; and his sins have hardly been commensurate with his suffering and illness. Although pain and the fear of death may have connections with one's view of life, this relationship has nothing to do with a legalistic balancing of the scales, in which the pain of punishment is directly related to the immorality of one's life. We have seen in On the Eve how Elena came to expect some relationship between the punishing guilt she felt, the misfortunes she experienced, and her attempts to find personal happiness and fulfillment. Tolstoi's alternative, as expressed through Ivan's final vision, provides a different view: someone with the right understanding of life is "really" immune to physical pain (although others may think the pain extreme) and need not be concerned about mental and moral suffering.

Before he leaves the funeral, Peter sees Ivan's two children, the daughter, Liza, looking "gloomy" and "angry," and the tearful Vasia; and in the hall he has a brief conversation with Ivan's servant, Gerasim. Peter's suggestion that Ivan's death was a pity elicits Gerasim's reply that it was God's will, and that all will end up that way (26:68). The word "pity" (expressed with the impersonal adverb "*zhalko*") will recur as a leitmotiv, losing, as the story progresses, its conventional meaning and strengthening its connections with authentic compassion.[15]

Although it is clear in the story that Peter has not seen the truth, he is obviously more receptive to it than others at the funeral, especially associates and fellow cardplayers like Shvarts (whose very name suggests the absence of the "light" of truth); he is also clearly more open to the truth than Ivan's wife. Even though in this version he is no longer idealized as in Tolstoi's early draft, Peter, obviously sensitive to the deeper meaning of Ivan's death, retains a limited susceptibility to understanding the error of his own ways.[16] Perhaps since his patronymic makes him the son of Ivan, he will some day see the light and carry the message, as did his biblical namesake (who, like Peter Ivanovich, had earlier missed three opportunities to admit the truth); for that matter, Ivan also has a symbolic biblical lineage: Ivan, whose name is the Russian version of John (the precursor of Christ), is by patronymic the son of Il'ia, or Elijah, the Old Testament precursor of the Messiah. The biblical resonance of the names in the story helps to generate an aura of seriousness and religious significance.

Thus the central issues the story will deal with—the falseness of conventional life, the meaning of pain and death, and the role of pity and compassion in authentic life—are suggested through Peter and his perception of Ivan's life and their society. This first chapter, which is both beginning and end, plays an important role in setting the context and establishing the values that will be examined. The final chapter, however, is even more important; for here Tolstoi deals with the moral concerns of the dying man, not just the values of those who have come to his funeral. It is here, in the last chapter, that Tolstoi distinctively marks his moral purposes with his depiction of Ivan's vital transformation. The amazing variety of readings this chapter has stimulated gives testimony to its key position in the story as well as its mysterious richness.

Though we are told in the beginning of the story and in the last chapter that Ivan screams for his last three days, other events—mostly psychological—in the last chapter push our awareness of his pain into the background. His screaming, which begins when he recognizes that the end has come and presumably continues without abatement until the end, is much less noticeable than in previous chapters. And the sense we have that it is somehow less testifies to the shift in emphasis Tolstoi has directed as we make the transition to his presentation of the positive side of his truth.

In each of the previous chapters we watch minute changes in Ivan's perceptions and temperament, his physical and psychological condition; subsuming all is his suffering. Now the pain has begun to move into the background, yielding its place to Ivan's revelations, which are of such importance that they will occupy the center of his consciousness. In fact, in his last hours Ivan seems unaware of his screaming; he is oblivious to his physical condition, undoubtedly because of his new view of life.

Ivan's mindset in this last period of his life can be seen as a stage of dying, the end of his depression and the beginning of his acceptance of death.[17] Paradoxically, the proximity of death is linked to recurring thoughts of childhood and images of birth. Ivan loses his ability to speak, a development that intensifies for the reader the physical pain he feels, the inefficacy of all verbalization, and the regressive quality of his experience. He tries to say something ("I don't want . . ." ["to die," presumably]) but instead merely howls with the sound of the final vowel of the word "want" (the long "u" sound of "*khochu*"). That Ivan's spiritual regeneration may lie in a return to the purity and innocence of childhood is suggested not only by the "babylike" sounds he makes as his defenses fall, but also by recurring thoughts of his childhood. In chapter 10, for example, he recalls the flavor of plums he ate as a child, and the smell of his striped leather ball: more and more he realizes that life then had been full, fresh, innocent, and untainted.

Tolstoi very accurately renders what many have observed about dying people: they are like children in their need for attention and their dependence on the care of others.[18] Screaming, of course, also fits the pattern of correspondences: that is how we come into the world and attract attention vital to our well-being. But also suggested is the inadequacy of language to convey the nature of his experience. Tolstoi, who used words so well, chose to make his moral statement in a different "language" here.[19] Tolstoi described the function of art as "laying the rails" for the correct feelings. These rails are laid by paradox, metaphor, and Ivan's sudden insight.

We are told that during these three final days, time did not exist for Ivan, that he continued to struggle in a "black sack" or "black hole," forced into it by an invincible power. But the source of his horror is ambiguous, both in his resistance and his yielding to the power forcing him deeper into the sack. The imagery suggests a high degree of disorientation, a life void of its customary points of reference:

> He struggled as one sentenced to death struggles in the hands of an executioner, knowing that he cannot save himself; and with each moment he felt that, despite all efforts in the struggle, he was getting closer and closer to what terrified him. He felt that his suffering came both from being shoved into that black hole and, still more, from not being able to crawl into it. What prevented him from crawling into it

was his claim that his life had been good [*"khoroshaia"*]. That very jus-
tification of his life enchained him and did not allow him to pass forward, and tormented him more than anything. (26:112)

Trying to rationalize a bad life has kept Ivan from advancing to a higher
state, though, paradoxically, this "advance" means "crawling" *("prolezt'")*
deeper into the hole.[20] The unconventional nature of Ivan's journey is cap-
tured in paradoxes, in the notion of advancing by crawling deeper. Recognition of what is really important in life is impossible with conventional perspectives. Seeing the truth through the abandonment of rationalization is
difficult and demands radical reorientation.

Ivan is still at the level of "torment" *("muchen'e")*, which will be contrasted
with a yet-to-come later state. There is a new development, however: now
his thoughts, not his physical condition, are causing him pain. All that is associated with his physical being recedes more and more into the background
as he sheds old ways of looking at the world.

Ivan's new orientation is intimately connected with the recurring image
of the black sack (alternatively, the black hole) from which he cannot escape.
The image possibly originates in his visualization of his illness: he has earlier
tried to make concrete what was causing him pain, vividly imagining the
"blind intestine" or cecum, which some of his doctors had identified as the
source of his ills.[21] The black sack also suggests the womb, an identification
that makes Ivan's pains analogous to labor pains. Labor pains can then be
linked with his recollections of childhood, his nonverbal communication,
and ultimately his "rebirth." Finally, the image of the black sack suggests
the intestine again, and a particular situation: Ivan wishes to escape from a
"constipated," restricted life. Tolstoi's linkage of scatology and eschatology
is not without philosophical precedent.[22]

Within the "sack" Ivan is subjected to surrounding pressures; he wants to
"crawl through," but something "did not allow him to pass forward" *("ne
puskalo vpered")*. The concept of "passing" from one plane to another is crucial. Shortly, in a slip of the tongue, Ivan will make a perhaps unconscious
request to pass on to the next plane: "Let me pass" (*"propusti"*). This is one of
a large number of verbs with the prefix *"pro-,"* which though relatively common as a Russian prefix, appears in this section with uncommon frequency.
Such a prefix, denoting actions and movements "through" something, as
well as movements that are "complete," underscores Ivan's need to "pass
through" to a different state. Multiple perspectives, all designed to intensify
the event's meaning, come to bear on Ivan's "passage." First, while in pain,
he feels a blow to the chest and side. The force impels him: "he fell through
[*"provalilsia"*] into the hole, and there, at the end of the hole, something lit
up." Now all that happens is beyond conscious control, and Ivan acts as if a
force is working through him.

The narrator compares the experience of falling and then seeing a light to the sensations of a person in a train who is confused about which way the car is going: first confusion, then orientation, a realization of the car's true direction. The train motif ironically closes what it began: it was on a train that Ivan first made the contact that led to his new job, a meeting that led to his move, his accident, his sufferings, his revelation, and his death.

Ivan's spiritual turnabout is expressed in vivid terms of violence and disorientation.[23] Coming to the truth is painful and involves radical reversals of former perspectives. Now Ivan understands that his past life was not right, and he explicitly says so:

> "Yes, everything was wrong ["*ne to*"]," he said to himself, "but that doesn't matter."
>
> "It's possible, it's possible to do it the 'right' way ["*sdelat' 'to*'"]. But what is the 'right' way?" he asked himself, and then grew quiet.
>
> (26:112)

The moment of revelation comes at the end of the third day, only an hour before Ivan's death. This explicit reference to time, with its biblical suggestiveness, marks and sets up expectations for the approach of a redemptive moment, a "resurrection." The imagery, however, suggests a new birth, and thus a clean slate or state of originary purity, rather than a resurrection, or returning to life from the dead. Rebirth evokes the black sack with the light at the end, the pressures to remain in the sack but also to escape, and the final liberation from constraint and emergence into the light. Moreover, present at this rebirth is the archetypal family—father, mother, and son. The perspectives are askew, however, for it is the father who is to be "born." The presence of other characters during Ivan's final moments expresses Tolstoi's belief that morality is a matter of compassionate actions and sincere feelings directed toward others. The relational, contextual, and interpersonal emphasis Tolstoi gives here to moral behavior is at odds with the customary representation of his ethics as bound by rule and logic.[24]

Ivan's son has crept (again a verb with a "*pro-*" prefix, "*prokralsia*") into the room to join his mother and father. Ivan places his hand on his boy's head, with powerful effect on all: the boy grabs the hand and kisses it, tearfully expressing his compassion. This is a crucial scene, wordless, with a focus on spontaneous action, direct and unmediated human communication, not conscious and imitative behavior according to social dictate or moral rule. With a biblical suggestiveness derived from the emphasis on compassion and Vasia's role (Christ urged people to become "as little children"), the scene makes vivid a significant feature of Tolstoi's religion.[25]

Disguised here is the general outline of Christ's crucifixion.[26] The central figure is condemned to death, and next to him are two others, also condemned (as mortals); Ivan's wife and son stand here as tokens for the two thieves. The analogy is reinforced by Tolstoi's choice of verbs. Vasia "crept" or, literally, "stole" into the room: the association with theft exists in both the Russian and the English. What happens next underscores the analogy, making it clear that Vasia represents the unnamed thief who suffered alongside Christ, the one Christ consoled (Luke 23:42–43). In Tolstoi's extensively revised version of the Gospels, Christ says that the thief by his action of ignoring his physical well-being and asking Christ to remember him in his "kingdom" is already in "paradise." Paradise as something this side of death, as a state accessible to the living, is a notion with important implications for our understanding of Ivan's final experiences. Here Ivan's son, who already knows authentic compassion, is already in "paradise." Whether he will remain there or be seduced by the world of the pleasant and the proper is an open question at the end of the story.

Vasia's intuition and compassion give him an unerring sense of what could help his father. And this help is nonverbal, silent, simply tears and the pressure of a hand. Emphasizing the simultaneity of events, Tolstoi repeats what has happened to Ivan in these moments: he has fallen through, seen the light, realized that his life has not been what it should have been. But in addition—and this is the new element—he recognizes that it is still possible to correct matters. Falling silent, he listens for an answer to his question about the "right" way of life. And at this point he feels his hand being kissed. Tolstoi presents the same temporally limited series of mental and physical events from different perspectives, reinforcing Ivan's realization and its connection with the authentic emotional contact represented by his son's compassionate gestures.

Rebirth is appropriately connected with the parent-child model. But here the roles are unconventional, the perspective and orientation are different; for it is the father and son, not the mother and son, who are emphasized. Now Ivan looks at his son and pities him. Vasia is the only one in his world whom he has pitied: earlier, in chapter 8, the narrator has said that Vasia "was always pitiable to him. . . ." And what is more, "besides Gerasim, it seemed to Ivan Il'ich that Vasia alone understood and pitied him" (26:105). The glow of compassion is now extended to include Praskov'ia as well; for as she approaches him, he feels sorry for her too. In practically all previous contacts with her in the story he has felt hatred for her; and we have learned that earlier in their marriage, he distanced himself from her emotionally because her querulousness and irritability during pregnancy were unpleasant to him, as they introduced into his well-ordered and rigidly controlled life an alien and threatening element. Immersing himself in his work and in his social games, he formalized the relationship with her so that Praskov'ia could not interfere with his "pleasant" life. But in the present, as his illness progressively worsens and as he comes closer to his "birth," she treats him as he has treated her, refusing to regard him as a suffering human being. He begins to hate her even more, as she represents in his mind his old way of life, the pleasure principle with all of its hypocrisy; and much of his anger, though displaced, is directed at her. Something has happened now, however, at the hour of his death; something in the situation has helped him to answer his question about the "right" way of life, and he no longer hates but instead pities her.

This "something" is not the product of logical, rational thinking; rather, a new way of looking at the world has come to Ivan at a time when he is receptive to it, when he is ready to abandon rationalization for his past way of life. The model for realizing moral truth in Tolstoi's writing at this time is not one that depends on or utilizes conventional moral arguments. Tolstoi directs that we look at the world honestly, and not through the elaborate defenses and rationalizations society has instructed us to build, and then wait for the truth to be disclosed. The lies have heretofore distorted the one true perspective.

Ivan's new understanding of life is reflected in a new interest in others, an attention not to his own personal well-being but to the feelings of those around him. He recognizes that he is torturing his wife and son and that his death will make their life easier:

> "Yes, I am tormenting them," he thought. "They are sorry, but it will be better for them when I die." He wanted to say this but did not have the strength to speak. "But why speak? I have to do something," he thought. With a glance he indicated his son to his wife and said:
> "Take him away . . . sorry for him . . . and for you too. . . ." He tried to say "Forgive" too, but said "Forward," and no longer having the strength to correct himself, waved his hand, knowing that whoever needed to understand would understand. (26:113)

The supreme moral attitude of compassion, the turn from the self to others, and the awareness of and concern for the suffering of others are emphasized repeatedly in the text, though English translations usually obscure this fact. The phrase "they are sorry" is too ambiguous in this context for "*im zhalko*"; better here is "they are sorry for him, they have pity for him." The expression exactly parallels Ivan's previous expressions of pity for his wife and son ("*Emu stalo zhalko ego*," and "*Emu zhalko stalo ee*"). The key word "*zhalko*" (an adverbial form for "pity" and "sorry for") when used with noun or pronoun objects denoting people, suggests having pity for someone.

What is unusual now is that Ivan's wife, with mouth open, tears on her nose and cheeks, and an expression of despair, is perceived by him as showing pity—and may indeed be experiencing such a feeling. Compassion has united Ivan, his wife, and his son. Sympathy and feelings of pity are fundamental to Tolstoi's religion and to his ethics, and his attempts to spread his religion to others depend on the potential infectiousness of compassion. The scene illustrates this potential in exemplary fashion: authentic compassion is shown in all its glory. Its effects, however, are not lasting for Ivan's wife; for in the first chapter she is shown to be once again in the world of the pleasant and the proper. The moment leaves its imprint only on Vasia, who has remained virtually untainted by society's evil influence.[27]

The didactic point of the story is transparent: examples of moral behavior have an infectious power, a power Tolstoi must rely on if his moral message is to be effective. The power can fade, however, once the example is gone and society's values have reestablished their dominance. The moral discussion focuses on behavior that is spontaneously and naturally moral: Ivan abjures talking, for he wants to do something. The need for action flows naturally from the feeling of compassion. Moreover, real compassion may be itself an action. The deed, not the words, is what is emphasized now. Action flowing spontaneously from the correct moral feeling has a much more important role than words and proper rituals.

The context makes it clear that Ivan has in mind not just action in general but completing an action already referred to ("*sdelat'*" is the verb); such an action could include dying, as well as showing compassion. But the verb has a mundane dimension as well. Ivan gives a concrete and very specific indication to his wife that she should remove their son from the room ("*Uvedi*," "lead him away"); but even in this case there is ambiguity, for the imperative could also suggest leading him away from the kind of life she and Ivan have lived, and from the values their society has supported. Ivan adds, again, that he feels sorry for her as well ("*zhalko . . . i tebia. . .*"). Feeling and expressing his compassion constitute Ivan's last actions.

Ivan's attempt to say "Forgive me" has been subjected to various interpretations. His conscious intention to ask for forgiveness has been embraced by those who have understood it as an appropriate response to his causing suffering in others; moreover, it would be the conventional thing for Christians to say, an expression of repentance. But there are other possibilities as well: the words point to Christ's, "Father, forgive them, for they know not what they do"; in this reading the attempt reinforces Ivan's Christ-like role. And perhaps what he planned to say is no longer as important as what he actually said under the influence of his new perception of the world.[28]

Ivan could not say "forgive" ("*prosti*") but uttered instead a word with the same first syllable ("*pro-*"): "*Propusti*," "Let me pass" (or possibly, "Let it pass"). The usual English translation, "forego," and to a lesser extent the word used in translating it above ("Forward"), obscures the possibilities inherent in Ivan's slip of the tongue: that he is asking to pass through into another state, to the light in the other realm, or, in effect, to death. On this reading what is shown is Ivan's unconscious assimilation of what Tolstoi would view as real moral understanding, understanding rooted in authentic religious feeling, not conventional religious doctrine. Ivan wishes his spirit to pass out of his body into another state, to merge with God.

Unable to correct what he said, Ivan nevertheless is confident that he has done what was required. Many English translations unjustifiably introduce

a capitalized pronoun, suggesting that God is the one who would understand. The phrase in Russian is ". . . *poimet tot, komu nado*," a very succinct
"that one will understand who needs to." There are no capital letters in
Soviet or pre-Soviet editions, although the possibility that God is the one
who will understand is not excluded. In any case, there is no reason to think
that the "one" referred to is a divinity. Praskov'ia, Vasia, and readers are
privy to what Ivan says, and if the message is compassion, then it has surely
been understood.

Insights in these last moments come quickly:

And suddenly it became clear to him that that which had been
wearing him down and which would not go away was suddenly and
all at once going away, on two sides, on ten sides, on all sides. He felt
pity for them, he had to do something so that it would not be painful for them. He had to release them and release himself from this
suffering.   (26:113)

Again pity and the need for active good are conjoined: releasing his wife
and son from suffering flows naturally from his feelings of pity. The verb
for "release himself" is "*izbavit'sia,*" with connotations of the biblical "deliverance from." Tolstoi's language aptly catches the exhilaration of freedom when everything that has been oppressing Ivan from all sides suddenly
falls away. Deliverance here is very concrete and of this world: it is an action
invoked and accomplished easily because it is derived from compassion.
Freeing others from suffering, which is a variation of doing unto others as
they would do unto you, is a notion shared by the conventional Christian
ethos and Tolstoi's Christianity. But Ivan's behavior is not so much obedience to the rule as it is spontaneous action in accordance with it. And this
spontaneity is an essential ingredient of Ivan's final experiences.

No longer subject to the power of the physical world, Ivan asks himself
what happened to the pain. He even apostrophizes it: "How good, and how
simple," he thought. "And the pain?" he asked himself. "Where was it?
Well, where are you, pain?"

The pain has diminished and almost disappeared. It is totally under the
dominion of Ivan's new consciousness of the "right" way, his new understanding of life. And when he senses it, he accepts it: "Yes, here it is. Well,
what of it? Let the pain be" (26:113). The parallel question, "Where is
death? Where is it?", leads to equally unexpected results:

He searched for his former habitual fear of death and did not find it.
"Where is it? What death?" There was no fear because there was no
death either.
Instead of death there was light.

"So that's it!" he suddenly pronounced aloud. "What joy!" (26:113)

In this simple experience Tolstoi expresses his alternative to the customary religious conception of "resurrection." It is a resurrection-rebirth that occurs before death, not after, and only after Ivan realizes how to live.

For him all this happened in a single instant, and the meaning of this instant did not change any more. For those present, his agony continued for another two hours. In his chest something rattled; his wasted body twitched. Then the rattle and the wheezing became less and less frequent. (26:113)

The sufferings *("muchen'ia")* have now turned into agony *("agoniia")*, the "predeath state of the organism." In this state, there need be no mental or physical suffering, and in Ivan's case there is none; thus, the English can be misleading, for our word "agony" usually has strong connotations of pain. Ivan is no longer suffering, nor is he even in the realm of time and space, the physical and the changing ("the meaning of the moment remained unchanged"). The pain and mental torment that have preceded Ivan's death are replaced in his consciousness by light and life. There is just one more step:

"It's all over!" said someone above him.
He heard these words and repeated them in his soul. "Death is over," he said to himself. "It is no more."
He drew in his breath, stopped in the middle of a sigh, stretched out and died. (26:113)

In Russian there is just a single word for "It's all over!": *"Koncheno!"* Having been uttered by someone "above," the word carries no little suggestiveness concerning divine origin. But because it provokes Ivan's response—his clarification that not life is over but, paradoxically, death—it is very doubtful that the word is God's. The meaning of Ivan's correction is clear: with his new knowledge of life, death no longer threatens him and no longer has any power over him. The solemnity and seriousness of the moment are enhanced by the religious connotations of the language and the context. It does not matter that the religious suggestiveness derives from a religion Tolstoi finds pernicious in its conventional forms. The feelings evoked by the scene are directed by Tolstoi.

The term *"koncheno"* is ripe with religious meaning. Ivan's final words, and the one uttered from above, parallel words spoken at Christ's death which suggested fulfillment of a divine plan ("It is accomplished!"). And of course this meaning is consistent with and finds its place in Tolstoi's ethics, which is also based on behavior according to a universal, "divine" plan.

There is every reason to believe that Ivan's life is part of the same plan as Christ's: to Tolstoi, Christ was a man who died as men do.[29] In his exegetical writings, Tolstoi denied any form of personal resurrection after physical death. When Ivan gives the completed action "It's all over" a more specific referent, changing it to "Death is over; it is no more," he is giving expression to his predeath "resurrection." Death is now a meaningless concept to him, for he has been born, in fact, into a new comprehension of life. Tolstoi has mapped out a new area for the application of the terms "life," "death," and "rebirth." Ivan's banishment of death and his rebirth are derived from his newly discovered religion; and in this new relationship (to Tolstoi, religion is one's relationship to the universe), he finds himself in harmony with the law of life, expressed as love and compassion for one's fellow human beings.

Death is a concept appropriate to the corporeal and the material sides of existence. It has no relevance to one who lives by the spirit. Tolstoi's new usage, translated into the old terminology, is that the rule of death over Ivan's life has been overthrown so that physical demands, including everything determined by or defined with concepts of space and time, no longer has any power.[30] His "rebirth" inheres in his new view. Convincingly orchestrating this rebirth required the use of an array of sophisticated artistic devices.

Knowing well the powers of art, Tolstoi used them to make his new picture of life, rebirth, and death convincing. Within the story's complex structure, there is a fascinating interplay of verbal elements that belies the usual claims made about Tolstoi's stylistic transparency and directness. We have already seen how he has manipulated conventional religious terminology to serve his purposes. If the music of Beethoven could lead to adultery and violence ("The Kreutzer Sonata"), then surely art's persuasive power could be utilized as a force for the good. His task was to put this power in the service of a higher moral purpose.

The devices he implemented in his moral strategy took a variety of forms. We have seen how he put the end of the story in the first chapter, how he suggested some of the major themes in the story through the perceptions of Peter Ivanovich, how he manipulated imagery (of the black sack, for example) to expand the meaning of Ivan's rebirth. In addition, phrases with one meaning in Ivan's early life—he was descibed as the "phoenix" of the family, and he received a medallion inscribed *"Respice finem"*—took on a deeper, ironic, meaning at the end of his life.

One of the most effective of Tolstoi's utilizations of language was his exploitation of the grammatical fact that the words for "pain" and "death" are both feminine and thus share the same pronoun *("ona")*. Interweaving linguistic and psychological phenomena, he linked both words in Ivan's consciousness by their common pronoun ("it" in English) and used its indefinite referentiality to suggest the indefinite but paralyzing horror and fear

Ivan experienced. Moreover, the interconnection of pain and death suggested an identical provenance, their common derivation from the same order or realm—the physical, the realm from which Ivan would eventually free himself. The preestablished connection of pain and death facilitated the natural turn from pain to death at the end of the story; both pain and death are by this time meaningless to Ivan, no longer oppressing him. And ironically, the victory over pain and death is a victory for "life," also a feminine noun.

Other key words linked both thematically and linguistically are "light" and "death." Thematically associated with the bottom of the black sack, "light" ("*svet*") is also the word for "world"—a meaning that connects Ivan's seeing the light with his coming into the world (i.e., being born). The expression "that world" ("*tot svet*") in Russian connotes a world beyond death, which in Tolstoi's philosophy means a life not in heaven but one lived on earth in accordance with God's plan. It is this life, which Ivan realizes he is now living, which moves Ivan to exclaim "What joy!"

The narrative account of Ivan's life had opened (chapter 2) with a statement from the narrator about Ivan's life being "most simple, ordinary, and horrible": "*Proshedshaia istoriia zhizni Ivana Il'icha byla samaia prostaia i obyknovennaia i samaia uzhasnaia*" (26:68). We discover in these simple, profound words that it was simple in the wrong way. His way of living was not right; for it was anchored in society's values, in the pleasant and the proper. And near death, he discovers that the right way to live is really very simple (though his reorientation was difficult). The right way entails pity, compassion, and living for others. Key words are again associated by sound texture, mostly by initial consonant clusters; and their linguistic connection underlines their ironic relationship: "*priiatno*," "*prilichno*" or "*prilichie*," and "*prostaia*" ("it is pleasant," "it is proper" or "properness," "simple") all lead, by way of "*provalilsia*," "*prokralsia*," "*prosti*," "*propusti*," and finally "*puskai*" ("fell," "stole into," "forgive," "let pass," and "allow") to Ivan's realization. Stylistic and structural devices all work harmoniously to present the moral message.[31]

Tolstoi's use of the devices listed above can be approached from several perspectives. His linguistic play with prefix, pronoun, and metaphor is surely related to his plan of undercutting civilized, conventional life in society, with its ossified and complacent evasions, its card games and empty posturing designed to conceal authentic life. Tolstoi leads readers to look at this reality in new ways, to understand simple expressions like "it's a pity" in terms of real compassion—to distrust language, for it represents society's power to conceal authentic values. He dethrones language in its conventional forms through Ivan, who rejects it in favor of acting, or fails to say what he means, and who ultimately creates new meanings out of conventional terms. Compassion, pain, life, and death are revalued, uprooted from comfortable points of reference in the world of the pleasant and the proper.

Language is a sphere of power to Tolstoi; and he will use it, turn it inside out, and create his own moral order and world (which he will call the real world). Tracing Christianity along its own fault lines with an iconoclastic severity, he will tear it from the hands of clerics and the grips of mystery and miracle, and embed it in an overarching philosophy more compatible with his own moral and metaphysical longings. His iconoclasm comes to a head in his reversal of customary distinctions and cherished dogmas: life, death, rebirth and resurrection. Challenging the conventional connections betweeen signifier and signified, exposing the flimsy basis of his society's linguistic and perceptual frames, he offers a new philosophy of life which he thinks captures the way things really are. In his quest for what is primary he never doubted that it existed, that there was an origin brimming with moral purity. Tolstoi took what people considered primary and made it secondary, derivative, and morally suspect. He revised, rephrased, and reformulated Christian dogma, using its semiotic system but altering most of its signifieds on the basis of empirically grounded common sense. What resulted, beyond his own apostasy, was a religion focused on this world, on actions and behavior.

Despite Tolstoi's insistent claims that his philosophy was in conformity with the demands of reason, the source of the good remained something vaguely mystical, a God within to which one must yield, an originary principle of love carrying overtones of Schopenhauer, Eastern religions, and mystical Christianity.[32] This suprapersonal foundation (which Tolstoi did not find in conflict with reason) supported a very practical moral edifice. Loving one another, having compasssion, giving of oneself for others—all this is eminently moral, and all this is possible in our everyday world. His philosophy of life is testable, for the consequences of perceiving the world the way he wants us to are observable in our behavior and authenticated in our personal experience.

If we want a reading of the story that coheres with what we know of the author and with other works by the author, then it is obviously necessary to consider Tolstoi's religious views, as he expressed them in a wide variety of writings from the late 1870s until his death in 1910. Striving for this kind of coherence does not, of course, amount to denying the significance of other frames of reference on other levels; thus an account of the story that examines it from a hermeneutic Heidegerrian perspective can be fascinating and illuminating,[33] even if such an approach carries with it concepts, assumptions, and terms quite unfamiliar to Tolstoi. Interpretations, of whatever cast, attain scope and power on the basis of what they do with whatever the text provides. Even moral-religious readings of a conventional sort can achieve a surface plausibility. But these sorts of readings, which run the usual risks associated with vague religious terminology and controversial theological conceptions, also come up against an even more formidable problem: it is hard to justify a reading based on notions we know the author inveighed against so persistently and vehemently for more than thirty years. One is then in the curious position of having to demonstrate that Tolstoi was an Orthodox Christian despite himself, and that, as V. V. Zenkovsky[34] maintains, he actually believed in the divinity of Christ and the truth of the Church and its sacraments.

But not all were willing to save Tolstoi for Christianity. The writer Vladimir Korolenko moved to the opposite position (which was equally unsatisfying), considering Tolstoi an atheist and Antichrist who concealed himself in religious rhetoric.[35] As George Kline observed, Tolstoi's radical reformulation of religious conceptions was bound to provoke opposition; and his habit of referring to his concordance and translation of the Gospels as "his" Gospels could only infuriate those steeped in the traditions of reverence for Holy Writ. Also infuriating was the apparent simplicity of Tolstoi's religion (Ivan says, "How good and how simple!"): Lev Shestov saw in this simplicity a potential compatibility with atheism, and Nikolai Berdiaev complained that there was no mystery, only rules.[36] What is missing in the vast literature concerned with "The Death of Ivan Il'ich" is a satisfactory reading in Tolstoyan terms, a reading that relates the work to the philosophical and religious issues he was struggling with in years following his "conversion."

Although they were expressed in different ways in his essays, letters, and fiction, Tolstoi's ideas about the "right way of life" remained much the same from the 1880s on. His work in this period, in particular his translation and exegesis of the Gospels, clearly presents his religious views. Especially rewarding for our purposes is his discussion and translation of chapters of John (14–16) that relate Christ's final discourse (24:734–37) and his commentary on Christ's final hours and the meaning of his death (24:790–98).

Tolstoi's religious views rest on a distinction between carnal and spiritual life. Taking cues from the Bible, but always with a care to avoid its "mystifications," he emphasizes the filial relation between God (the Father) and people. Those who fulfill God's basic teaching to love one another manifest the presence of God within them. "Life" is to be found in the proper understanding (he uses the term "comprehension") of God's teaching and the filial relationship between God and people. A person who has comprehension lives spiritually, somehow beyond the limits and demands of physical existence. Life in this exalted spiritual sense cannot come to an end the way physical life does; for death, as well as our concepts of space and time, have no power over the spirit. Thus Christ, like Ivan, has no fear of death; both have the right notion of life. And Christ's teaching of love and sacrifice of one's life for another, which he expressed in the Sermon on the Mount, should be obeyed not as slaves blindly obey a master but as free people who understand what the meaning of life is.

Tolstoi underlines the primacy of love,[37] which is the source of life. It is

God's plan that we love one another and act in behalf of the good. No one can know God, but people can nonetheless discover that love is the identifying mark of authentic life. People with the customary "comprehension" or understanding of life avoid pain and suffering and fear death as something alien, a violence from the outside. Death and suffering as they are customarily understood appear pointless and unfair, threatening, as they do, our very being and our right to exist. Ivan passes through the stage in which he deeply feels the injustice of his suffering, the unfairness of his dying when he has done nothing wrong. Only when he rejects this legalistic concept of life and death (a concept that exercises considerable control over Elena Stakhova in *On the Eve*) with its notion of unfair and incommensurate suffering, does he conquer the power of this suffering and his fear of death.[38]

Tolstoi opposes to the customary view of life one that he ascribes to Christ. This view does not focus on justifying or accounting for death, endeavors that preoccupy conventional Christianity and all religions that promise that something better than present-day life will be given to people after they die. Tolstoi's focus is rather on the positive qualities of life, of which the most positive is the potential to love. This potential exists in everyone, but not all recognize it. If people would recognize love in themselves and yield to its power, "unite" with it, they would have no need to be concerned with death. Life is a gift, it is not "naturally" given, nor is it something people are in any way entitled to; it is given for a purpose, associated with love and goodness, which Tolstoi believes he has discovered. Individuals do not and cannot have eternal life in any personal sense. Death and suffering are problems only to those who do not realize that life itself is an extraordinary gift of love.

Tolstoi's support for his view is borne, if not by logic and philosophical rigor, by the energy of his conviction and the comforting force of his terminology. His unconventional definitions of familiar terms map out a fairly familiar world: it is obvious that here in his religious writing as in his story he is building on the familiar only to mold it to a shape of his making, which he hopes will capitivate readers. He argues that we should see our lives as something precious given to us by a higher power for a purpose that we can discover by using our reason. If we adopt his picture of life, a gift that raised us out of nothingness, we will not complain of the cruelty and unfairness of death. Ivan's horrible suffering before he realized the "truth" should not be understood as punishment for having lived the wrong way; the reward-punishment model is not appropriate for assessing the way one lives. Ivan's initial pain and fear of death are merely indications that he has not had the "right" view, not punishment for having the "wrong" one.

Ivan's joy before his death is, ultimately, the product of a chain of realizations, all deriving from a newly found sense of compassion. The transformation of grief into joy reflects an analogy used by Christ speaking to his disciples (in Tolstoi's version of the Gospels):

When I am no longer in the carnal life, my spirit will be with you. But you are like all people and will not always feel the strength of this spirit in yourselves. Sometimes you will weaken and lose this strength of spirit, and you will fall into temptation, and sometimes you will again awaken into true life. Hours of enslavement of the flesh will overcome you, but this will only be temporary; suffer and be born again in spirit, as a woman suffers in the pains of birth and then feels joy that she has brought a man into the world; you will experience the same when you, after enslavement of the flesh, rise up in spirit: you will feel then such bliss that there will be nothing left for you to desire. (24:753)

The metaphor of sorrow passing into a joyful birth is obviously relevant to Ivan's experience. After much inner struggle Ivan rejected the customary comprehension of life—he let go of it—and he no longer conceived of life as avoidance of the unpleasant. He was eventually given or led to the "right" direction by his son's gesture of pity and love. He felt the good as having a powerful source, love; and he "united" with this source. In giving himself up to it, he vanquished death's grip, together with all the power of the earthly and the physical. Just as the woman gave birth after labor, Ivan labored and was reborn.

The key to moral behavior is first attaining "comprehension" and then yielding to the force of love it discloses (24:737); when one yields totally, one's actions are good because they flow spontaneously from a divine source within and are not the products of abstract reflection and deliberation. The polarities Tolstoi established, which he elaborated in his later essay, "On Life" (1886–1887), placed truth, life, and submission to a higher force at one end of the axis and the physical, animal, and personal life at the other (26:363–66). Again and again until the end of his life he would demand if not the "renunciation" of personality, its submission to a higher consciousness authenticated by reason (26:375–82).

Ivan's life and death are a vivid illustration of the lessons of love, self-sacrifice, and submission to "the God within"—lessons Tolstoi elaborated on in his exegetical writings and essays. Acting in accordance with God's plan means acting compassionately as the thief next to Christ did in Tolstoi's account of the crucifixion: "The thief had pity on Jesus, and this feeling of pity was a manifestation of life, and Jesus said to him: you are alive" (24:781). Authentic life, pity, and love are all intertwined. Right actions can be explained by reference to God's divine plan. God's plan stipulates our helping to realize divine goals, and helping in this way yields great joy.

The fundamental beliefs of other religions point to the same divine plan. To Tolstoi, the truths of other religions helped to prove that Christ's example was indeed a divine exemplification of the plan, not that Christ was a divinity. Using his empirical sensibility and his findings in the study of other religions, Tolstoi excised what he took to be irrelevancies and superstitions in Christian dogma. Above all, he appealed to common sense and reason, thereby undercutting the basic objection to moral theories based on revelation.

Though Tolstoi had no use for religion as an incentive for doing what is right—a system that is ultimately a form of egoism—he nonetheless utilized religion and religious example as well as the concept of a divine plan in establishing a foundation for his own moral theory. He found necessary a divine, nonhuman basis for his theory of right and wrong; for Tolstoi, God and his plan were concepts consistent with reason.

Faintly perceptible in Ivan's final hours are features of a conventional Christian conversion.[39] Tolstoi follows the outlines of the traditional Christian final rite, but he gives it a new content based on his own religious and moral views. Ivan recognizes what has been wrong in his past life and chooses to act differently. Instead of a priest, there is his son showing compassion. Instead of verbal refrains and incantations, there are compassionate actions. Instead of asking for forgiveness, Ivan asks to "pass through." And instead of being guided through a time of terror, Ivan touches his son, in a gesture of authentic compassion.

By now it is clear why it is misleading to say Ivan, after his accident, becomes conscious of his sinful ways, becomes contrite, finds redemption through God's grace and the example of Jesus Christ, and ultimately finds salvation. This would be the interpretation of conventional Christianity, which Tolstoi explicitly rejected in favor of his own religious views. The Christian framework can be imposed only with great difficulty, for there is no mention of Christ, sin, contrition, grace, and redemption; in fact the role of the Christian church (represented by the priest who comes to see Ivan) is hardly flattering: the Church's aid to Ivan is ineffective, and its role in the story remains insignificant.[40] Finally, it is doubtful whether any kind of conventional Christian interpretation can be made without ignoring or distorting not only Tolstoi's views as expressed in his essays but also, and more importantly, passages in the text.

The problem is that the story's religious suggestiveness—its numerological references, its biblical terminology, its references to a voice above Ivan, its use of names (Peter Ivanovich as well as Ivan Il'ich—John, son of Elijah), its parallels with the story of Christ (including peripheral parallels such as the "son" bringing the message of true life, the "son" as one of the "thieves," and the filial nature of compassion)—all this lends itself easily to "Christian" readings. But, as indicated above, Tolstoi uses the religious suggestiveness to enhance the seriousness of his statement and at the same time subtly to divert conventional views into new channels.

Although it is undeniably true that there are indirect allusions to Christ, they are deeply embedded, pointing to ironies that are far from obvious.

Part of the subtext is readily apparent: both Christ and Ivan are condemned to death, both are in the hands of executioners, both suffer three days of torment (and wounds in their side), both experience a "resurrection," both exemplify their love by willingly yielding up their lives, and both conquer death.[41] Beyond the obvious is the parallel filial relationship: Ivan's early apostrophe to God (chapter 9): "Why do you torment me?" (which echoes Matthew 27:46, "My God, my God, why hast Thou forsaken me?"); Ivan's attempt to say "Forgive [me]"; and the expression from above, "It's all over!" ("*Koncheno!*" in both the story and Tolstoi's translation of the Gospels).

The surface similarities may be misleading, however. In his translation of the Gospels (24:781) Tolstoi renders the verses from Matthew as "My God, my God, in what hast Thou left me?" (which he elucidated in a note as "in what, in what kind of exhausted body have you held my spirit?") and thus changes a complaint to a query suggestive of the spirit-flesh dualism he comprehends. Ivan, however, is made to echo traditional translations of Matthew in his words. But in what actually happened to him—his feeling of being in a black sack—it is Tolstoi's version of Christ's words that wins, in appropriateness, in the end. Finally, Ivan's slip of the tongue, with its emphasis on passing through rather than seeking forgivenesss, indicates the presence of something more powerful beneath the surface, a more authentic kind of "religion," a force acting upon the individual's psyche and carrying him away with it.

But the most striking deviation of all from conventional Christianity is the concept of rebirth or resurrection. To Tolstoi there is no personal life after death, and both Christ and Ivan prosaically illustrate this fact. Ivan may have said that death is finished, but the narrator had the last word: "he stretched out and died." Nothing could be more alien to Tolstoi's concept of morality than the notion that virtue will be rewarded in heaven with eternal life and vice punished in hell. Once again, Tolstoi disputes the picture of justice as fairness, as a strict balancing of actions with their appropriate rewards and punishments:

Perhaps it is fairer to suppose that awaiting a person after this worldly life lived in the exercise of personal will is an eternal personal life in heaven with all kinds of joys; perhaps this is fairer, but to think that this is so, to try to believe that for good deeds I will be rewarded with eternal bliss, and for bad deeds, eternal torments—to think this way does not contribute to our understanding of the teaching of Christ; to think this way means, on the contrary, to deprive Christ's teaching of its main support. All Christ's teaching promotes this goal: that his disciples, after understanding the illusoriness of personal life, will renounce it and convert it into the life of all humanity, the son of man *["syna chelovecheskogo"]*. The doctrine of the immortality of the personal soul, however, does not urge us to renounce our own personal life but affirms personality forever.

According to the Jews, Chinese, Hindus, and all peoples of the world who do not believe in the dogma of the fall of man and his redemption, life is life as it is. People live, copulate, have children, raise them, grow old, and die. Children grow and continue the life of their parents which uninterruptedly leads from generation to generations exactly like everything in the existing world; stones, the earth, metals, plants, animals, stars, and everything in the world. Life is life, and we must use it as best as we can. (26:398–99)[42]

Immortality is impersonal, a spiritual potential dwelling in people, sometimes referred to as "truth" or the "spirit of truth" by Tolstoi. Christ "saved" people only by illustrating with his life the power and truth of his message: there is no fear when one is in the power of the good, when God's plan is manifested through one's being. Thus the peasant servant, Gerasim, has no fear of death and no fear or discomfort in dealing with someone who is dying. In contrast to people around Ivan, he accepts pain and dirt as a matter of course. Healthy, strong, uncomplaining, and brimming with vitality, he casually accepts the most disagreeable functions in helping Ivan through his final days. Like a parent caring for a baby, he does not judge Ivan but only serves him, easing his final days. Gerasim is an illustration of the positive ideal—someone living totally, and unconsciously, the "right" way.

There is an extraordinary spirit of defiance—of the conventional, of traditional authority—in Tolstoi's moral elevation not only of a peasant, but of an ordinary man like Ivan, whose banal, venal, and shallow life leads to a Christ-like revelation and death. The conventional Christian perspective is not Tolstoi's, and it is hardly plausible in this story. Even though other kinds of readings are possible,[43] religious and moral interpretations have dominated critical discussion. And these interpretations, insofar as they adhere to conventional religious and moral categories, have been misleading, often relating only superficially to the text.

The tale makes concrete and personal what Tolstoi's moral and social commentaries exposit, expand upon, and generalize. In their generalizing role, his essays elaborate on and thereby enhance the significance of Tolstoi's personal experiences; art also enhances this significance, and it does so by means of the feelings it generates. But feelings too can be interpreted and experienced in various ways. Tolstoi left the task of generalizing the personal to his readers, who read with their own frames of reference, through their own religious and philosophical glasses. Their feelings too were affected by their presuppositions; emotions generated and communicated are also part of a context that depends on interpretation, on what is brought to the text by the reader. Tolstoi relied on the power of the example he was giving to convey the appropriate moral truth—but more importantly to lay the rails for the proper emotional responses to questions about the meaning of life. These emotional responses, however, have varied widely.

The very demands of fiction, and especially moral fiction (which must be alert to heavy-handedness and overly specific reliance on special doctrines), conditioned the open texture of the story. The danger of the open texture of the moral example is that it can yield multiple and diverse readings that may fail to do what Tolstoi wanted. He may have underestimated the ability of people to mold and distort what is alien and discomforting. On the positive side, the story's enduring value may very well reside in its broad suggestiveness, in its insights into predeath experience—characterized by Tolstoi as including a rejection of materialism, loss of fear for death, an absence of pain, and a feeling that one is moving toward the light—whatever the specific nature of the philosophy of life projected through Ivan.[44]

Tolstoi believed that the artist's responsibility was to promote feelings that would bring people together and make them recognize that love and compassion are reasonable, that they function as the source of what is good in life. To convince people of the power of these emotions and the benefits of yielding to the tremendous impersonal source within that nurtures them, he presents a vivid example of how an ordinary man can emerge victorious in a confrontation with death. In a contest that mortals can never win, the only option is to yield to the very forces aligned with death; by reevaluating what has seemed negative as now positive, one can salvage a victory. Whether or not Tolstoi's efforts were mere wishful thinking or self-delusion, his attempt to change the rules of the game left its lasting imprint: "The Death of Ivan Il'ich" continues to be vital to generation after generation, its moral revelations from a man on the edge of death serving as a seemingly never-ending source of provocative readings.

GOR'KII'S "TWENTY-SIX AND ONE"

It seemed to us that we were playing some kind of game with the Devil, and our stakes were Tania.

WHEN MAKSIM GOR'KII heard that the octogenarian Tolstoi had abandoned home and family to make what was to be a final pilgrimage, this is how he responded:

Well, now he is probably taking his final leap in order to give his ideas the highest possible significance. Like Vasilii Buslaev, he loved to jump, but always in the direction of strengthening his own holiness and seeking a halo. This is inquisitional, though his teaching is justified by the ancient history of Russia, and by his own sufferings of genius. Holiness is attained by flirting with sin, by enslaving the will to live. People want to live, but he tries to persuade them: "That's nonsense, our earthly life!" It is very easy to persuade a Russian of this: Russians are lazy creatures who love nothing better than resting from inactivity.

The normally respectful, and keenly perceptive younger writer, who justified his remarks by referring to his many conversations with Tolstoi, could also be critical of the sage of Iasnaia Poliana. What Gor'kii betrays here is, in addition to an aversion to Tolstoi's elevation to the status of a religious idol, an impatience with Russians who were forever ready to rationalize their inactivity and inability to shape life. The critical edge was there when he denounced the foundation of Tolstoi's philosophy:

He always lavished great praise on immortality on the other side of this life, but he preferred it on this side. A writer who was national in the truest meaning of this notion, he embodied in his enormous soul all the defects of his nation, all the mutilations, all the ordeals of our history we have borne; his obscure preaching of "non-activity," of "non-resistance to evil"—the preaching of passivism—all this is the unhealthy ferment of old Russian blood, poisoned by Mongolian fanaticism and is, so to speak, chemically hostile to the West with its tireless creative labor. What is called Tolstoi's "anarchism" essentially and fundamentally expresses our Slav opposition to a State system—again a truly national characteristic, ingrained in our flesh from old times, a tendency "to disperse in separate directions."[1]

It was dedication to an active life that Gor'kii demanded and extolled: passivity has no cherished role in his pantheon of virtues. What he found fault with in Tolstoyism he associated with the worst traits of his people; heroes like Ivan Il'ich do not live in Gor'kii's works. In the story to be considered here, the "active life," brimming with healthy and youthful vitality, is portrayed with surprising effectiveness against a background of passive and sickly endurance of things the way they are. But the sharpness of this contrast and the moral implications it carries have not been appreciated by most critics of the story.

As a writer, Gor'kii nowadays hardly has the stature of Tolstoi; it seems difficult to believe that at the turn of the century he ranked in popularity with Tolstoi for his fiction, for his social and political views, and also for the moral intensity that informed them. Gor'kii lived a long life (1868–1936) and was a prolific writer. What has remained of value, however, at least outside the Soviet Union (where he ironically suffers from the very idolatry he feared would swallow up Tolstoi), is not his long string of novels nor his plays—with the possible exception of *The Lower Depths* (1902)—but his memoiristic and autobiographical writings—his accounts of Tolstoi, for example, or of the people who played important roles in his life (in *Childhood*, *Among People*, and *My Universities*).[2]

In postrevolutionary Russia Gor'kii occupied a peculiar position, straddling two worlds: he was sympathetic with the aims of the Revolution, friendly with and respected by its leaders, yet not so ideologically intransigent as to ignore the precarious position of numerous political victims of the new age, talented outcasts of the "enemy" class whom he helped to survive in the early 1920s. For much of the 1920s he lived in Germany and Italy, returning only after persistent urgings by Stalin, to whose causes he lent his support in the 1930s. Gor'kii's early aid to starving and embattled talents did not mitigate for many the moral obloquy of his support for tainted causes like the White Sea forced labor project or the establishment of Socialist Realism. That he may have been, and probably was, killed by Stalin's orders in 1936 is to some a kind of justice, an ironic turnabout and final balancing of the scales.

Evaluated more soberly in the West, the "father of Soviet literature" is praised most often for his prerevolutionary fiction, his engaging autobiography and fascinating reminiscences of Tolstoi and other writers. He is not regarded as a master stylist: only rarely was he able to restrain his verbosity, limit the metaphysical posturing of his exotic characters—mostly those "at the bottom" of society—and portray them forcefully and effectively. But his characters have had an appeal: many of them were understood to symbolize the indomitable spirit of rebellion. Living on the fringes of society, having willingly abandoned civilizing constraints in favor of the dangers of life on the edge, they become larger-than-life forces of rebellion against conventional life and values. A smuggler like Chelkash (in the story of the same name) intensifies his sense of life by taking risks, by engaging in psychological warfare with others. The story's basic contrast between life bound tightly by conventions and rules and life lived spontaneously, actively, and openly, with no heed to social conventions, is also depicted in what many regard as Gor'kii's best work of fiction, his frequently anthologized "Twenty-six and One" (1899; sometimes translated as "Twenty-six Men and a Girl").[3]

Despite its fame (Mirsky praised it highly), this little masterpiece has been critically neglected.[4] Studies of the story have tended to emphasize the author's vivid descriptions of the plight of the twenty-six pretzel makers and have given very little prominence to the heroine of the story, a sixteen-year-old maid named Tania who works for embroiderers in the same building that houses the pretzel factory.[5] Tania works under much better conditions than the bakery workers of the basement factory; and her status, too, is considerably higher: there is no question of the story's symbolic associations between material and spiritual conditions. Part of its moral edge is clearly its implicit condemnation of stifling and inhumane working conditions—conditions highlighted by contrast with the more humane setting of the embroiderers and of other bakers who are yet to be introduced.

But the kind of moral issues we are concerned with here lie in a different realm. They are the issues most intimately related to the emotional high points of the story, episodes of intense feeling that usually bring insights and moral clarity to characters. In this story, however, the characters do not see clearly what has happened to them; they do not recognize the moral implications of their actions. For reasons they are only vaguely conscious of, they have put their values to a test. Why they take such a risk and act out their roles in such a drama is never clear to them. Once they take the risk, they demonstrate their potential for an active, more authentic life. But in the end they fail to take advantage of the opportunity given them for appreciating the moral significance of their condition.

The insights the story provides pertain to the twenty-six and the one, the moral plight of the former and the moral stance of the latter. The workers are given their chance to see and understand—they take a bold step out onto the edge—but they fail. Tania, too, takes a chance; but she emerges victorious, morally and spiritually. The role of Tania badly needs reassessment in terms that direct attention to the moral and psychological implications of her relationship with the twenty-six. Tania, the "One" of the title, is *central* to the meaning of the story and its moral dimension; and recognizing the importance of her role enhances our understanding of wider implications of the work and its place in the author's creative development.[6] A proper appreciation of her role will also help us understand how opportunities for moral enlightenment may be missed, even though all the necessary conditions are met.

The story focuses on various developments in the relationship of Tania and the twenty-six workers. In the beginning we see her making daily visits to the workers in their basement habitat (we are told little of their lives outside the factory). When she visits them, the men give her freshly baked pretzels, and in time they all become infatuated with her. With her long chestnut hair and gleaming white teeth, she appears before the men as a goddess: the men look up to her reverentially and give her pretzels as an offering. A new person enters the picture, an ex-soldier working as a roll baker in another section of the building. He too, unlike the other roll bakers and embroiderers, enjoys visiting the twenty-six; for his visits give him an opportunity to tell his jokes and build his ego at the bakery workers' expense. His boasts about his sexual conquests and ability to seduce anyone begin to irk the men, to exasperate them; and in the end they are provoked into offering their goddess and object of worship, Tania, as a sexual challenge. The soldier agrees to the test and in several weeks manages to seduce her. The twenty-six react violently to the loss of their bet and, more importantly, to their goddess, who could not live up to the high standards they had imposed on her. They berate Tania, but she maintains her composure and responds to their curses with invective of her own. Strong and seemingly unflappable, she proudly walks out of their life, leaving them in hopelessness and gloom.

The two points of high emotion are the bet itself and the workers' confrontation of Tania after they lose. The point of view is that of the workers; and the story is told by one of them, presumably by Gor'kii himself, who also worked in such a bakery when he lived in the city of Kazan'.[7] The narrator, though he has obviously escaped the confines of the basement bakery, makes no attempt to separate himself from the other workers. His point of view is theirs to the end, though he ventures several psychological generalizations in the narrative that demonstrate his sophisticated awareness of the general picture. Moreover, by the very act of writing, he shows to some degree a mastery of the situation and the feelings it aroused.

Gor'kii's conservative contemporaries were quick to see moral implications of the story, but what they saw was only on the surface. Some critics understood the story as, if not pornographic, at least amoral in its apparent refusal to condemn Tania and the ex-soldier,[8] as if the men in their bet were totally blameless. But the threat the story represented to contemporary moral standards on extramarital sex was only one aspect of the story's moral dimension.

Another aspect is obviously the depiction of working conditions. Marxist critics, both in Gor'kii's time and later, have rightly pointed to the power of Gor'kii's description of the basement factory, with all its filth and oppressive routine. It is easy, but perhaps misleading in the end, to exaggerate the prominence of the alienating, demoralizing, and dehumanizing effects of labor in the story. While not denying that the story can be read this way, we can all the same insist that there are other ways in which it can be read that do not deny the hypnotic power of exploitive labor to distort human perceptions and emotions. Tania can be understood as more than an illusory hope the workers desperately reach out to, more than a token who highlights the negative aspects of their situation. To say that the pretzel makers do not respect themselves and for that reason do not allow her the right to be wrong and make mistakes on their own is to beg many questions and to make many questionable assumptions, not the least important of which is the view that suffering gives its victims the right to make others suffer—a pervasively held sadomasochistic trap that has virtually come to be viewed as intrinsic to the Russian soul.[9] A Marxist view of Tania, centering on the workers, their relationship to her, and their plight, is not likely to do her justice, nor adequately to appreciate her role.

If we focus on psychological polarities in the story—strong and weak wills (so often displayed in Gor'kii's early fiction), the differences in attitudes and behavior, the contrasts between lethargy and activity, the will to live and apathetic resignation—we end up with an axis of openness and repression that may not have anything to do with the workers' working conditions but everything to do with their psychological makeup. The story raises issues that go beyond worker alienation; it points to ways in which alienation might be overcome, ways in which the men might achieve some measure of autonomy and authenticity in their lives within the economic system that exploits them. Moreover, in showing how disastrous their idealization and even idolatry can be, the story suggests that proffered solutions to the workers' plight may not be what they promise, but only more of the same—sedatives or opiates perpetuating enslavement. The story shows how the workers, through their idealization of Tania, find a very promising way of coping with their otherwise unendurable lives. Their efforts to cope in this way ultimately fail, and their failure reflects on the ameliorative powers of idealism in general.

Tania is idealized by the workers; through her they rise, at least temporarily, above their oppressive working conditions. Critics who have focused on her as a personification of rebellion against conventions (and with the imposition of bourgeois moral values, a girl with "a proclivity to evil")

are partly right, for she openly violates all sorts of group standards. She ignores implicit prohibitions of her own group (the embroiderers) in visiting
with the pretzel makers, she violates society's moral code in her sexual behavior, and she violates the implicit standards the twenty-six have imposed
on her behavior.[10] It is apparent that this story is about codes, implicit rules
of behavior, both internal and external, that hold tremendous power over
some but not all. Perhaps this is why such a wide range of contradictory
judgments surrounds interpretations of the men and their actions, as well as
Tania: readers' codes are intimately engaged and threatened. And out of
these complex interrelationships of moral assumptions comes a wide range
of conclusions about what losing the wager meant to the men.

The story in its subtlety and complexity obviously goes far beyond conventional moral judgments; the propriety of Tania's involvement with the
ex-soldier is clearly not the focus. The real issue here, as in most of Gor'kii's
early stories, is struggling against the routine and conventional, exerting
one's will against environmental controls, and through these efforts giving
expression to authentic and truly human emotions. The starkness of the extremes Gor'kii depicts here—the subhuman regimen of the men in a sunless
world serving a monstrous and insatiable oven versus the brightness introduced into this world by Tania and her friendly openness—is one of the
story's most striking features. And the characterization of Tania in this situation, just as Gor'kii's previous depictions of tramps (bosiaki), reflects his
positive conception of and attraction to "uncommon" types, those who do
not accept the status quo and who have the ability to break free from constraints of the norm.

Although the heroine of the story is not a tramp, there is no question she
falls within the category of Gor'kii's types who challenge conventional morality, who assert their will, and who derive strength from confrontation
with adversity. She dominates the story; and, while she does exemplify the
men's desperation, she is in no sense a secondary personage.

The range of emotions experienced by the men draws our attention to
central issues in the story. From the outset we are provided with a
psychological spectrum—what we can expect from the bakery workers and
from Tania. Her appearance on the scene is prepared for by an introduction
of the men and the conditions under which they work. Some notion of their
potential for authentic human feeling is given early, by their spontaneous
turn to song in order to break the routine of their labor. In the words of the
narrator, the singing would "revive our hearts with a quiet tickling pain,
irritate old wounds, and awaken our longing" (9). The songs do not, it
should be noted, bring pleasure alone: "pain" and "old wounds" are connected with their longing; the nostalgic and masochistic notes sounded here
are significant for later developments. In any case, wishing for something
better in their life provides a transition to Tania's appearance.

Tania brings the men pleasure merely by appearing: she greets them, takes the pretzels they offer her, and leaves them in "pleasant" discussion. From the very beginning their affection is tinged with solicitude, an element that bodes ill for future events: their advice, even if it is unheeded, implies a desire to impose their will on hers, to set the standards for her behavior. There can be no question that the men want something or someone to idolize, and the deity they have chosen is Tania. Tempers quickly flare if someone questions her role. They insist that everyone love her without qualification, and they regard anyone who goes against them as an "enemy" (12).

Their intolerance of heresy with respect to their idol is paralleled by their dislike—which the narrator attributes to envy of better working conditions and social status—of the roll bakers. The ex-soldier, a new roll baker, is exempt from more direct manifestations of this envy; for he, like Tania, socializes with the twenty-six and treats them as fellow human beings. Their good feelings toward him are tempered, however, by apprehensions about his womanizing. They take pride in Tania's indifference to him and even feel "elevated" by it, loving her all the more for scorning him (15).

The situation to this point has been artfully constructed; all that remains is to make what was unstated specific. The turning point occurs when the ex-soldier, drunk, visits the men and begins his customary boasting. The chief baker of the twenty-six, whom the narrator later characterizes as more intelligent than the rest, angrily belittles the soldier's sexual victories. He expresses his fury with an image—the soldier has been dealing with saplings *(elochki)*, and Tania is a full-grown pine *(sosna)* (15).

The other workers are fascinated with the challenge and grow animated and noisy. After the wager has been made, with a two-week limit, their solicitude for Tania turns to curiosity (both "burning and pleasing") about her fate. They are eager and confident, and for a while they fear that they have not wounded the soldier deeply enough and that the match will be called off. As the tension mounts, their behavior changes. They begin to work nervously, to argue with each other, and also "to become more intelligent, to talk better and at greater length" (17). They give their game cosmic dimensions, envisaging it as sport with the devil, with Tania representing their stake in the outcome. The soldier's attempts to win Tania over give them a feeling of "elation" *(vozbuzhdenie)*, so that they live more intensely and in sway of this intensity unwittingly do extra work.

Although they continue to be affectionate toward Tania, their curiosity, "cold and sharp like a steel knife" (18), complicates this emotion. And as the two-week deadline approaches, they examine Tania for evidence of weakness. When the day of truth comes, they meet her silently instead of amicably. The head baker, now sullen, does not hurry to give her the customary offering of pretzels; and she, surprised by her reception, becomes "pale and nervous" and then suddenly leaves (19). This new attitude toward her, marked by the withholding of the daily "offering" or sacrifice, presages their misfortune. The narrator has admitted earlier that she existed for them only because of the offering. What is curious now is that all act as if the wager has been lost and that their idol has fallen. Their attitude toward her has completely changed.

The effects of making the bet should be emphasized. In contrast to their previous existence (before Tania), when their only respite from routine was in nostalgia and song, the pretzel makers now experience a wide range of intense emotions—curiosity, eagerness, confidence, fear, nervousness, elation, and finally sullen resignation (even before Tania "loses" the bet for them). Taking a chance with their "idol" has obviously resulted in a new spirit and vitality that humanizes the men and provides a vivid picture of their potential.

One way of interpreting the head baker's sullenness is that the men have obviously realized, even before proof of the seduction has been offered, the uncomfortable truth that Tania is not a goddess but a normal human being. Deprived of their comforting illusion, they lose their spirit ("We felt sad and uneasy . . .", [19]) and dejectedly watch through their basement window as the soldier follows Tania into a cellar in the yard. Her troubled face (*ozabochennoe*) upon entering is contrasted, however, with her shining eyes and smiling lips (". . . *glaza u nee siiali radost'iu i schastiem, a guby—ulybalis'* . . .", [20]) as she leaves. The soldier is not visibly different when he emerges; and, having played his role, he quickly disappears from the story.

When Tania reenters the yard, she is met with verbal abuse and derisive whistling. The twenty-six come out, circle her, and begin to taunt her. She remains silent, momentarily taken aback. The emotion they have invested in their idol is unleashed in the form of rage. Seeking revenge for the pain they feel and attribute to her betrayal of their values, they come close to attacking her (the narrator asks himself why they do not beat her). One of them grabs at her sleeve, a violation of an unwritten code. But their numerical and physical superiority is no match for the power she has: her eyes flash (*sverknuli*), she straightens her hair, and then she calls them "unhappy convicts" (*arestanty neschastnye*), no longer using the affectionate and compassionate diminutive (*arestantiki*) with which she used to greet them on her daily visits. Walking upright, beautiful, and proud (*"priamaia, krasivaia i gordaia"*) through the circle as if the men did not exist, she drops all signs of compassion and calls them "rabble" and "vipers" (*"svo-oloch'. . . . gaady. . ."*, [21]). They are stunned into silence and left alone in the dirt and the rain.

Reading the story through a frame that associates what is positive in life—what makes for authentic living—with strongly felt emotions (both painful and pleasurable) and what is negative with all that constricts, confines, and limits people necessarily promotes Tania's position. The curiosity, elation, suspense, and rage experienced by the men all derive from their relationship with Tania and the confrontation that terminates it. The point, which Tania exemplifies in her own behavior and which the men exemplify when they risk their cherished beliefs, is that human beings are alive when they feel strongly. We know that what Gor'kii viewed as positive in the character of his fellow workers at the Kazan' bakery was the gleam of sadness in their "bloated faces" and the anger and resentment they would sometimes show. Their worst quality—what he tried to eliminate in his efforts to educate them—was their "patient endurance" and "hopeless resignation,"[11] traits often associated with the ability of Russians over the centuries to adjust, endure, and survive no matter what enslaved them.

His personal experiences with the men in the Kazan' bakery give us a fascinating perspective on the story, for what he left out of the story (but included in his autobiography) is extremely suggestive:

It was difficult there physically, and even more difficult morally.

When I sank down into the basement factory, a "wall of oblivion" grew up between me and the people, whom it was necessary for me to see and listen to. None of them approached me in the factory, and I, working fourteen hours a day, could not go to Derenkov's on weekdays; on holidays either I slept or I stayed with my fellow workers. Part of them from the first days began to view me as an entertaining jester, some regarding me with that naive love of children for a person who is able to tell them interesting tales. The devil knows what I said to these people, but, of course, it was everything that could inspire in them a hope for the possibility of another easier and more sensible life. Sometimes I succeeded in this and seeing how their swollen faces lit up with a human sadness, and their eyes flamed up with resentment and anger—I felt festive and with pride thought that I was "working with 'the people,'" I was "enlightening" them.

But of course more often I experienced my own impotence, lack of knowledge, and inability to answer even the simplest questions of life and everyday existence. Then I felt I had been thrown down into a dark pit where people swarmed like blind worms, striving only to forget reality and finding that state of forgetfulness in taverns and in the cold embraces of prostitutes.

Visiting public houses was obligatory each month on payday; they dreamed aloud about this pleasure a week before the happy day, and after living through it—they talked to each other for a long time about the delights they experienced. In these conversations they cynically boasted about their sexual energy, brutally jeered at the women, spitting in disgust as they talked about them.

But—it is strange!—behind all this I heard—and I wondered at it—sadness and shame. I saw that in the "houses of consolation" where for a ruble one could buy a woman for the whole night, my comrades acted embarrassed, guilty—this seemed natural to me. And some of them behaved unduly free and easy, with a daring in which I felt a deliberateness and falseness. I was terribly interested in the relation between the sexes, and I watched all this with special intensity. I myself had still not enjoyed the caresses of a woman, and this put me in an unpleasant position: both women and my comrades taunted me maliciously. (16.37–38)

For the story Gor'kii made many modifications. There are no references to the life of the workers outside the factory. The sexual dynamic is present, however, though it is transferred to another plane: the sexual boasting of the men is projected onto the soldier, the idealization of sexual experiences is projected onto a Madonna-like teenaged girl to whom they can give gifts with no sense of shame. It is only when she shows signs of being a real person that they display the anger and hatred for real women that lurks behind their idealization. Without their comforting ideal they sink back into that hopeless state in which the young Gor'kii had found himself as well and which he described in terms of despair, a dark pit infested by blind worms, ignorance, and apathy.

The narrator of the story offers several generalizations to bring home the impact of idealization—what it means and can do to people who grasp it as their only hope. Early on, for example, the narrator notes that human beings respect every form of beauty (10) and cannot live without something to worship. Gor'kii's conviction that people need something to worship ultimately led to his philosophy of "God-building" (*bogostroitel'stvo*) which he expressed artistically in his later "Confession" ("Ispoved'," 1908).[12] Working people, Gor'kii thought, were natural "God builders," with their enormous vitality and creative energy, their sense of spiritual kinship with each other, and their cohesion as a group. But directing "God-building" energy into conventional patterns of religious belief involving transcendent deities was not, to him, the answer. From the story of the twenty-six we can conclude that idealizing individuals leads to disillusionment. There are no obvious implications concerning an appropriate object of worship, although in later years he would suggest ideal forms of social organization. What is offered in the story is a dramatic illustration of the human need for something to worship and hold in reverence.

The narrator offers other comments on human psychology: people desire to impose their love on those whom they love without respect for their integrity (11). This coercive love is at the heart of the story, for the men in their solicitude for Tania and in their very idealization of her bind her with the ropes of a special code of behavior. The love they offer her does not allow her the freedom to make her own choices, to live her own life. But there is something positive here as well: the love Tania inspires in the men, and the hatred her behavior subsequently invokes, makes them human enough to curse. As the narrator observes, the men in the bakery rarely cursed before (and there is always a reason to curse a comrade) because they were "half-dead," like "statues," their feelings stifled by the burden of their work. Their cursing represents an assertion of their humanity.

One additional generalization concludes the narrator's explicit psychologizing: he notes that some people derive vitality from a mental or physical disease that they cherish (16). Though made with special reference to the soldier and his sexual prowess, the remark also carries implications for the twenty-six. People with this cherished "disease" may not enjoy it and may even complain about it, but they can attract attention with it and even inspire compassion. Boredom or poverty can lead to the acquisition of a vice that will function as a cherished disease. The soldier's self-esteem is wrapped up in his "disease": that is why he is so offended that the twenty-six have doubts that he can succeed with Tania. But the workers also tie their self-esteem to idealization, which resembles and functions as a disease. In idealizing and idolizing Tania they set themselves up to lose their self-esteem, and with it their vitality and reason for living. It is clearly their miserable life that predisposes them to acquire this vice of idealizing a pretty girl. Thus the narrator's comments about vice, like his comments about other features of the human condition, serve to define a psychological framework through which we can perceive what develops.

Imagery brings out very effectively the negative features of the men's situation. The bakery is a prison, and they are inmates or convicts on one level and a whole series of depersonalized entities on another: machines, stone statues, sheep, oxen, but also (more positively) the foundation for the building. The workers' surroundings are ominously animated; what is underlined is the pernicious and demonic character of exploitive labor: boiling water "purrs" in a melancholy way *(zadumchivo i grustno)*, a shovel "scuffles and throws," "darts in and out," and, in a most striking fashion, the oven of the bakery is described as the head of a monster *(skazochnoe chudovishche)* with a mouth and jaws, "pitiless and passionless" vent-eyes that stare at the workers, and scorching breath; in its superiority to them it is even capable of hating them *(". . . prezirali ikh kholodnym prez'reniem mudrosti . . ." [3])*. [13]

Into this world of dehumanized and alienated workers and animated means of production, Tania comes and quickly becomes a "little idol" *(bozhok)*. As if counterbalancing the hatred of the demons, she offers friendliness, kindness, and smiles to the miserable workers. A set of images emphasizes her elevated, superhuman status: she is viewed as a substitute for the sun (which they never see directly) and a falling star (9–10): in view of what happens, perhaps it is significant that she is a "substitute" and not a real sun and that the star is "falling." When she comes for pretzels, it is a ritual *(sviashchennyi obriad)*, with the pretzels as offerings or sacrifices *(zhertvy)*; she is always four steps above the workers (11), a spatial suggestion of her exalted position in their lives. Her identity as a personal object of worship to them, as an idol *(idol)*, as a holy being *(sviatynia)*, and as a vessel containing their "best," is explicitly noted by the narrator. Only at the end, when she "descends" with the soldier and then confronts the twenty-six in the yard are Tania and the men on the same level—a sign of her lost divinity and transcendence.

The imagery of the story leads suggestively to interpretations at various levels; the language of religious doctrine seems most promising as a place to begin our exploration of the story's rewarding meanings.

As in "The Death of Ivan Il'ich," much here suggests religion. But in this case, more than Christianity alone is implicated. At the beginning of the story the language of the narrator establishes a climate of paganism, referring to the workers as slaves *(raby)* and the central oven as a furnace idol that they serve. This relationship is overturned as the story develops, with the worshippers adopting a new deity described in terms of light (against the darkness of the workers' plight); moreover, there is a new ritual—a daily visit and an offering—and a new code of behavior concerning both what this god will or will not do for them and also how they may relate to her (there can be no physical contact). There are religious overtones in the plot as well. The deity's power is challenged as the Messiah undergoes a test arranged with the help of a disciple (the head baker), disappoints all the disciples by showing all too human qualities, but in the end rises above them, though not in any supernatural sense. Here is where we find a mundane alternative to Christian dogma: Tania has risen above the twenty-six because of her spirit and vitality, which have given her a moral sureness; the workers, however, remain trapped in the language and behavior of submission.

In terms of Christianity, Gor'kii appears to be paying his disrespects to its conventions by suggesting that despite its considerable power to evoke strong emotions, inspire fidelity, and provide amelioration and consolation, it does not offer authentic life. The deceptive promise of security it offers but cannot deliver proves in the end to be disastrous for believers—reality, when it breaks through illusion, strikes with a vengeance. Idealism founded on the transcendence of individuals may easily be destroyed if challenged, and in the wake of this destruction the fragile spirit of believers will be shattered.

The workers are no better off at the end of the story than they were at the beginning: the same rituals and routines are carried out in a lifeless world. It seems clear that they are enchained by these routines, but there is reason to think that their submission to them is both internal and external. Life in the factory before Tania had interesting surface similarities: feeding the oven of capitalism, which was also an untouchable source of light and warmth, was an idol-centered ritual to which they had become habituated. The same psychological weaknesses that tie them to their miserable lot in the factory determine their submissive and ritual-bound relationship with Tania. Even though their slavery is now illumined not by the oven but by a different kind of "light," it nonetheless remains slavery. What "elevates" them is challenging and testing their cherished beliefs, questioning the values by which they have been living. Tania serves both as the object of their idealization and as a model for a healthier approach to life. Their idealization of her gives Gor'kii the opportunity to show the liberating possibilities in challenging the status quo. He does not show, however, how the men can learn from their experience and overcome the internal constraints that predispose them to submission.

What makes the story so fascinating is what it suggests about the different ways of thinking that enslave people. Gor'kii may have been referring subtextually not just to Christianity of a conventional sort[14] but also to Sophiology which, as a doctrine, became known to the public through the poetry of Vladimir Solov'ev in the late 1880s and 1890s. Solov'ev gave particular prominence to a feminine deity, the divine Sophia of Eastern Orthodoxy, known also as Holy Wisdom and the Maiden of the Resplendent Gates. Characterizations of the one who "tarrieth at the Entrances" suggest Tania in her relationship to the pretzel makers and her customary appearance at the basement door.[15] Such a parallel, of course, has ironic power. Gor'kii shows that lowly factory workers, like Symbolist poets (on whom Solov'ev had considerable influence), can create feminine deities to serve and revere. What is more, even workers can appreciate what Symbolists regarded as the purist of artistic forms—music. Early in the story we are told that the men can move the walls of their prison by evoking thoughts of freedom and space with their singing (9). Gor'kii has clearly democratized the powers of spontaneous artistic expression and suggested as well the power of art to improve reality by loosening the bonds of slavery.

Not only Christian perspectives may be applied to the story's patterns: its "paganism" provides hints of other meanings accessible through the appropriate frames. For example, a Freudian view of the story presents a fascinating new angle on the head baker's bet and on the intense anger of the men after being "betrayed" by Tania. Without invoking or relying on perhaps tenuous hypotheses about Oedipal relationships, it is still possible to use insights Freud had in his work on group psychology or in *Totem and Taboo* to explain the ritualistic nature of the men's approach to Tania, their attitudes toward her, the code of behavior they implicitly recognize with regard to her, and the ambivalence (affectionate and hostile impulses) they betray both in making the bet and in awaiting its resolution.

Psychological theory could undoubtedly elaborate on the connections between their elevation of Tania, their forbidden, erotic impulses toward her, their voyeurism, and their hostility. It could be argued, for example, that the soldier they have goaded into accepting the bet (which they admit is like a pact with the devil), is merely their representative, one they can identify

with and in this identification experience vicariously the goals of their re-
pressed desires. The prohibitions—for example, against touching (27)—the
jealousy, the expiatory offerings, the ambivalence of the men, and on
another level, the conflicting impulses to elevate and to dethrone Tania
might easily find a place in a psychoanalytic frame. In such a way, the bet
could be understood as an impulsive "discharge" of accumulated tension
caused by two conflicting and mutually inhibiting sources.

Like children who spend hours building and then derive pleasure in destroying what they have built, the men, by betting on Tania's fidelity to
them, assert their mastery over and control of the situation they have arranged. Freud talked about the need people have to reenact experiences that
were painful to them, to arrange (unconsciously) for variations on themes
related to what they once were unable to deal with or live with and master.
If Tania indeed is part of their "arrangement," it is not difficult to define her
role. She is obviously a parent-figure, a nurturer—although the men reverse the roles by offering her the food and thereby assert their active role in
the reenactment—who brings them light and comfort. And the bet is a
chance for jealous siblings to participate in a contest for favored position
with the mother. Their imprisonment in the basement factory has predisposed them to regression and the selection of Tania as a mother-ideal.

The bet can also be understood as an expression of their need for growth
and autonomy, if development is seen to derive from challenge and risk.
The head baker senses the need for autonomy, and impulsively takes the
initiative in putting the idol to the test. But when the bet is lost, so is the
fetishistic substitute (for parent, religion, or both) that made miserable conditions tolerable. The bet marked going out on the edge, and this experience
brought with it a new, clearer picture of the world. The price of autonomy
was, in the case of the men, too high. Once regressive bridges were burned,
their plight seemed hopeless. Deprived of their idol and venting their anger
in a way that suggested the hatred of children for parents who have not lived
up to their own rigid moral code, the men sink even deeper into morose resignation. Moral clarity and a less illusory picture of reality do not guarantee
spiritual commitment to rebellion and action.

Gor'kii himself, in another text, drew attention to a similar pattern of experience. In his autobiography he told of his painful feelings, his hurt and
resentment, when his mother remarried and eventually abandoned him;
and he told of other events in his grandfather's house which destroyed any
illusions he had of his mother's power to help him. [16]

The promising lines of thinking that emerge by applying a psychoanalytic grid, though surely productive, need not be taken as the final answer to
the story's central problems. For there are questions that can be dealt with
in more ordinary terms with more conventional concepts. Much critical interest, for example, has been focused on sexual morality as it is portrayed in
the story. There is surely little basis for concluding that the story condemns

sexuality, notwithstanding our knowledge of the author's strong negative views of sexual profligacy and his preference for maternal types. Tania's age, her inquisitive and lively nature, and most of all her openness to new experience at the expense of restrictive social conventions predispose her to amatory experimentation with the ex-soldier. Tolstoi, as Gor'kii reports in his reminiscences, was quite frank—and even brutally vulgar—in his assessment of a young girl's sexual needs, much to the discomfiture of the keenly sensitive Gor'kii:

> When he [Tolstoi] wanted to, he could become tactful, sensitive, and gentle in a particularly nice way; his talk was fascinatingly simple and refined, but sometimes it was painful and unpleasant to listen to him. I always disliked his opinions about women—he was extremely "common" then, and something artificial, something insincere, and at the same time very personal sounded in his words. It seemed as if he had once been hurt and could neither forget nor forgive. The evening when I first got acquainted with him, he took me into his study—it was at Khamovniki in Moscow—he sat me opposite to him, and he began to talk about *Varenka Olesova* and "Twenty-six and One." I was depressed by his tone and even taken aback, he spoke so plainly and harshly in efforts to demonstrate that chastity is not natural in a healthy girl.
>
> "If a girl has turned fifteen and is healthy, she wants to be embraced and touched. Her mind still fears the unknown and what is incomprehensible to it—and it is this people call chastity, modesty. But her flesh already knows that what is incomprehensible is unavoidable, lawful, and demands that the law be carried out, in spite of the mind. But this Varenka Olesova of yours is described as healthy, but she feels cachetic—that is not true!"
>
> Then he began to speak about the girl in "Twenty-six and One," pronouncing one after another "indecent" words with a simplicity that looked like coarseness to me, and even offended me. Later I came to understand that he used "unmentionable" words only because he found them more precise and to the point, but at the time it was unpleasant to me to listen to his speech. I did not object; suddenly he became attentive and kindly and began to question me about how I lived, what I was studying, and what I read.[17]

Regardless of what this passage indicates about the psychology of both Tolstoi (who here does not find chastity and modesty "natural" to a girl) and Gor'kii (who seems unusually sensitive) and their respective inhibitions about sexually explicit language, the point remains that the older writer contrasted the health of Tania with the sickliness of the more modest Varenka Olesova. Moral categories apparently were not introduced into this discussion, but Tolstoi's other writings in his later years (such as "The Kreutzer Sonata") leave little doubt about his feelings on sex.

Health obviously wins out over moral inhibitions in Gor'kii's story, for Tania emerges from the experience with the soldier not like Anna Karenina, spiritually and physically sullied, but radiant and happy. The very same traits that allowed her to break conventions and associate with the twenty-six workers—most notably, that independence of spirit that allows people to see others as people regardless of social status—ironically lead her into conflict with the men. It was their adherence to and imposition of a rigidly defined behavioral code that determined their reaction to her actions. Even if we read her association with them less charitably—she uses them to get favors and adulation—the strength of her character is still unquestionable. Though her motives may not be pure, she shows no fear in going after what she wants.

In a manner that suggests some awareness of Nietzsche's *Beyond Good and Evil*, Gor'kii has placed Tania beyond conventional moral categories, has promoted her "free spirit" as well as the strong emotions she arouses, and through her has advanced the view that people must learn to live without comforting illusions, whether about moral absolutes or transcendent deities.[18]

Whatever the underlying motives or psychological explanation of the wager, it plays a positive role in the story and is obviously a key support to Gor'kii's defense of the independent spirit. Challenging the soldier is a spontaneous gesture on the part of the oldest and most intelligent baker; the challenge is made in a moment of anger, ostensibly a reaction to the soldier's boasting, but probably also relates to a concern all the men had about the reality of their idol.[19] They admit they wanted to test her: their insecurity about her transcendence has been indicated by their overreactions to suggestions that Tania might not be worthy of the special treatment they give her. Their desire to test her combines at least to some extent with resentment over the bravado of the soldier and envy of his success. But from this challenge they make to the order of things come a new vitality and new attitudes toward life. While waiting for the outcome to their bet, the workers come alive, experiencing feelings they had not known before.

The story is existential insofar as it presents human beings in situations where their actions lead to new, more intense feelings. In much the same way that Dostoevskii's Underground Man purposely brings about his own suffering in order to savor the experience of it, Gor'kii's bakery workers participate in a test that allows them to suffer tormenting doubts and thus feel alive. Indeed, the focus is on the experiences themselves; it is not important whether they relate to existentialist authenticity or repetition compulsion, whether they are positive or negative by conventional standards. We know that Gor'kii at this time was most concerned with the psychological implications of confrontations between strong wills and conventions. The generic subtitle of the work, "Poema," calls attention not only to the lyrical aspects of the story but also to its epic qualities: strong wills and emotions are truly heroic in a situation where oppression, routine, and suffocating restrictions are the norm.[20]

What makes the story problematic from this perspective is then the conclusion: the workers cannot maintain this vitality in the face of their lost ideal. They sink, in fact, even deeper into alienation from the rest of humanity. The insight they are offered—that challenging the norm and taking risks can lead to growth and autonomy by enhancing life and giving it meaning—is lost on them. It is only Tania who embodies the epic spirit of the story, since her vitality and her strength stand out in relief against the workers' dejected acceptance of their "sunless" world. Her apostasy predominates, despite the fact that the story represents the men's point of view, their milieu, their predisposition to idealize, and their ideal destroyed by reality. The possibility that she too will find disappointment in the future hardly diminishes her role.[21] Nor does the view that the workers will have a more optimistic future because next time they will be able to choose better ideals.[22]

What rescues the story from moral nihilism is the free and healthy Tania, not the workers' chances for renewal, which can only be tenuously supported in the text. The spiritual death they suffer gives testimony to the suffocating power of social and economic pressures, as well as their own psychological limitations. The risk they take in testing their values leaves them *in extremis*, on the edge, and in this new position they experience fuller lives. But after their experience comes not a new sense of liberation but a more intense hopelessness—and with it resigned submission to the forces around them. Why this should be is related to their choice of ideals: an individual cannot carry the weight of such idealization.

In Tania, Gor'kii presents a model of authentic behavior and the kind of courage that is necessary if, for example, social conditions are to be changed. Though she is a young girl and though she shows no signs of social or political consciousness of broad issues, she nonetheless gives clear indications of having the psychological attributes without which action is impossible.

The author does not provide an explicit program of social action in this story. Instead he presents, through the characters, a view of human psychology and the obstacles that confront people who wish to change their lives. And beyond that, he promotes, by suggestion and primarily through the character of Tania, the values of remaining open to experience, receptive to emotions, and fearless in the struggle with social conventions that are inimical to the human spirit. He shows both the problems with traditional morality, which the men have internalized, and the external morality of capitalism and the society they grew up in. Tania, like the men, is subject to both internal and external demands, but she demonstrates a new configuration, an alternative to the repression and regression that hold them where they are. As the bearer of positive moral and psychological attributes she can hardly be denied a claim to significance in the story.

PASTERNAK'S LYRIC "SUMMER"

And the fall, till now howling like a bittern,
Cleared its throat: and we understood
That we were at a feast in an ancient prototype—
At Plato's feast during the plague.

ONE OF THE AMAZING things about Boris Pasternak's long career as a poet, novelist, and translator was his ability to survive, to endure the vicissitudes of different Soviet regimes without sacrificing his integrity and without yielding to that despair which destroyed some of the most talented of his generation—Vladimir Maiakovskii, Sergei Esenin, and Marina Tsvetaeva. Indeed, Tsvetaeva marveled at the optimism and hope Pasternak displayed in adversity.[1] He showed moral courage in the face of public pressure and the displeasure of authorities in later years when *Dr. Zhivago* was published abroad and subsequently when he received a Nobel Prize. But even before this, in the dangerous 1930s when, as Osip Mandel'shtam's fate so clearly illustrated, words could easily lead to Siberia and death,[2] Pasternak managed to balance prudence and principles; for he possessed a fine sense of the limits to which he could go. The poem we will discuss in this chapter brilliantly illustrates Pasternak's skill at expressing dangerous ideas within these limits.

Once again we see a dissatisfaction with maintaining the status quo, with remaining passive in the face of life's pressures for moral conformity. Once again we find a willful challenge to fate and a decision to stand apart with one's own moral convictions. What led to this decision was adopting a new moral perspective, which had grown out of a revelatory experience. The experience was described in a powerful and remarkably allusive lyric poem written in 1930—at a time when Stalinism was first achieving its distinctive character.

"Summer" *("Leto")* is a poem in ten amphibrachic tetrameter stanzas, eight of which are quatrains and two of which (the fifth and the sixth) are sextains. It is a poem about the poet's recollection of an intense emotional and intellectual experience, one that took place in 1930 (the poet included

the date in published versions of the poem). The experience—and the revelation that was intimately bound up with it—are given toward the end of the
poem. The movement of the poem may be seen as crescendo and decres-
cendo: the poet's recollection of his summer in the country proceeds from
seemingly haphazard observations about the natural setting and the weather up to a dramatic climax—his vision or realization—and finally to
speculation on the meaning of the vision. Throughout the poem one senses
a close relationship between sound and meaning, between phonetic and
semantic properties:[3]

Лето

Ирпень—это память о людях и лете,
О воле, о бегстве из-под кабалы,
О хвое на зное, о сером левкое
И смене безветрия, ведра и мглы.

О белой вербене, о терпком терпеньи
Смолы; о друзьях, для которых малы
Мои похвалы и мои восхваленья.
Мои славословья, мои похвалы.

Пронзительных иволог крик и явленье
Китайкой и углем желтило стволы,
Но сосны не двигали игол от лени
И белкам и дятлам сдавали углы.

Сырели комоды, и смену погоды
Древесная квакша вещала с сучка,
И балка у входа ютила удода,
И, детям в угоду, запечье—сверчка.

В дни съезда шесть женщин топтали луга.
Лениво паслись облака в отдаленьи.
Смеркалось, и сумерек хитрый маневр
Сводил с полутьмою зажженный репейник,
С землею—саженные тени ирпенек,
И с небом—пожар полосатых панев.

Смеркалось, и, ставя простор на колени,
Загон горизонта смыкал полукруг.
Зарницы вздымали рога по-оленьи,
И с сена вставали и ели из рук
Подруг, по приходе домой, тем не мене
От жуликов дверь запиравших на крюк.

В конце, пред отъездом, ступая по кипе
Листвы облетелой в жару бредовом,
Я с неба, как с губ, перетянутых сыпью,
Налет недомолвок сорвал рукавом.

И осень, дотоле вопившая выпью,
Прочистила горло, и поняли мы,
Что мы на пиру в вековом прототипе—
На пире Платона во время чумы.

Откуда же эта печаль, Диотима?
Каким увереньем прервать забытье?
По улицам сердца из тьмы нелюдимой!
Дверь настежь! За дружбу, спасенье мое!

И это ли происки Мэри арфистки,
Что, рока игрою, ей под руки лег
И арфой шумит ураган аравийский,
Бессмертья, быть может, последний залог.
1930

SUMMER

Irpen'—this is a recollection of people and summer,
Of liberation, of escape from bondage,
Of pine needles in the intense heat, of the gray
    mustard plant
And the cycle of calm, good weather, and haze.

Of white verbena, of the viscid tenacity of
Resin; of friends for whom are inadequate
My praises and my eulogies,
My glorifications, my praises.

The scream of piercing orioles, and their appearance
Turned the trunks yellow, like a golden apple and coal,
But the pines did not move their needles out of laziness,
And rented corners of rooms to squirrels and woodpeckers.

The chests of drawers grew damp, and a change of weather
The wood frog prophesied from a twig,
And the beam at the entrance sheltered the hoopoe,
And there, behind the stove, was a cricket, for the
    children's pleasure.

On days of meeting six women were trampling the meadows.
Clouds lazily grazed in the distance.
It grew dark, and a crafty maneuver of twilight
Brought a lit-up burdock with the semi-darkness,
With the earth, the towering shadows of Irpenki
And with heaven a fire of striped material.

It grew dark, and putting the vast openness on its knees,
The enclosure of the horizon made a semicircle.
Summer lightning raised antler-like horns.
And from the hay they arose and ate from the hands
Of friends who upon arriving home, nevertheless,
Locked the door from petty thieves.

In the end, before leaving, stepping through a pile
Of fallen leaves, in a delirious fever
I ripped from the sky, as from lips drawn
Together with a rash, the thin covering of unexpressed
    utterances.

And the fall, till now howling like a bittern,
Cleared its throat; and we understood
That we were at a feast in an ancient prototype—
At Plato's feast during the plague.

From where does this sadness come, Diotima?
With what assurance can we prevent oblivion?
Down the streets of the heart, out of unpeopled darkness!
The door's open! To friendship, my salvation!

And are these the schemes of Mary the harpist,
That by fate's game the Arabian hurricane lay under her
    hands
And sounds like a harp,
Perhaps the last promise of immortality?
1930

The poem does not yield its meanings easily, for much is only suggested, as if challenging us to provide all-embracing meaning.[4] And one feels so strongly throughout the poem the pressure of the sound texture on meanings, the close cooperation of sound and sense, that to provide coherent meanings without taking into consideration phonetic properties is an impoverishing distortion.

Pasternak's poetry is distinguished, at least in part, by the complexity of its sound instrumentation and by the variety of ornamental devices used. There are two problems of interest to us here: the poem's moral significance and the role sound instrumentation plays in enhancing and even determining this significance.

Although it has often been noted that musical effect is not the only function of Pasternak's rhymes,[5] establishing semantic and thematic correlations on the basis of similar patterns of sound nonetheless calls for caution. Repetition of combinations of sounds takes a variety of forms in his poetry—anagrams, anaphora, alliterative sequences, consonance, and assonance. If correlations can be established between these devices and a number of lexical items, irrespective of their thematic importance, one cannot responsibly claim that the poem links sound and sense in a significant way. If, however, particular clusters can be distinguished on the basis of frequency of occurrence and association with thematically important expressions, there is likely a strong connection between sound and meaning in the poem.[6]

To assess whether the patterns of ornamentation serve more than a melodic function entails first determining whether patterns of sound repetition can be associated with what carries thematic weight and, second, whether these patterns can be distinguished from other sound patterns presumably associated with euphony or musicality alone. By isolating and analyzing sound patterns that relate to the thematic fabric of the poem one can demonstrate the poet's significant use of sound.

"Summer" has been analyzed before, with claims made about sound and sense. Krystyna Pomorska, for example, maintains that the last stanza, "with the concluding ideas on art and immortality[,] has the heaviest and most meaningful sound repetition."[7] In support of this thesis she points to the "central function" of the sounds of the "key" word *rok* ("fate") in the second line, its paronomastic relation to the word *igra* ("game" or "play"), the occurrence of the sounds of *rok* in all their combinations *(rok, gro, ork)*, and the paronomastic relation in the third line of this stanza between *arfa, uragan*, and *araviiskii* ("harp," "hurricane," and "Arabian"). The transliterated stanza follows:

> I eto li p*roiski* Me*ri* a*rfi*st*ki*
> Chto *rok*a ig*ro*iu ei p*od ruki* le*g* (/l'*ok*/)
> I *arf*oi shumit u*ragan* a*ra*viis*kii,*
> Bessme*rt*'ia, byt' mozhet, poslednii zal*og*. (/zal*ok*/)

The relation Pomorska emphasizes is an interesting example of Pasternak's manipulation of sound combinations, but is not really to the point; for the three words do not in themselves seem more "meaningful" (nor are they "heavier") than combinations found in practically every other line of the poem. The connections Pomorska makes between *rok* and *igroiu* in the second line of this stanza are also a bit strained because they rest on the identification of the third sound as a velar stop (g/k). It will be shown that "a play of fate," though important within the stanza, does not have as significant a role in the general interpretation of the poem as other expressions.

Dale Plank has stated that in this poem form leads to meaning along the path made by the final syllable of the first word of the poem, *Irpen'*.[8] Plank takes the sound *en'* (variant *eni*) to be the major recurring rhyme in the poem, one that gives particular significance to the first line, in which Irpen' is said to be a "memory about people and about summer." All the words rhyming in *en'* are associated with the name of a place, so both as a word and as a place Irpen' evokes memories: "Thus, when the poet says, 'Irpen" is a memory of . . .' he tells us with his rhymes that he is also saying [that the word] . . . 'Irpen' . . . is a memory of. . . ." That is, the cue is as much the word, with its properties, as it is its referent, the place. Rhyme is here shown to be a ticket to the scenes of memory" (p. 112).

This satisfying argument depends, at least partially, on the undemonstrated claim that *en'* is the major recurring rhyme. It serves in end-rhymes in eight lines, which is a frequency equal to or greater than any other end-rhyme (*-y* also occurs in eight of the forty-four lines). The total number of repetitions of *en'*, including end-rhymes, is fifteen; but an additional nine might be admissible if the similarity of sound criteria were relaxed to allow unaccented forms, forms with unpalatalized *n*, and inversions: *Irpen', smene, verbene, terpen'i, voskhvalen'ia, leni, otdalen'i, teni, irpenek, doleni, po-olen'i, mene, osen', uveren'em, spasen'e, smenu, zhenshchin, lenivo, zazhzhennyi, repeinik, sazhzhennye, sena, neba, nedomolvok.*

Furthermore, the cluster *en'* occurs at least once in every stanza (if we allow the unpalatalized *n* in *smenu* in the fourth and the inversion *neba* in the seventh stanza). The only other cluster repeated with a comparable frequency is *pa/po* (seventeen occurrences, with some variation). This sound combination, however, is very common in Russian as a preposition and a verbal prefix *(po-)*, and there is no easy way of specifying its thematic connections; the most significant nouns it is associated with are "praises," "weather," and "friends."

Because of the highly associative character of Pasternak's poetry—and the "murkiness" of this poem in particular[9]—not all of the puzzles can be solved, and much depends on interpretation, our assessment of the relative importance of the poem's themes. Although it is clear that Plank's thesis can be supported in the text, there are reasons against limiting our attention to the rhyming element *en'*. That it occurs so often in the poem—even in the place name that begins the poem—is not totally unexpected, for *en'* is a relatively common derivational suffix. A much more striking element is that an anagram of the first three letters of *Irpen'* is *pir*, the word for "feast." Although the order of component sounds *p*, *i*, and *r* may vary, and the three may be separated by other sounds, the sound cluster occurs sixteen times, with at least one occurrence in each stanza: (1) *Ir*pen', (2) te*rpen'i*, (3) *pron*-z*i*tel'nykh, (4) za*p*ech'e — sve*r*chka, (5) *rep*ein*i*k, *irp*enek, (6) *pri*khode, zapiravshikh, (7) peretianutykh, pred, (8) prochistíla, piru, prototipe, pire, (9) prervat', (10) proiski.

Although the word rok ("fate") and the suffix en' are undeniably significant in the poem's sound structure and meaning, they are not as significant as the word pir ("feast"). It will be shown that by placing "feast" in the formal and thematic center, we can give "Summer" a reading which captures the close relationship between sound and meaning and does justice to the poem's moral dimension.

The first stanza of the poem presents, in reverse order, a summary of the whole poem: the reader learns that Irpen', a summer resort area near Kiev, is the source of memories the poet will relate, memories of people, summer, freedom, a flight from bondage, trees and flowers of the countryside, and changes in the weather. The bondage he is fleeing is unspecified, but we can hypothesize that the experience at the end of the poem represents the "liberation" from bondage. The changes in weather, too, have metaphorical potential, perhaps as emotional gauges. All this will become clearer in later stanzas.

Botanical observations continue in the second stanza, but people also take a significant role. The poet praises his friends—in fact, cannot praise them enough.

Beginning with a transferred epithet, "the scream of piercing orioles" (whose appearance against a tree trunk is brilliantly described as a "golden" apple and coal turning the trunk yellow), Pasternak takes us into a realm where animals have human qualities, a fairly frequent event in his poetry.[10] A frog prophesies a change in weather; and pines are lazy, although they rent out corners of rooms to woodpeckers and squirrels.

Difficulties arise in the fifth stanza with the first two lines: "On meeting days six women trampled the meadows." What is the "meeting" ("convening," "arrival")? And who are the six women trampling the meadows? The lazily grazing clouds of the second line suggest one idea: the women may be peasant women grazing their cattle in the meadow, and the daily feeding might constitute a "convening" of sorts. On the other hand, the use of the antonym "departure" in the seventh stanza suggests that the "meeting" or "convening" involved people; for the poet here explains what he himself does "before leaving" ("pred ot"ezdom"). A plausible construction then is: on days the poet and his friends met or came together, peasant women could be seen in the field (either grazing their cattle or making hay). On a connotative level, then, appears the association of the women who routinely graze their cattle with old Russian patterns of behavior, ingrained habits. And also present are associations of "meeting" days with political meetings, a connection that will become more meaningful.

The next four lines of the stanza center on the "craftily maneuvering" twilight, the play of light and dark, fire and shadows, on earth and in the sky. Nature here takes on a conspiratorial stance, as if concealing something threatening. In the sixth stanza, following the repetition of the verb form *smerkalos'* ("it grew dark"), an image of entrapment is presented. The vast openness is put "on its knees" by the horizon, which forms a semicircular enclosure. The image, which is intensified by the approaching darkness, echoes the bondage and the tenacity of resin referred to earlier. The imagery suggests that people can handle this natural "enslavement": bolts of summer lightning raising antler-like horns that rise up from the hay and eat from the hands of friends. The realized metaphor (suggestive of people feeding reindeer) leads, within the same sentence, to a surprisingly prosaic, and puzzling, conclusion: these same friends (of other people, of animals, of things) can appreciate and do not fear the grandiose spectacle of nature but all the same show caution by locking their doors when they go home, for they fear petty thieves. Entrapment, submission, fear of something crafty and mysterious but also characterizable as "petty thieves": all this is balanced by reference to friends, who nurture and give shelter, and non-threatening natural phenomena.

The seventh stanza begins the climax of the poem, its revelation. Several cues indicate the central role of this stanza. The first words are "in the end," and we are told what happens before the poet's departure (where "departure" is semantically related to "escape" of the first stanza). In a feverish state, perhaps of inspiration, the poet experiences a revelation which is metaphorically keyed to ripping a covering from the sky and removing a rash from lips drawn together. What "covers" and "binds" are "incomplete utterances" or "reservations" *(nedomolvki)*. What could not be expressed before now can be expressed. With this metaphorical "ripping away" the hitherto ineffable, or partially expressed, becomes expressible, and the poet has a new "freedom." The nature of his vision is explored in the following stanzas.

At the moment of enlightenment a personified autumn (for now the season has changed), previously "howling like a bittern," suddenly "clears its throat." The implied thunder and rain correspond with the poet's sudden realization: ". . . we understood / That we were at a feast in an ancient prototype— / At Plato's feast during the plague." This realization is central to the poem's meaning; it was signalled grammatically by the use in the three preceding lines of three perfective verbs *(sorval, prochistila, poniali)* while all the verbs in preceding stanzas were imperfective. More important, the notion of a prototypical feast leads us to hypotheses about earlier puzzles.

What is needed now is a frame, a perspective for bringing disparate threads of meaning and association into a coherent pattern. Obviously, such a pattern will make use of the explicit reference to Plato and prototypes. The "meeting" *(s"ezd)* now takes on more concrete referents. The "we" referred to is obviously a group of friends at Irpen' in the summer of 1930. When members of the group would meet, they did as Socrates and his friends do in Plato's *Symposium*. The characters of Pushkin's miniature tragedy, "Feast during the Plague," do the same: they eat, drink, and talk about love, friendship, poetry, and immortality.

There is a historical dimension to the prototype which cannot be accidental: the great plague of Athens occurred in 430 B.C. (and was described by Thucydides, a believer in prototypes); Pushkin's "Feast" was written in the fall of 1830, the year of the cholera epidemic in Russia; and Pasternak's poem and the experience it relates belong to 1930. It should not be difficult to identify the counterpart of the plague in Russia at this time.

In general terms the plague could be Stalinism and what it meant to individuals: but the plague could also refer to events associated with the collectivization of the peasantry, which had been taking place in late 1929 and in early 1930. Within a sociopolitical framework a number of references and allusions in the poem become more meaningful: peasants fleeing to the cities to avoid collectivization (line 2), overcrowded conditions in the cities (line 12), Stalin himself (the *"drevesnaia kvaksha,"* or "wood frog," who prophesies the future in line 14), peasants hiding food from authorities (lines 27–28), the sinister nature of collectivization and the craftiness of those who ordered it (the natural imagery of lines 19–22), the gradual enslavement of the peasantry (lines 23–24),[11] tactical changes in Communist party policy in response to widespread discontent (lines 4, 13, 14), and the Sixteenth Party Congress (26 June–13 July 1930), which endorsed Stalin's restrictive measures against individual farming (line 17).

The word *zagon* ("enclosure," line 24) suggests the phrase *"zagoniat' v kolkhozy"* ("to drive [peasants, like cattle] into the collective farms"), and enslavement is certainly suggested by the first letters of the last stanza, *BIChI* ("whips, scourges"). Feeding the "lightning" ("horns") in the hay and locking the doors from "petty thieves" may then constitute sheltering runaway peasants from forces of the Party who have come to steal their land.

Oppositions between bondage and liberation abound in the poem from beginning to end: the resin and its tenacity, the calm of good weather, the immobility and laziness of animals and clouds, the darkness and submission of the openness, the locked doors, the bound lips, and the "unpeopled darkness," are all opposed to "flight," the storm, the screaming orioles (of resistance), the fire (of the burdock and the horizon), the lightning, the departure, the poet's delirium, the ripping apart of drawn lips, the howling fall, the feast, and the poet's ecstatic decision to "open the door" to friendship.

Thus the poet's realization, in lines 29–36, could refer to a particular sociopolitical development (as well as his own personal situation as a witness). It is not difficult to understand how the prototype of the "feast during the plague" could have been suggested: the poet may well have seen peasants, fearing collectivization and expecting the worst, drinking heavily and feasting on cattle they were slaughtering to prevent confiscation by the collective.

Even in these early years of collectivization, the magnitude of the human loss it entailed must have been apparent to the Pasternak and his friends. At Yalta, Stalin admitted to Churchill that ten million peasants had died as a result of collectivization (including those who died during the 1932–1933 famine). In the period of January to March of 1930 alone, the number of collectivized peasant families increased from four to fourteen million; efforts to collectivize the peasantry were then suddenly relaxed (with Stalin's calling off of his assault on the villages, a move indirectly expressed in his speech "Dizziness from Success"), so that by May the number had declined to fewer than six million.[12] Images in the poem of peasants in the field herding their animals, of "meetings," of confinement and restriction, of "crafty maneuvering," of finding shelter, and of feasting within the historical context specified by the date given at the bottom of the poem all point to Stalin's disastrous civil war in the countryside and its effects.

Although the social and historical context referred to by this date makes the poem important as an obloquy on state policy, the poem's personal dimension is also important for the moral implications it offers. The poet has described a vision he experienced at a country home in late summer of 1930; the vision is essentially a perception of himself, his friends, and peasants in the area in a prototypical situation as participants in a feast during a plague—and in this case the plague was the menace of Stalin's policies to individuals and humanity.

Whether political or personal, the bondage undoubtedly stems from fear. On a personal level this is a fear of going about with an open heart, befriending people, helping them. The image of the open door in the ninth stanza is in marked contrast to the locked door in the sixth. The choice for the poet is opening himself up to friendship or remaining restrained and cautious toward others, submitting to the darkness.

Those who avoid risks out of fear risk spiritual isolation and sadness. Thus the poet seeks advice, in the ninth stanza, from the archetypal instructor, Diotima, whom Socrates calls "a woman wise in this love and many other kinds of knowledge."[13] But because she is an instructor in the art of love, her advice is not surprising: love and friendship are the poet's salvation. His vision is a realization that his situation has historical precedents, and he seeks and accepts wisdom from them.

Immortality, which is semantically associated with salvation, is the central issue of the last stanza. The topic arises in the *Symposium* and in Pushkin's "Feast," but this stanza refers specifically to the latter. The "Arabian hurricane" finds its source in Pushkin's "hymn" to the plague, a poetic evocation of a principal theme of these studies:

> Est' upoenie v boiu,
> I bezdny mrachnoi na kraiu,
> I v raz"iarennom okeane,
> Sred' groznykh voln i burnoi t'my,

I v araviiskom uragane,
I v dunovenii Chumy.[14]

There is rapture in battle,
And at the edge of the gloomy abyss,
And in the raging ocean,
Amidst the threatening waves and stormy darkness,
And in the Arabian hurricane,
And in the winds of the Plague.

All of these threats to life—battle, the edge of the abyss, the ocean in a storm, the hurricane, the plague—offer an "ecstasy" or "rapture":

Vsë, vsë chto gibel'iu grozit,
Dlia serdtsa smertnogo tait
Neiz"iasnimy naslazhden'ia—
Bessmert'ia, mozhet byt', zalog,
I schastliv tot, kto sred' volnen'ia
Ikh obretat' i vedat' mog.

All, all that threatens with death
Conceals for the mortal's heart
Inexplicable delights—
Perhaps a promise of immortality,
And happy is the one who amidst the turmoil
Could find and come to know them.

In Pushkin's little drama, and for the character who expresses these lines, that which "threatens with death" may hold the key to immortality; in Pasternak's poem, however, the Arabian hurricane, the plague, or standing on the edge of the abyss may offer the last hope of immortality.

It is a source of wonderment to the poet that the skilled hands of Mary the harpist (the singer in Pushkin's poem) can subdue the hurricane and make it sound like a harp. Mary in the poem offers a selfless, all-sacrificing love.[15] Her harp, of course, carries associations of the Aeolian harp and is undoubtedly a metaphor for poetry. Mary, in turn, may be associated with the poet or the poetic muse; and on the same mythological level, the hurricane (or the plague, or the edge of the abyss) may be associated with Thanatos ("death," or "deathwish"), the brother of Eros. The flight from bondage, then, consists in the poet's resolution of a dilemma—his realization that friendship, love, and his poetic vocation are all related and derive significance of a special sort from life-threatening situations. Not just art alone (for "last" implies the possibility of others) but friendship too can offer immortality.

The importance of the sound structure in conveying Pasternak's optimistic and basically hopeful message should now be clear. The poet's recognition of a prototypical *"pir,"* or "feast," marked his revelation. There are no preexistent semantic links between the words *Irpen'* and *pir*. Their sound relation is suggested by their thematic relation, but theme and sound reinforce each other. And because repetitions based on the sound clusters of *Irpen'* are so pervasive in the text, the double role of this place name as a reference to verbal and geographical sources of memories is enhanced.

From a distinctive chain of sounds a pattern is outlined, though it is not driven home until the eighth stanza. Just as the poet's experiences at Irpen' are a source of moral vision—a vision that through the suggestiveness of Pasternak's poetry can be understood as criticism of Stalin's policies—so the sounds of the word itself are keyed to the elements of that vision. The pattern of sounds links the place to the feast and to history and thereby serves as an essential component in determining the moral force of the poem. The poet has effectively incorporated the sounds of *Irpen'* into the phonetic and thematic structure of the poem so that both word and theme seem indissolubly united in sound and sense.

Pasternak was not afraid to take chances for his beliefs. In particular, writing *Dr. Zhivago* and submitting it for publication in his own country were famous acts of courage. Even in 1931, under Stalin, he dared to write "A Century More" (*"Stolet'e s lishnim . . ."*), in which he asked for an end to the executions; this poem had the political significance of Pushkin's appeal to Nicholas I for mercy toward the Decembrists. Pasternak's lyric "Summer" contained no such appeal: its condemnation of state policy is indirect, safely encoded in the poem's texture. It provided a commentary on the inhumanity of the times and also, for him, a way coping with the barbarity of the times.

The poet's vision crossed cultural and temporal boundaries, and his reorientation derived from radically different sources. Risking death—or rather deciding to risk death—led to a revaluation of former values and a new moral clarity, all steeped in and indebted to literary tradition. What is striking here is the mixture of allusions—Plato and Pushkin—and the almost mystical harmony of the ages—"plagues" of 430, 1830, and 1930. And even more striking is the manner in which the optimistic message emerges. The chaos and puzzling haphazardness of the imagery in the opening stanzas of the poem yield to harmony and lucidity as the poet makes evident his historical allusions and draws moral truth from feverish lips. And just as Evgenii found sudden clarity in his vision of the Bronze Horseman's culpability, the poet (and his friends) suddenly "understood" that they are not alone, that their feelings about art, death, and immortality have support.[16] The young Iurii Zhivago, after losing his mother, also pondered this link: "In answer to the desolation brought by death to the people slowly pacing after him, he was drawn, as irresistibly as water funneling downward, to dream, to think, to work out new forms, to create beauty. More vividly than ever before he realized that art has two constants, two unending concerns: it always meditates on death and thus always creates life."[17]

One can speculate on the motivation for the problems the poet raises: if indeed he and his friends witnessed the results of Stalin's collectivization policies, they may have felt some guilt for their own lives, dedicated to art, poetry, and music. Though the times were hard for all and artists, like others, were being organized into collective units, the violence against the peasantry was then of a different order. By taking a risk, by advocating openness—and even perhaps by sheltering runaway peasants—the poet and his friends also become vulnerable, for open hearts, sincerity, and truthfulness to self can, often do, jeopardize security. Surely their own vulnerability to the terror would serve to assuage feelings of guilt and limit their complicity.

SOLZHENITSYN'S *CANCER WARD*

If you remember your collar size, then you must forget something—
something that's more important!

NOT UNEXPECTEDLY, most of the commentaries on *Cancer Ward* have focused on Oleg Filimonovich Kostoglotov, the novel's hero, who is on a quest for life's meaning among other patients and medical personnel of a cancer clinic in Tashkent. Early in the novel, Kostoglotov relates an experience of death and dying:

> This fall I found out for myself that a person can cross the threshold of death even while the body has not yet died. There is still something there circulating in your blood or being digested, but you have already, psychologically, passed through all the preparation for death. And you have experienced death itself. All that you see around you, you see as if from the grave, unfeelingly. Though you have not counted yourself a Christian, and you have even been the opposite sometimes, here suddenly you note that you have already forgiven everyone who has wronged you and you have no malice toward those who have persecuted you. You are simply indifferent to everything and everyone, you feel no need to correct anything or to regret anything. I would even say: you are in a natural state of equilibrium. Now I have been taken out of it, but I don't know whether or not to be pleased. All my passions will return—both the good and the bad ones.[1]

Clearly, Kostoglotov will give readers a distinctive point of view, for he has crossed the dreaded "threshold" and, unlike Ivan Il'ich, has returned to world of the living, uniquely experienced in the life of the dead and the dying. *Cancer Ward* explores how this experience has affected Kostoglotov and his values. What will be explored here are crucial stages of his quest, some of the value systems he considers, and some of the characters who shape his responses to life and efforts to understand it.

Though Kostoglotov's primacy as a moral spokesman is unquestionable, he is not the only one to raise issues of ethical import, nor is he the only one to come close to death. Other characters who have not shared his experience in life have different views about life's values. Consigned to the camp system for imprudent words about Stalin, he has formed a distinctive perception of life, one that gives the novel much of its power. But his perspective is complemented by that of others who have lived on the "outside" during the horrors of Stalinism, and who have suffered in far different ways.

The characters who surround Kostoglotov, with their varied backgrounds and experience, test, broaden, and reaffirm his moral convictions. Solzhenitsyn provides one character who manages to combine all these functions, the former academic and librarian Shulubin. More than anything, Shulubin represents moral sensitivity; but this sensitivity is combined with spiritual weakness and cowardice. Fiercely condemning himself for betraying his own principles in order to survive, Shulubin argues for a rigid code of culpability and elevated moral standards. This man, a citizen whose courage was insufficient, has gone along with the judgment of the crowd; he has not spoken out against wrongs he has perceived. His character allows Solzhenitsyn to offer insights into the nature of moral fortitude and, more important, on the complex factors underlying assessments of culpability.

Shulubin enhances the novel in surprising ways. He demonstrates that all people, no matter what their behavior might suggest, have an innate moral sense. And he systematically articulates the manner in which people can lose sight of what is of value. Even more important, by reaffirming the rightness of Kostoglotov's basic attitude toward people—his concern for others and his understanding of their limitations—Shulubin sharpens the focus and deepens the presentation of "mutual affection," the novel's moral focus. Finally, what Shulubin brings to the novel is a radically different experience from that of Kostoglotov and a penetrating analysis—based on his personal experience—of collective culpability for the crimes of Stalinism.

Solzhenitsyn has been quite outspoken on the Stalin years. His more recent fiction deals with World War I and the Revolution; but his earlier novels, *One Day in the Life of Ivan Denisovich*, *The First Circle*, and *Cancer Ward*, and his nonfiction (most notably, *GULag Archipelago*), have been part of a program of making public what happened during Stalin's reign.[2] But in direct moral probing in his essays and speeches Solzhenitsyn is less restrained and skillful than in novelistic presentation, through characters such as Shulubin, of what life was like then. Though commentators have not overlooked the importance of Shulubin, his role in the novel has not been examined in any detail.[3]

Despite the importance of other characters, Oleg Kostoglotov is the center of attention for most of the work: he has forged his soul in extremis, having spent time first in the labor camps and then in exile, during which he fell into the grips of a cancer so debilitating that he nearly did not make it to the ward for treatment. Like Solzhenitsyn himself, who is a very autobiographical writer,[4] Kostoglotov has undergone a change in vision in the camps, and emerged with a radical new perspective on life and the values he formerly held. The novel is very much Kostoglotov's quest to find what he has missed while in exile, to experience life anew, and to explore the perspectives of others who were not in the camps. Shulubin becomes one of his closest friends, providing him with psychological and moral insights. With both Kostoglotov and Shulubin, the imminence of death is a positive force, compelling a reassessment of old values, dogma to most people in their society. The moral apostasy of Kostoglotov and Shulubin comes from different experiential sources, but it nonetheless unites them in the same positive value—mutual affection and caring.

Shulubin appears late in the novel, which portrays in two parts the manner in which a group of cancer patients with various backgrounds and sophistication deal with each other, their disease, and their treatment within the confines of a hospital in Tashkent (the capital of Uzbekistan, a central Asian republic of the USSR). Part 1 of the novel follows closely Kostoglotov's daily quest for the truth about his cancer and the methods of treating it. This quest, however, is part of a larger search for the answers to his questions about values to live by. In the course of his search he becomes romantically involved with two women, one a nurse, Zoia, and the other a doctor, Vera Gangart. His relationship with the former is primarily a physical one; with the latter the relationship is largely spiritual.[5] The two forms of love have as their reference Plato's *Symposium;* and they set forth a central preoccupation of the novel: the relation of the physical to the spiritual and the importance of each within one's system of values.

Among other patients of the hospital is a government official named Rusanov whose Stalinist sympathies, opportunistic behavior, and limited moral perspective make him a foil to Kostoglotov, the former camp prisoner and current political exile and cancer patient. Standing with Kostoglotov in moral sensitivity is the former agronomy professor, Shulubin, who acts as a prism, focusing the major moral concerns of *Cancer Ward*, giving Kostoglotov's moral quest a broader scope and coherence. It is with Shulubin that Kostoglotov has his longest and most philosophically substantive conversation: a colloquy on the hospital grounds (chapter 31), the day before Shulubin is to have a serious operation. Their talk ranges over such problematic issues as guilt, betrayal of principles, courage, responsibility, and social organization. This conversation is crucial to the ideological structure of the novel and carries considerable moral weight.

Shulubin appears late in the novel, in part 2. He enters at the same time as Chalyi, a cheerful black marketer who is temperamentally and ideologically as dissimilar to Shulubin as Rusanov is to Kostoglotov. Indeed, in part 2 these pairs mark a moral polarity: self-deluded optimism, egotism, and materialism on the one hand, and openness, genuine compassion, and spiritual depth on the other. The clear contrast between Shulubin and Chalyi is marked by the language they use as well as the literary taste and sophistication they exhibit in their conversations: Shulubin quotes some of Pushkin's most serious poetry; Chalyi revels in salacious verse.[6]

The initial description of Shulubin emphasizes his stooped and crooked body, his worn face, and his enormous round and bloodshot eyes. Solzhenitsyn's characters reveal themselves, the moral quality of their lives, in the way they carry themselves. In the novel *One Day in the Life of Ivan Denisovich*, the tall old man who appears for only a page represents an ideal, a paradigm for survival with dignity: he does not bend when he walks or sits, and he brings his food up to his mouth instead of bending down to it. Spiritual steadfastness has its physical component: a stooped frame can suggest complicity, guilt, and culpability—associations with bending under pressure. One of the most positive figures in *Cancer Ward*, the old and kindly Dr. Oreshchenkov, a man who refuses to bend to the regime and its orchestrated pressures, walks with no stoop at all, despite his advanced age.

Not just Shulubin's physical appearance is enigmatic but also his mannerisms and the way he looks at everything and everyone with an "attentive and unpleasant gaze." Moreover, his eerie presence and his refusal to communicate freely with the other patients create a constrained atmosphere, as if death itself were mysteriously hovering over them. Rusanov, who dubs him an "eagle-owl" (*filin*), feels that Shulubin's stares are a reproach to him. And this reaction suggests that Shulubin is a reminder of uncomfortable truths, truths that disturb Rusanov's conscience. The nascent moral sensitivity stirred in this obtuse civil functionary bears testimony to Shulubin's moral function in the novel and also supports Kostoglotov's observation that people still have an moral indicator somewhere deep inside themselves that works in spite of damaged circuits.

Though Shulubin is an unpleasant reminder to Rusanov, Kostoglotov is able to view him differently and likens him to an exhausted actor who has just taken off his makeup. This image has a significance unknown to Kostoglotov: Shulubin has indeed taken off the mask he has worn for years in society; no longer does he present a face that shows compliance and cooperation with whatever the authorities desire. In the cancer ward, facing death, Shulubin no longer feels the need to hide behind a mask. He is one of the few characters who are willing to face squarely the truth of their situation, as well as their past and their prospects for the future. His imminent death has put all other matters in perspective and has led to a rearrangement of his former priorities: now honesty has become a principal value, and in his conversations with Kostoglotov he demonstrates his ability to face and express the truth.

Kostoglotov probes the reticent Shulubin, using his camp skills for quickly establishing friendly relations with people. What he discovers pertains to several subjects—Shulubin's medical history, his professional life, his personal life, and his ethical views—all approachable from a moral perspective.

His medical problem alone raises a number of moral issues. What is uncovered over the course of several chapters is that Shulubin's rectal cancer went undiagnosed because of the irresponsibility of doctors he had consulted when the tumor was yet in its early, more treatable stages. As a direct result of this irresponsibility—the squeamishness of physicians, as one of the cancer ward surgeons expresses it—Shulubin now requires a colostomy, which he feels will make him so radically changed as to separate him from the rest of humanity. By linking a life of repression and conformity with rectal cancer, the novel offers a tragic irony: Shulubin's life of conformity with the group will eventually result in his isolation from the group. Also ironic is the excremental nature of his ailment and the fact that what was "hidden" before will now be exposed, no longer internal. Thus Shulubin not only represents the cumulative effects of guilt but also serves as a reminder and result of the blameworthy behavior of others.

Rusanov intuitively senses that Shulubin is a threat, a reminder of his own culpability; he must, therefore, conceive of Shulubin as a "reproach" and "enemy sentry": Shulubin reminds him of and "guards" an uncomfortable truth, a truth built on the close proximity of death, as well as the knowledge that something important has been betrayed or violated.

Shulubin, though reticent at first, comes to voice his ethical views actively in ward discussions. He expresses himself forcefully, knowledgeably, and with no little drama. He energetically questions the young geologist (and Party member) Vadim, asking his reasons for becoming a geologist; later he vigorously opposes those in the group who try to justify a differential wage scale in Soviet society. Both by opposing conventional perspectives and probing beneath conventional pieties, he shows courage. Not only does he unmask the egoism that underlies such ideals as "serving humanity" and human knowledge, he also exposes the contradiction between a privileged leadership elite and Lenin's early ideas (and the ideals of the Revolution). These arguments are sociopolitical, not personal; but they suggest the reformist zeal of someone who has found the truth and has abandoned earlier fears. What they also suggest is Shulubin's conviction that behind the surface of the language of conventional values in Soviet society lies another, contradictory, value system, rooted in materialism and personal gratification.

Though his "public" words point to significant issues in the ideological fabric of the novel, Shulubin's private conversations with Kostoglotov identify the novel's principal moral issues. The most important conversation is one that takes place on the hospital grounds two days before Shulubin's operation. He is understandably pessimistic about the outcome of this operation that will separate him from humanity; he views it as a kind of death. He and Kostoglotov begin their discussion with the question of who had the worse life. Shulubin insists that his cancer is worse and his life has been harder, using an analogy: "The people who drown at sea or dig in the soil or look for water in the desert don't have the hardest lives. The one with the hardest life is the one who walks out of the house every day and bangs his head against the top of the door because it's too low" (407). The concept here has appeared before in Solzhenitsyn's works; it is a response of those who have not experienced the camp horrors but who have suffered a different kind of horror. Nerzhin, in *The First Circle*, remarks that it's not the sea that drowns you, but the puddle. The seemingly trivial pressures of everyday living, especially if they are morally tainted, can have cumulative effects of enormous proportions. Tolstoi succinctly expressed the incremental effect of culpability in the epigraph to *Power of Darkness:* "If the claw is caught, the whole bird is lost." This increase is one of the most insidious features of "minor" moral infractions, and Shulubin's life demonstrates vividly how small compromises lead inexorably, in a sensitive person, to overwhelming guilt.

Kostoglotov's imprisonment and subsequent exile in perpetuity are not as bad, Shulubin says, as his own life of lying and constant compromise. For fear of losing his prestigious position with the Timiriazev Agricultural Institute (and positions he fell to after this), he had to bow to pressures to conform. For fear of losing his comforts, his family, and his life, he had to accede in the state-directed condemnation of heretics; he had to expose others, applaud the verdicts of rigged trials, and demand firing squads. He fully recognizes his complicity in these moral outrages but, besides himself, he indicts all those who did not object, who stood by and let evil flourish.

Always sensitive to the feelings of others, Kostoglotov offers Shulubin a salve for his conscience, expressing reservations about universal culpability. Many Russians in the 1930s simply did not know what was going on, and for this reason their tacit or even zealous support for the State was certainly not so reprehensible as that of the cognoscenti. But Shulubin holds his position rigidly: the naiveté of young people perhaps could be excused (Kostoglotov's Zoia is an example of such a young person), but adults knew the truth about the trials and the purges and the enemy agents and the deported nationalities. People knew but chose safety and security and dared not refuse to cooperate. If people knew and said nothing, they betrayed their principles and their humanity. In later discussions he suggests that self-delusion too played a role.

These matters are by no means unique to *Cancer Ward;* Solzhenitsyn has treated them often in earlier works. One of the major themes in all of his writings has been the priority of ethical considerations in human affairs. In his novels, he often offers situations in which an individual's principles and desires—for security and comfort in particular—come into conflict with morality prescribed by the state. In *The First Circle* the protagonist Nerzhin

chose not to cooperate with the authorities in the *sharashka*, the special re-
search prison where he was serving his sentence, even though to help them
with their new project would mean to shorten his term and hasten the re-
union with his wife. The government official Volodin, in the same novel,
risks his materially privileged way of life by choosing to do what is decent
and morally appropriate: he will not let evil come about through him. Fully
aware of the risks involved, he nonetheless acts and by his action answers
the question he had asked himself: "if one is forever cautious, can one remain a human being?"

Shulubin exemplifies, vividly and convincingly, the fact that a person
who would sell principles in exchange for security always buys an illusion:
nothing gained through so great a sacrifice is adequate recompense. The
price one must pay to live is a major theme of the novel. It is something
Kostoglotov painfully struggles to determine, especially toward the end
when he must balance his life against a medicine that will affect his sexuality. But Shulubin has finished his soul-searching. His quest is over, and he
has reached a certitude about what is essential. Both the depth of his characterization and the boldness of his assessment of collective responsibility for
the crimes of Stalin make him an unusually strong figure in Solzhenitsyn's
gallery of characters.

In a world peopled by victims, survivors, and their warders, Shulubin
has managed to remain outside the camp system. The novel poses the question of whether he should be considered culpable, sharing in the complicity
with those who helped to perpetuate and extend Stalin's power. Harboring
no illusions about his cowardice, Shulubin admits that he knew what he was
doing was wrong. He faced the truth and was willing to talk about it only
when he was pushed into a corner, almost entirely destroyed by the system
and disease. Challenging fate does not lead to his moral awareness: he has
never really lost it. The threat of imminent death has forced him to turn to
his past and analyze what went wrong in his life. Not unlike Ivan Il'ich,
Shulubin comes to recognize how he has destroyed his own integrity by
clinging to false values.

Shulubin's moral vision is sharpened by the nearness of death and the
realization that he has nothing left to lose. It is principally disease, however,
that has pushed Shulubin to do something he has not done before—to con-
fess his sins to someone and to speak out not only against his own past behavior but the behavior of his generation. To some degree he has defeated
his former fears, emboldened by the realization that there is nothing left to
lose. But even now, he admits he might not speak openly outside the ward.
The hospital offers him a sanctuary, an island of freedom where he can express what has lain festering within him throughout his adult life.

Moral apostasy comes late to Shulubin. Though always morally sensitive, he has nonetheless deluded himself for years, keeping his doubts to
himself, rationalizing when he could that what he did was for his family.

The doubts grew, however, and, the novel suggests, had devastating psychic and physical consequences. Shulubin has put himself in the baseless void of someone who yields to societal values without vocal protest, knowing well that these values had a flimsy foundation.

Supporting and deepening the resonance of this novel are literary allusions, most explicitly to Tolstoi, but to other Russian writers as well.[7] Several ward discussions in part 1 are devoted to the question posed by Tolstoi's story "What Men Live By." But Pushkin, not Tolstoi, serves as Shulubin's source of moral support, once when Shulubin presents his views on collective responsibility for the crimes of Stalin and again, at a more personal moment, when he is thinking about his own death.

The first time he invokes Pushkin, he does so with the purpose of describing the only three categories into which he believes history will justly distribute people: traitors, tyrants, and prisoners. Pushkin's poem reads as follows:

> So the sea, that ancient killer, has enflamed your genius?
> You praise with your golden lyre the awesome triton of
>   Neptune.
> Do not praise him. In our vile age gray Neptune is an ally of the
>   land.
> In all elements, man is tyrant, traitor, or prisoner.[8]

Cutting judiciously to sharpen his argument, Shulubin reduces all this to the aphoristic: "In our vile age, in all the elements man is tyrant, traitor, or prisoner."

Though the context has been changed, the general idea of Pushkin's poem is preserved. We know the original poem had a concrete politicohistorical reference. Pushkin had been concerned about the well-being of Nikolai I. Turgenev, who though in London at the time of the 1825 rebellion, had close ties to the Decembrists. Having heard a rumor, later proved unfounded, that Turgenev had been arrested in London by a representative of the tsar's police and was being returned to Russia by sea for punishment, Pushkin was understandably concerned and sent this poem to his friend Petr Viazemskii, who had just finished a poem eulogizing the sea. Thus Pushkin's admonition against praising the sea—for it could, as an ally of "the land" (Nicholas I's police), serve tyranny—has a polemical and political significance. Drawing the conclusion of Pushkin's poem out of its former historical context, Solzhenitsyn applies it to other circumstances, with obviously related issues of moral complicity: tyranny, treachery (in the sense of betrayal of principles), and imprisonment are the only options available "in our vile age."

Other Solzhenitsyn characters have viewed the world with a similar moral rigidity. For example, in *One Day in the Life of Ivan Denisovich*, Aliosha the Baptist suggests that if Orthodox priests in Russia had truly stood up for what they believed, they would be prisoners, not lackeys (by implication, traitors). When the imprisoned Henry David Thoreau met Ralph Waldo Emerson's question, "What are you doing in here?" with "What are you doing out there?" he showed the same uncompromising quality. Kostoglotov is not prepared to accept so large a category for traitors but would prefer to restrict this label to those who were actually engaged in evil, the denouncers and the informers.

But Shulubin has no time for fine discriminations and ignores Kostoglotov's distinction. He obviously regards this conversation not as a dialogue but as a forum for the presentation of his views. It becomes clear that Shulubin wants a sympathetic listener, not a balanced discussion; topics replace each other at a furious pace, each new one presented with a frenzy and enthusiasm born of desperation—for each time may be Shulubin's last opportunity to express what he has kept within for so long. Critics are correct in sensing Shulubin's pedagogical tone; but before condemning him, we should keep in mind the urgency of his situation.[9]

Not only the actual wrongs of his compatriots but their motivation as well occupy Shulubin's deliberations on culpability. And behind both actions and motives he finds fear: a fear so strong that it made people oblivious to the demands of their conscience. Admitting that he himself had been subject to that fear of living in apostasy, "outside the community" as a nonconformist and rebel, he blames the atmosphere of Stalinism, which forced people to acquiesce in actions they knew were wrong and to rationalize this acquiescence.

Like the poet of "Summer," Shulubin uses historical precedents to support his views. Here the model is not Plato but Francis Bacon, the early seventeenth-century English philosopher. Reasoning, according to Bacon, could be sabotaged by four different types of errors, which he called the Idols of the Tribe, the Cave, the Marketplace, and the Theater. To draw hasty conclusions at the expense of contradictory evidence is to submit to the Idol of the Tribe. Idols of the Cave are the idiosyncratic qualities and traits of individuals that keep them from thinking correctly. Idols of the Marketplace are errors of communication associated with the imprecise use of words; often these words, together with their deceptively loose meanings, are associated with old, possibly outmoded philosophical and theological systems. Bacon's last category, Idols of the Theater, includes unquestioned dogmas tainted with superstitious theology.

Shulubin's account of Bacon's Idols, and his illustrations, are designed to be applied to contemporary Soviet reality—its taboos, myths, and ideological dogmas. And of course, it is difficult for Kostoglotov to rule out the literal application of the word "Idol" to Stalin himself: he envisages a bluish idol in a smoke-filled cave, with savages roasting meat nearby; an idol in the lobby of a theater, or on a curtain, or on the square. One of the most striking features of the Stalinist years was the ubiquitous representation of the leader himself—his symbolic presence in every phase of Soviet life. We may take Solzhenitsyn's insistence, in another context, on the literal meaning of "idol" as an indication that both applications have validity, that "Idol" need not refer to Stalin alone.[10]

Shulubin's definitions are not precisely those of Bacon, but they are consistent with the philosopher's terminology and examples. He defines Idols of the Theater, for example, as authoritative political and scientific opinions that people are inclined to accept without thinking on their own. Here Shulubin is obviously condemning mindless obedience to Party dogma and directives. Idols of the Marketplace, in Shulubin's interpretation, are errors in communication made when people use terms, formulas, and slogans indiscriminately—terms such as "traitor" and "enemy of the people." He implies that he himself has worshiped both kinds of idols. Kostoglotov too, when he is in the actual marketplace, will have his problems with Idols, especially those having to do with communication based on shared values. Generally speaking, the Idols foster and sustain a blindness to all but the state's values.

Shulubin closes his account of contemporary flaws in reasoning with a reference to the power that ensures obedience to the Idols. His description of this power serves as a prelude to his disturbing autobiography:

> And over all idols there is the sky of fear, the sky of fear overhung with gray clouds. You know, sometimes in the evenings thick, gray-black, low clouds gather, even without a storm; it gets gloomy and dark early, and the whole world makes you feel ill at ease; and all you want to do is hide under your roof, close to a fire and your family. For twenty-five years I lived under such a sky, and I saved myself only because I bowed low and kept silent. (411)

What compelled his silence was fear for his personal safety and the well-being of his family, his wife, and his children. But fate has punished him: his wife dies and his children grow up callous and insensitive. His hopes for domestic inviolability and security have had the wrong foundation, one constituted not by moral principles or the promptings of his conscience but by an untrustworthy state morality that offered only temporary security. Though aware of higher values, he acceded to the mundane.

Shulubin's betrayal of higher spiritual values is reflected in his very appearance. From the outset, Kostoglotov thinks he resembles a large bird with clipped wings. The resemblance is more than accidental; for here, as in Turgenev's novels, the bird, with its natural inclination for soaring at great heights, is an apt image for spiritual aspirations. Unfortunately, Shulubin-as-bird is tragically hobbled and must linger, painfully, in close proximity to the earth.

Kostoglotov is not the only one to note Shulubin's affinity to birds. Rusanov, for example, sees him as an eagle-owl, and this too is not accidental. The lexicographer Vladimir Dal' calls the raven and the eagle-owl birds of "ill tidings"—their cries mean misfortune. To Rusanov, who fears that his past victims will return to punish him, Shulubin represents misfortune, whether as eagle-owl or reproachful sentry.

Other images and literary allusions occur to Kostoglotov as he characterizes this guilt-ridden moralist. His perception of Shulubin as a bird changes, for example, when Shulubin speaks of his daughter. Now he is no longer a bird but the mad miller of Pushkin's (and later Aleksandr Dargomyzhskii's) "Rusalka" ("The Water-Spright"). But even here, Shulubin cannot escape his image: the miller in his grief at losing his daughter says he is a raven, not a miller. The miller's sadness at his loss and also his guilt—for he takes on much of the blame for his daughter's death—suggestively enhance the picture of Shulubin and his fate.

Shulubin is a graduate of one of the best schools and a leader in his field. He has done all he was supposed to do in bad times, compliantly confessing his mistakes when called upon to do so. Gradually withdrawing into less conspicuous and controversial positions, he descended the ladder, forced by circumstances and his quest for security into the role of a provincial librarian who burned books at the request of the state.

Having condemned himself, he turns his moral logic against all who have never been prisoners, finding them tyrants or traitors. He poses the question of culpability: how can a nation collectively lose its nerve? How can the bravery of early revolutionaries (and he was one) turn so quickly to cowardice? Why did such well-known and respected communists as Nadezhda Krupskaia (Lenin's wife) and Sergo Ordzhonikidze say nothing, when their words could have meant so much? Shulubin's criticism of himself and others who tolerated the lies is based on a philosophical system that he only sketches at the end of his lecture to Kostoglotov. There can be no doubt that this system has acquired a special significance now that he is under cancer's assault. His perceptions on the edge of the abyss have gained a new clarity, and his values—like those of Kostoglotov, who also has experienced life on the edge—have acquired an urgency and immediacy.

Previously, Shulubin has exhibited his new priorities in his conversations with other patients, particularly with the young geologist, Vadim. Merely by speaking out, Shulubin demonstrates a courage he has never before shown. Now, in his dialogue with Kostoglotov, he makes explicit what had been only implicit; and he provides a historicophilosophical context for his views.

What is suggested are possibilities worthy of exploration, a framework, and some of the principal terms. Shulubin advocates a socialism founded on ethics and the primacy of ethical considerations. He believes (and Solzhenitsyn in his publicistic work in the West has indicated that his own views are similar)[11] that considerations of right and wrong doom capitalism (which is based on greed) from the outset. Marxism too is flawed, for it gives priority to economic considerations before ethics. A socialism founded on ethics, however, will promote love and mutual affection as the highest motivating forces. Decidedly against happiness as a goal, on the grounds that it is too hard to define, Shulubin promotes mutual affection as the most worthy goal of social organization.

Invoking the names of three important non-Marxist thinkers, Shulubin builds his case for an ethical socialism. Nikolai Mikhailovskii, Petr Kropotkin, and Vladimir Solov'ev all believed in the primacy of ethical considerations. Shulubin does not provide any analysis of their contribution to ethics or social theory; he merely suggests that they are relevant. It is easy to speculate on what Shulubin found so appealing in these pre-revolutionary thinkers, whose views have never been endorsed by Soviet authorities.[12]

Kropotkin, for example, promoted the notion of mutual aid as the basis of all ethical principles; he conceived of morality as an evolutionary stage of the instinct of human sociability and an unconscious recognition of the close dependency of an individual's happiness upon the happiness of all. Shulubin invoked these ideas when he criticized Vadim's appeal to "what was interesting" as a criterion for choosing a vocation, since others less fortunate than he, without such a choice, worked long hours in tedious, repetitive work for the benefit of all. They could not afford the luxury of choosing a life based on "what was interesting." Kropotkin urged that we foster those feelings which induce human beings to unite for the purpose of attaining common ends by common effort, for these feelings are in harmony with our basic desires for unity and mutual sympathy. Furthermore, he believed that certain facts of animal life tended to support his position on mutual aid and sympathy. It is in his perception of the kinship between animal and human lives that we can see a connection with the novel's suggestive animal imagery (especially that of birds): the book is dense with animal references reminding us of our close ties with the animal kingdom.[13]

Mikhailovskii's insistence on the primacy of ethics (at a time when positivism, sociologism, religious mysticism, and Marxism were the dominant intellectual movements) and the importance of individual responsibility and moral judgment, as well as his emphasis on compassion ("Compassion lives in me and consumes my soul."), conscience, and honor all suggest the major ethical concerns of *Cancer Ward*. As for Solov'ev, there is possibly a metaphysical role (by way of Pushkin): as Shulubin lies in the recovery room, he quotes Pushkin's line, "Not all of me will die," reminding Kostoglotov of their previous conversation about immortality: "Sometimes I feel quite distinctly that what is inside me is not all of me. There's something else, very elevated, quite ineradicable, some little fragment of the World Spirit. Don't you feel that?" (453–54).

The immortality Shulubin hopes for is presumably based on or related to Solov'ev's notion of a "World Spirit."[14] In Solov'ev's philosophy, love is the key to immortality, for it enables one to unite with this transcendental "spirit." In view of the thematic prominence of love in the novel, Solov'ev's views seem especially appropriate.

Shulubin's rigid moralism and metaphysical transcendentalism are obviously to stand for a perspective Kostoglotov must consider and respond to. He is one among several of the characters whose views are portrayed positively and sympathetically. His perspective helps define one group of relevant issues for Kostoglotov—that individual happiness may not be worth pursuing, that helping others is a value in itself, that preserving one's life may not always be worth the price one has to pay, and that people easily delude themselves, succumbing to various "Idols." This last issue, the issue of delusion, whether of self or others, leads directly into the thematic center of the novel; for delusion, together with falsehood, are the major causes of moral blindness.

Shulubin plays much more than a peripheral role in the novel, for the issues he raises relate directly to the novel's fundamental concerns. Moreover, his character and his remarks establish a moral tone and frame through which other characters may be seen. His presence, his illness, and his views connect themes that define the novel's moral dimension.

First of all, his presence has made some in the ward uncomfortable, perhaps reminding them of death or former guilts. Second, his illness demonstrates the close connections between physical and moral health. Ailments have an eerie relationship to character and behavior: Rusanov and his cancer of the neck (he had "given it to people in the neck"), Podduev and his tongue, and now Shulubin, with an affliction that he believes will separate him from the rest of humanity.[15] The notion of a link between physical health and character is explicitly raised several times but is not limited to the patients. In fact, it is expressed most vividly when one of the principal surgeons, Dontsova, finds that she is suffering from the very disease she has dedicated her life to treating. As the kindly old Dr. Oreshchenkov, whom she has consulted, remarks, "It's the truest of all tests for a doctor to suffer from the disease he or she specializes in" (396).

This fascinating irony of fate is itself part of the framework of binary oppositions that structure the novel's ideology: medicines and X rays are both poisonous and curative, life is poised against death, truth struggles with falsehood, sight against blindness, the physical against the spiritual. Surely the novel's emphasis on the human qualities of animals is part of the same primitivistic scheme where things are not what they seem, and opposites gradually shade into each other.

Dr. Oreshchenkov is living proof of the close connection between many of these polarities, but especially between the physical and the spiritual. His life seems to symbolize their synthesis and balance—spiritual and physical equilibrium, peace, tranquility, health, and fulfillment are suggested by his name (Dormidont Tikhonovich—sleep, quiet), words, and demeanor. Moreover, the narration of Oreshchenkov's life testifies to his moral courage. Concern for values and for young people, a desire to treat each patient as an individual (he is very much opposed to specialists), a desire for simplicity, and a determination to defend his principles (which include the right to maintain a private practice) are all expressed in his words, actions, and gait. Not only does he strengthen associations between the physical and the moral, but he also gives support to one of the most pervasive metaphors in the novel: "sight" as a gauge of moral sensitivity.

Oreshchenkov's eyes never wander. He gives full attention to patients and visitors, always observing; for his eyes are "the chief instrument he used to study his patients and students, to convey his decisions or wishes." And he diagnoses without X rays, relying on a finely tuned instinct, as if using mechanical means meant yielding up his judgment to others. His cultivation of simple, unaided vision is linked with his philosophy of life, according to which the meaning of existence lies in preserving "unspoiled, undisturbed, and undistorted the image of eternity with which each person is born" (403).

Oreshchenkov stands in marked contrast to the other physicians, who to various degrees use euphemisms, indirection, and subterfuge in dealing with their patients. Nowhere does the tension of this dual vision become more pathetic than in the case of the radiotherapist, Dontsova, who suffers (ironically) from radiation sickness and cancer (the novel does not say exactly what kind, though she suspects it is cancer of the esophagus). She knows and anticipates every step of her diagnosis and treatment but fights this knowledge within so that she can maintain her cherished belief that patients should be kept from the truth at all costs.

The parallels between medical and "civilian" reality are transparent: "protecting" people from the truth is not a technique used only in the medical world. Kostoglotov is constantly combating lies; whatever the intentions behind them, they still entail blindness. Closing one's eyes to reality results from mindlessly accepting scientific opinions—bowing, as Shulubin would say, to the Idols of the Theater.

The novel argues that yielding to the Idols affects the family as well as the person who has yielded. Shulubin's children (and other young people in the novel, such as Vadim and Rusanov's daughter) are easy targets of the state's educational programs, which have promoted unity by encouraging the facile use of political labels, compliance with the desires of authorities, and the hatred of common enemies. Obviously, actions based on concern for family security can be counterproductive. Furthermore, although fear for the well-being of one's family may motivate compliance, the novel strongly suggests that human greed and the desire for material comforts and immediate gratification also wield considerable power in shaping attitudes toward the state.

Again and again the novel returns to the issue of truth versus the lie, whether the lie be delusion, rationalization, or benevolent euphemism. The question is sharply raised when Kostoglotov is speaking with the the the orderly Elizaveta Anatol'evna. She is the exiled wife of an incarcerated musician whose sin was speaking too openly about Stalin. Kostoglotov advises her to tell her young son the truth about their reality—that the whole family has been wrongly tainted by a society filled with taboos and intolerant of criticism—though he is well aware that doing so is not easy. Earlier he himself has withheld the truth from a terminal patient with a heart tumor out of a sense of consideration and sympathy for the victim. The novel poses the question whether these kinds of lies are different from those used by the doctors in their relationships with the patients. This crucial issue of facing the truth—and making others face the truth—though clearly presented with a bias toward candor and openness, is nonetheless given in all of its complexity.

Though lies may be told with the best of intentions, these very intentions are based on the assumption that the people being lied to are like children, to be protected from discomfort. And the lies quickly become second nature, working their way into consciousness so that in the mind of the teller they lose all resemblance to lying. Then, as unquestioned articles of dogma, they perpetuate infantile dependencies in adult situations. Vadim, for example, clearly links Stalin and the state with his own father, who was all-wise and all-powerful and whose authority could not be questioned. Even Vera Gangart, an otherwise mature woman, shows this childlike dependence (on her mother and her mother's values) and neurotic response to her reality, especially in personal matters. Solzhenitsyn gives considerable attention to her, detailing with obvious symbolism the decorating in her apartment (pictures suggesting isolation, imprisonment, and mourning); how she experienced life (she as it were "wore a mask" and "saw through goggles" for many years); and most telling of all, how, alone at night, she curls up like a child in her mother's armchair and listens to "Sleeping Beauty."

When Kostoglotov at the end of the novel realizes that he cannot live his life with her, because to do so would be to live a lie, his realization is linked with his seeing the bedding of her communal apartment hanging indecorously over the railings, with sexually suggestive contours: "If it hadn't have been for that pillow—with one corner of it all crumpled, and two corners hanging down like cows' udders and one sticking up like an obelisk—if it hadn't been for that pillow he could have grasped the situation and decided on something" (484).

After deciding against living a platonic life with Vera, he can become honest with himself and admit that his sexual feelings for her would make their relationship ridiculous and hypocritical. His longing to regress to earlier times (expressed repeatedly in imagery that likens him to a dog obedient to and grateful for affection from his mistress) when there were no problems and when everything he did was all right, when a wise and protective parent figure was there to console and protect him, is understandable considering the radical new orientation to reality he must take after facing imprisonment, exile, and death. He emphasizes his desire for "animal" simplicity at the beginning of this chapter (479) but remains fully aware of the fact that "real" life is not like this. Indeed, such a view of life is no more mature than Vadim's exalted respect for authority. Oleg and Vera's closest moment together occurs as he undergoes a transfusion, with her standing nearby, massaging the line carrying blood into him. In this unusual and tender scene of symbols and displaced sexuality, the most important point is that Oleg cannot see her. His "blindness" portends the failure of their relationship.

Facing and telling the truth are not easy, for people do not easily reject what has comforted them and made their lives secure. Furthermore, there are fears to overcome; to tell or even listen to the truth entails a risk. Kostoglotov knows from his experience that the risk is worth it and that life at any cost is not a philosophy to live by. Again Volodin's line, from *The First Circle*, is relevant. About to take a courageous and risky step to save another's life, he asks, "If one is forever cautious, can one remain a human being?" This is Shulubin's plight: he has been cautious; and his caution, he believes, has led to his disease, the treatment of which will in turn lead to separation from the human community. What makes his case more tragic is that his sight remains unimpaired throughout most of his unfortunate life. His visual and moral acuity did not correspond to his courage, however, and the consequences of caution are illustrated in his fate.

Sight and blindness are the central metaphors of the novel. They are linked in numerous ways with moral concepts, but the thread originates in Genesis, the book of the Bible with which the final two chapters of the novel ("The First Day of Creation" and "And the Last Day") resonate: eyes being opened are here related to the perception of good and evil (Genesis 3:5–7; and 21:9). And vision is the central moral issue of the novel's last chapter. On his walk through the zoo, Kostoglotov, feeling like a zoo animal himself, comes upon an empty cage of a Macaque Rhesus. The sign on the cage reads that an evil person threw tobacco in the monkey's eyes, blinding it. And this image of the monkey blinded by evil haunts Kostoglotov through the last line of the novel.

Shulubin again is an obvious referent; not only has Kostoglotov seen other monkeys that resemble him, but the Macaque's fate suggests Shulubin's "tobacco-colored" eyes. The issue of blindness, however, goes beyond

Shulubin into the fabric of the novel's ideology, relating concerns for the truth and also for the origins and nature of cruelty. The novel is populated with victims of cruelty, both animal and human. The line between them, in fact, is blurred by design. Not only are there the zoo animals, toward which Kostoglotov—and Solzhenitsyn—might be predisposed because of their imprisonment but there are also numerous dogs, all pictured in very human ways. Oreshchenkov's St. Bernard is almost human, and the Kadmins' dog, a particularly friendly one who lived with Kostoglotov's friends in exile, plays an especially telling role: it is killed by a gunshot wound to its eye and, like the monkey, is a victim of senseless violence against sight. Imagery and symbolism of arbitrary violence and animal affinities abound, exposing a complex picture of life and truth.

The concern for animals reflects Kostoglotov's camp experience, when human power, which ordinarily issues from our abilities, is obliterated by the sheer animalism of the struggle for survival. Camp experience compels a reorientation, an understanding of the basics of living, if one survives. And the need to survive provides a clearer sense of one's kinship with animals. Coming to terms with one's biological nature, stripped of civilized accretions, strengthens our sense of animal affinities and fosters concrete thinking. There is no theory, no experimentation, in the camps. And this can lead to personal growth as awareness of animal affinities moderates pride and helps people to come to grips with the biological nature of their humanness. Kostoglotov's rejection of Zoia, and especially of Vera, shows his understanding that human beings are both biological and spiritual. Further, his image of Shulubin as a hobbled bird, a spirit chained to the earth, suggests his recognition of the duality in human nature.

Encompassing and unifying the animal motifs is the blinded monkey, the preeminent animal symbol. Beyond his blindness, this creature's fate brings into focus crucial moral issues. First, the monkey has been blinded by an "evil" person. Describing this act in moral terminology is in accordance with the ethical views expressed by Shulubin. "Sight," as we have seen, is connected with moral sensitivity, historical awareness, and an ability to see the Idols for what they are, to understand ways in which society and the state present their version of reality. Late in the novel Kostoglotov says "a hard life deepens the ability to see" (475), thus linking victimization and moral vision. In this respect, the blinding of the monkey becomes a composite image of willful deprivation of the individual's means of discriminating truth from falsehood and good from bad. Once a live being is maimed, it can depend only on public values.

The "evil" done to the monkey is extremely important, drawing together the themes of victims, human and animal affinities, and the importance of love. For the novel concerns itself with victims of random evil; connections between the capacity to love animals and to love people; people who love animals (the Kadmins, Oreshchenkov, and Kostoglotov), people who resemble animals in their approach to life (in this sense, we think of the zoo animals, such as the noble antelope, the squirrel running nowhere in its cage, and the blinded monkey); and, related to this, the common plight of people and animals (blindings, maimings, imprisonment, and other forms of victimization).

There are, however, problems with accounting for human motivation with the concept of "evil." Though it is simple, direct, and in harmony with "ethical socialism," which rests on the priority of ethics, it unavoidably suggests a simplistic, overly clear world. One could argue, for example, that Kostoglotov's obsession with the problem of evil represents in its simplicity a sentimental longing for what cannot be, an attachment to a pastoral vision of a world where good and evil are clearly differentiated, a nostalgia disguised as hope for firm moral categories that will make life outside the camp easier to live. Simple political-ideological labels also make the world black and white, and because they do so, they encourage categorical solutions to moral problems. Though on the surface "evil" looks adequate as a concept, its application to the real world is not as simple as the sign over the monkey indicates. For if there is any lesson in Shulubin's story, or in Kostoglotov's venture "outside," it is that reality cannot be encompassed in easy categories, that there are no privileged access points or perspectives. Shulubin may be right in positing the primacy of ethics, but ethics will not provide simple solutions to the kind of problems Oleg Kostoglotov encounters. The use of the epithet "evil" may indicate that ideological labels have been abandoned in favor of those that are more fundamental, but it hardly indicates the simple solutions to all moral dilemmas.

The overwhelming impression of the last chapters of *Cancer Ward* is that Kostoglotov will have many problems adjusting to conventional life. It is not an easy world that awaits him, and his difficulties in coming to terms with it give us an appreciation of its complexity. Because he has had a hard life, he sees things differently; and because he sees things differently, he finds it difficult to adjust to ways of life that most others take for granted.

A number of surprises await Kostoglotov as he emerges from the cancer ward into the ordinary world. He experiences new pleasures of sight and taste but also disappointments about values: he is shocked by the unexpectedly high price of necessary material goods (food, medicine, clothes), a clear sign that his values are not in harmony with those of the rest of society. And this disharmony is brought home even more forcefully to him when he sees a man buying a shirt by shirt size:

What was this? People were rotting in trenches, people were thrown into mass graves, into shallow pits in the permafrost, people were being taken for the first, second, and third time into the camps, people were growing numb in prison trucks, people were straining themselves with picks to earn money for patched-up padded jackets—and here there was this fine fastidious fellow who can remember not only his shirt size, but also his collar size?!

It was the collar size that really hit Oleg! He could not believe that a collar had its own separate number! Stifling a wounded groan, he immediately left the shirts. A collar size too! What's the point of such a refined life? Why return to it? If you can remember your collar size—then you are bound to forget something! Something more important!

He simply grew weak over this collar size. (469)

It is no wonder later that, leaving the department store, he thinks back to his conversation with Shulubin: "And he dragged himself from this accursed temple into which he had recently run with such stupid greed, obedient to the idols of the marketplace . . ." (472). Even he is susceptible to those idols. Somewhere in the city, he realizes, he has lost his "pure *(tsel'nuiu)* morning soul" (472).

His previous experience, as well as Shulubin's example and theories, have made Kostoglotov sensitive to the gulf between his values and those of others. It is clear that people who have experienced life's extremes have a different, and often superior, vision of what is truly important in life. Solzhenitsyn presents human beings with their own "moral indicator," their own potential to see reality. But clouding their vision are idols, myths, prejudices, and lies that urge conformity, distort reality, and obscure direct apprehension of good and evil and right and wrong.

Even unobscured, moral judgments are not always simple. If Kostoglotov has learned anything, it is that neither truth nor telling the truth is simple. Self-serving lies are at one end of a scale which leads gradually to the merciful fabrications and euphemisms with which physicians shield their patients from painful realities. Kostoglotov longs for a world of certainties and directness, one in which a poison is labeled as a poison and not disguised as a "treatment." What Kostoglotov learns through his venture outside the ward/camp is that reality in general shuns easy categorizations and that there are no privileged perspectives. He is betrayed time and again by his senses, and his own expectations are constantly striking against the alien conventions that structure the social realities of Tashkent. The fact that he cannot recognize himself in the mirror in the department store points up his own alien status—he is out of tune with the world outside, the world of material goods, social proprieties, expensive shashlik, and shirts with neck sizes.

Claims of the body and the spirit are weighed, considered, and reconsidered by Kostoglotov when he visits the department store and the zoo. Wherever he goes, he attempts to come to terms with his new life by dealing with his basic needs as he feels them. Dealing with food and clothing is difficult for him, but not nearly so difficult as dealing with his sexual urges. Indeed, he links his concern over sexuality with his highest spiritual need, the need for truth. Thus, he realizes that joining Vera would mean deluding himself into thinking that a purely spiritual relationship with a woman can be fulfilling. Her idealism entails ignoring the demands of the physical organism. Because he is acutely aware of his sexual drive, he will not delude himself or Vera into thinking it can be ignored.

Deprivation in the camps included (for most) sexual deprivation; thus it is not surprising that sex, and having children, should be an important topic for Kostoglotov. He has been deprived of everything for years and now has a new freedom. That very peculiar relationship he has fostered with Vera is not without a sexual component, despite their solemn talk of a purely spiritual relationship. His ambivalence is betrayed by the very imagery he uses: on the one hand he is a dog at her feet, but simultaneously he lavishes physical tenderness on her. She is both an unapproachable Madonna, a spectral vision of purity and light ("Vega," he calls her), and at the same time (as he admits in his farewell letter) the object of his erotic desires. The truth remains one of Kostoglotov's principal concerns, and the truth—about himself as well as society—must be faced without blinders.

The novel suggests another perception of reality, one that is more comprehensive and more in harmony with human life: this perspective is one that rests on being truthful and, above all else, caring for others. Thus, despite his dedication to the truth, Kostoglotov, knowing that another patient is terminally ill, refuses to tell the patient this one truth. Shulubin's notion of mutual affection is the ethical heart of the novel, but Kostoglotov lives it by word and deed.

But another major theme, more problematic, is reflected in the ending. This time it is that on the last day of creation it is time to rest, just as Kostoglotov does, dangling his feet over the edge of the shelf in the train car. Obsessed with the problem of evil, he mimics the blinded monkey, burying his head in his rolled-up coat. What we should not lose sight of in evaluating this scene is that it is "the last day of creation"; and Kostoglotov, who has been "creating" his own values, may be more tired than dead.[16] His future is sure to include passion and potency, although not without some risk. (He has been prescribed a drug that would endanger his libido, but he has not been able to afford it.) Furthermore, the novel suggests in its final image of him, feet dangling over the edge of the bunk, that he has achieved a kind of balance and that he will perhaps come to understand that equilibrium pictured so well by the narrator in our final glimpse of Oreshchenkov in his rocking chair, poised between heaven and earth.

The categories of good and evil may seem simple, but they obscure a complex reality that offers no easy answers to moral questions. And seeing the truth is very painful. Kostoglotov has admitted while at the zoo that it would not be right to let the animals go, for they had no knowledge of "rational freedom." His position, having been deprived of freedom for so many years, is comparable. The moral apostasy he represents is the result of his victimization by Stalin and disease: he has known the extremes, and his experiences have tempered his moral sensibility so as to separate him from conventional society.

Shulubin is also condemned to live apart from society. His own culpability has given him special insight into the malaise, the massive self-delusion and cowardice that prevents people from doing what is morally right. He is punished not only by his conscience but also by disease; nonetheless, he has faith in a transcendent reality, a world spirit that promises him immortality.

Though his hope is immortality (expressed through Pushkin's rendering of Horace, "Not all of me shall die"), one could argue that what is expressed is the hope of the man who has not lived, whose life has been spent in an attempt to conquer death by trying to avoid it. Shulubin, who first sought a secure material reality, is still the seeker, now in search of another, spiritual reality. Indeed, he has not lived, though he has deluded himself that his actions were helping him to live: his hope was his family, for whom he sacrificed everything. In the end he is sick and alone, and disease has forged a link with his moral life. Having accepted whatever the state has given him all his life, he has come to realize the true value of this "gift," symbolized by cancer of the rectum. An excretory malady connotes a perverse balancing of the scales: what has been kept secret within him must now become public, visible to all; what had been concealed—actions taken out of fear of being ostracized by the society—are now made real outside his body, externally. Ironically, they will separate him from the very group with which he sought identity.

The narrative of *Cancer Ward* moves between different perspectives, presenting sympathetically various alternatives to Kostoglotov, who is concerned that without a firmly planted understanding of life's goals, he will not survive but will, like the Chu River, run out into the sands. Shulubin helps to define the relevant moral issues: that individual happiness may not be worth pursuing, that helping others is a value in itself, that preserving one's life may not always be worth the price, and that people delude themselves and succumb to various "idols" that lead them morally astray. Finally, Shulubin convincingly presents the perspective of a segment of society in the Stalinist years which has unwillingly supported what they knew to be wrong.

As examples of moral apostasy, Shulubin and Kostoglotov are unique to the twentieth century, for the concentration camps and mass atrocities of our age diminish the moral outrages of previous times. Terence Des Pres, in his study of survivors of twentieth-century atrocities, re-echoes a common theme of this book while discussing *One Day in the Life of Ivan Denisovich:* "Extremity intensifies experience, purifies it, forces men to the essence of their encounters with reality. Only sex (and how like sexual climax Shukhov's ritual is) comes close in that it too may issue in the physical intuition of a goodness at life's core."[17]

The point, however, has not been to demonstrate how adversity, a "hard life," and experience on the edge of the abyss lead to transcendence or the "goodness at life's core," even though such a point would be satisfying. Shulubin may achieve a vision of transcendence and immortality, but Kostoglotov clearly does not. His concerns are more pragmatic: with balancing needs and desires in this world and refining his understanding of the meaning of life. His is a struggle not just to survive but to understand the meaning of survival and to carry on with a mature, strong sense of autonomy that allows him to make decisions with his eyes open. His heroism is in carrying on. It is his vision as well as Shulubin's that have been the focus of our interest. Having survived life-threatening experiences, both men stand apart from their society, challenge the values that reign there, and question the assumption that conventional reality is the only reality.

The challenges of Shulubin and Kostoglotov are not unlike those of the characters studied earlier in this book. Revelations and visions which in themselves or in their consequences constitute moral apsotasy are a unifying theme in all these studies. What is more important, however, is the particularity of the literary situations explored. These literary situations individually carry distinctive moral implications which I have examined and clarified with a variety of critical tools.

In using various critical approaches to illuminate the moral dimension, I have tried to enhance appreciation for and understanding of some of Russia's best literary texts. This sampling of six Russian masters and masterpieces represents some of the varied approaches to the literary rendering of moral matters. Present and future readers searching for new meanings that relate to their own concerns and values should expect of these works new avenues of exploration; the texts are seemingly inexhaustible in their riches.

NOTES

CHAPTER 1

1. I am using the terms *moral* and *ethical* as they are used in most contemporary philosophical literature, i.e., as virtual synonyms. Moreover, I am using them in their "classifying," rather than "evaluating," sense. Thus to call standards, problems, or judgments moral is not generally to evaluate them positively or to endorse them (e.g., as in "He is a moral man.") but merely to set them apart from other kinds of problems, judgments, and standards. Although moral and ethical are regarded as synonymous here, I am aware that there is at least one kind of situation in which preserving the distinction might be useful: Ethical, when used in the Aristotelian sense of "that which is consistent with living a good life, or the best sort of life," is a term that encompasses what are often considered prudential issues, as well as moral ones. All uses of ethical in this particular sense will be noted.

2. Michael Holquist, "The Irrepressible I: The Role of Linguistic Subjectivity in Dissidence," *Yearbook of General and Comparative Literature* 31 (1982): 30.

3. On the dangers of exaggerating the influence of the censor, see Nicholas Rzhevsky, *Russian Literature and Ideology: Herzen, Dostoevsky, Leontiev, Tolstoy, Fadeyev* (Urbana: University of Illinois Press, 1983), 10–11.

4. See Richard Rorty's essay, "Nineteenth-Century Idealism and Twentieth-Century Textualism" in his *Consequences of Pragmatism (Essays: 1972–1980)* (Minneapolis: University of Minnesota Press, 1982), 139–59.

5. Wayne Booth gives a stimulating discussion of the issues surrounding ideological (and moral) criticism in "Freedom and Interpretation: Bakhtin and the Challenge of Feminist Criticism," *Critical Inquiry* 9 (1982): 45–76. I share Booth's preference for pragmatic moves in the very complicated area of ethical, political, psychological, and ideological criticism (see Booth, 54n.).

6. See Edward Wasiolek, "Wanted: A New Contextualism," *Critical Inquiry* 1 (1975): 623–39. His remark on Burke (639) comes in a summary of his program for turning attention from ontologies to strategies and making the most of "the systematizing and structuralizing functions of the human mind that take precedence over events that are independent of our constitutive faculties."

Wasiolek's comments are clearly in harmony with Rorty's on the virtues of pragmatism:

What is distinctively modern in modern literature depends for its effect upon straight men, and especially upon philosophers who defend "common-sense realism" against idealists, pragmatists, structuralists, and all others who impugn the distinction between the scientist and the poet. The modern revolt against what Foucault calls "the sovereignty of the signifier" helps us to think of creation of new descriptions, new vocabularies, new genres as the essentially human activity—it suggests the poet, rather than the knower, as the man who realizes human nature. ("Problem About Fictional Discourse?", *Consequences of Pragmatism*, 136–37.)

7. See, especially, Tynianov's "O literaturnom fakte" (1924); the work is included in his *Arkhaisty i novatory* (Leningrad: Priboi, 1929). For a discussion of Tynianov's criticism, see Sandra Rosengrant, "The Theoretical Criticism of Jurij Tynjanov," *Comparative Literature* 32 (1980): 355–89. Also see Victor Erlich, *Russian Formalism*, 3d ed. (Yale University Press, 1981), 251–71.

8. Wasiolek, 633.

9. Waclaw Lednicki, *Pushkin's "Bronze Horseman": The Story of a Masterpiece* (Berkeley: University of California Press, 1955), 2–3.

10. Steven Marcus, *Representations: Essays on Literature and Society* (New York: Random House, 1975), 310.

11. This terminology is from Roland Barthes; see "Writers, Intellectuals, and Teachers," in *A Barthes Reader* (New York: Hill and Wang, 1982), 388.

12. John Gardner, *The Art of Fiction: Notes on Craft for Young Writers* (New York: Alfred A. Knopf, 1984), 31.

13. Stanley Cavell makes a similar point about the capacity of literature to render the particularity of moral conflicts, their context and their consequences, and to present the human condition so as to make people appreciate the different positions on moral matters that can be taken. See his *The Claim of Reason: Wittgenstein, Skepticism, and Tragedy* (New York: Oxford University Press, 1979), 326.

The problem of morality perceived abstractly as obedience to principles and morality perceived pragmatically and concretely in examples is not limited to the philosophical disputes of pragmatists and antipragmatists. Carol Gilligan, for example, has made a strong case against traditional developmental psychology, demonstrating that its assumptions have been tied to a Kantian conception of morality and have tended to bias analyses of the way children develop their moral sensibilities. Though her basic argument (that notions boys have of morality—which emphasize objective principles and a formal logic of equality and reciprocity—have been unjustifiably regarded as superior, or more advanced, than those of girls of the same age) is not relevant to my discussion, her specification of those conceptions considered to typify females—e.g., notions that give importance to context and are distinguished by compassion and tolerance—supports Cavell's observations on literature, especially in regard to its role of emphasizing the concrete particularity of moral dilemmas within their social, historical, and psychological context; see Gilligan, *In a Different Voice: Psychological Theory and Women's Development* (Cambridge: Harvard University Press, 1982), 100.

CHAPTER 2

1. George Ivask, "The Vital Ambivalence of St. Petersburg," in *Texas Studies in Literature and Language* 17 (1975): 249. Waclaw Lednicki, in his *Pushkin's "Bronze Horseman": The Story of a Masterpiece* (Berkeley: University of California Press, 1955), provides an excellent discussion of the role of the city itself in Pushkin's poem, as

well as the literary and historical factors involved in the poem's genesis. Also see Donald Fanger's important examination of the myth in *Dostoevsky and Romantic Realism* (Cambridge: Harvard University Press, 1965), 103–6. For a discussion of the building of St. Petersburg and its cultural significance, see W. Bruce Lincoln, *The Romanovs: Autocrats of All the Russias* (New York: Dial Press, 1981), 239–70.

2. Nicholas's objections are discussed by Valerii Briusov, "Mednyi vsadnik," in *Pushkin*, ed. S. A. Vengerov, vol. 3 (St. Petersburg: Brokgauz i Efron, 1909), 470–72; T. G. Zenger, "Nikolai I—redaktor Pushkina," *Literaturnoe nasledstvo* 16–18 (1934), 522; Roman Jakobson, "The Statue in Puškin's Poetic Mythology," in *Puškin and His Sculptural Myth*, trans. John Burbank (The Hague: Mouton, 1975), 27; and B. V. Tomashevskii, "Pushkin i Peterburg," *Pushkin. Issledovaniia i materialy* III (Moscow-Leningrad: AN SSSR, 1960), 3, 43. For documentation on some of the principal interpretations of the poem's hidden meanings, see Dora Burton, "The Theme of Peter as Verbal Echo in 'Mednyj vsadnik,'" *Slavic and East European Journal* 26 (1982): 24. For documentation of poetic sources, see L. V. Pumpianskii, "'Mednyi vsadnik' i poeticheskaia traditsiia XVIII veka," *Pushkin. Vremennik Pushkinskoi komissii* IV (Moscow-Leningrad: AN SSSR, 1939), 91–124.

The edition of the poem used here is that found in Alexander Pushkin, *Polnoe sobranie sochinenii v desiati tomakh*, vol. 4 (Moscow: AN SSSR, 1963), 377–98. The English translation (based on this text) is by Walter Arndt, in *Pushkin Threefold* (New York: E. P. Dutton, 1972), 400–27. I have used Arndt's linear translation, with brackets omitted. His "form-true" translation is on pp. 131–44.

3. Pushkin had difficulties because some of his manuscripts were found among papers of the Decembrists. Also, sections of his "Andrei Shen'e," which were suggestive of Russian political conditions, were found circulating in manuscript; see "Pokazaniia po delu ob elegii 'Andrei Shen'e,'" in *Rukoiu Pushkina*, ed. M. A. Tsiavlovskii, L. B. Modzalevskii, and T. G. Zenger (Moscow-Leningrad: Academia, 1935), 743–48; also see George Gutsche, "Pushkin's 'Andrei Shen'e' and Poetic Genres in the 1820s," *Canadian-American Slavic Studies* 10 (1976): 189–204. For a discussion of Pushkin's political verse see, e.g., Efim Etkind's "Svoboda i zakon: Zametki na temu 'Pushkin i nasha sovremennost','" in *Russian Language Journal* 35 (1981): 12–17.

4. For a general summary of what took place in this meeting in 1826, see Iu. M. Lotman's recent biography, *Aleksandr Sergeevich Pushkin: Biografiia pisatelia* (Leningrad: Prosveshchenie, 1983), 137–42; see also Walter N. Vickery, *Alexander Pushkin* (New York: Twayne Publishers, 1970), 57. Nicholas apparently gave Pushkin reason to think that a "new Peter" had taken the throne (Lotman, 139). One could hypothesize that Evgenii (Pushkin) was deluded into thinking that he was on equal footing with Peter (Nicholas), only to realize subsequently that he was to be persecuted by the tsar.

For an historical account of the Decembrist uprising, see Anatole G. Mazour, *The First Russian Revolution, 1825* (Stanford University Press, 1965). A discussion of Pushkin and the Decembrists is given in V. E. Vatsuro and B. S. Meilakh, "Pushkin i deiatel'nost' tainykh obshchestv," in *Pushkin: Itogi i problemy izucheniia*, ed. B. P. Gorodetskii, N. V. Izmailov, and B. S. Meilakh (Moscow-Leningrad: AN SSSR, 1966), 168–97; also see Aleksandr Slonimskii's "Pushkin i dekabr'skoe dvizhenie," in *Pushkin*, Vengerov ed., 503–28, and N. Eidel'man, *Pushkin i dekabristy: Iz istorii vzaimootnoshenii* (Moscow: Khudozhestvennaia literatura, 1979).

5. Charles Corbet provides an account of the poem's Decembrist connections in his "Le symbolisme du Cavalier de Bronze," *Revue des études slaves* 45 (1966): 129–44. Also see D. D. Blagoi's "Decembrist" interpretation (which he later modified substantially), given in *Sotsiologiia tvorchestva Pushkina* (Moscow: Federatsiia, 1929); a summary is provided in *Pushkin: Itogi*, 402–3.

6. Iu. N. Tynianov discusses Pushkin's titling of his historical narrative poems, focusing attention on the relationship between "secondary figures" (like Evgenii) and the ostensible heroes (designated by the titles) and Pushkin's new conception of genre; see his "Pushkin," in *Pushkin i ego sovremenniki* (Moscow: Nauka, 1969), 153–54. Pumpianskii (93; see n. 2) discusses the title and subtitle as reflections of the poem's two principal concerns.

7. See Roman Jakobson (31) on the semiological role of the statue.

8. Pushkin's views of St. Petersburg, as reflected in his correspondence, are considerably more negative than these lines would suggest; see Jakobson, 24; and Lednicki, 57–68.

9. Jakobson, 35.

10. On the poem's break with the odic tradition, see Pumpianskii, 91–124.

11. Roland Barthes uses the idea of the "naturalized" in explaining myth: concepts become conventional, "naturalized," and understood as facts and essences ("Myth Today," in *A Barthes Reader*, ed. and with an introduction by Susan Sontag [New York: Hill and Wang, 1982], 131):

> What the world supplies to myth is a historical reality, defined, even if this goes back quite a while, by the way in which men have produced or used it; and what myth gives in return is a *natural* image of this reality. And just as bourgeois ideology is defined by the abandonment of the name "bourgeois," myth is constituted by the loss of the historical quality of things: in it, things lose the memory that they once were made. The world enters language as a dialectical relation between activities, between human actions; it comes out of myth as a harmonious display of essences. A conjuring trick has taken place; it has turned reality inside out, it has emptied it of history and has filled it with Nature, it has removed from things their human meaning so as to make them signify a human insignificance. The functon of myth is to empty reality: it is, literally, a ceaseless flowing out, a hemorrhage, or perhaps an evaporation, in short, a perceptible absence.

12. Lednicki's monograph is an excellent source for a summary of readings of *The Bronze Horseman;* a comprehensive, general account of the numerous perspectives that have been taken on the poem; and a discussion of the numerous issues the poem raises. For more recent summaries of criticism relating to the poem, see Armin Knigge, Puškin's *Verserzählung "Der eherne Reiter" in der russischen Kritik: Rebellion oder Unterwerfung* (Amsterdam: Adolf M. Hakkert, 1984); G. V. Makarovskaia, *"Mednyi vsadnik": Itogi i problemy izuchenii* (Saratov: Saratovskii universitet, 1978), and V. B. Sandomirskaia, "Poemy," in *Pushkin: Itogi i problemy izucheniia*, 398–406. Also see the new edition of the poem, *Mednyi vsadnik*, ed. N. V. Izmailov (Leningrad: AN SSSR, 1978), which contains the text, variants, documentary materials, and a survey of interpretations.

13. Lednicki, 52.

14. On this issue see Lednicki, 48–51; also see Victor Erlich, "Puškin's Moral Realism as a Structural Problem," in *Alexander Puškin: A Symposium on the 175th Anniversary of His Birth*, ed. Andrej Kodjak and Kiril Taranovsky (New York: New York University Press, 1976), 175.

15. Lednicki, 52.

16. Erlich, 174.

17. Erlich, 175.

18. Burton, 12–26.

19. The notions of pride deflated and happiness frustrated connect this poem with Pushkin's "miniature tragedies." See Victor Terras's "Puškin's 'Feast during the Plague'

and Its Original: A Structural Confrontation," in Kodjak and Taranovsky, 217.

20. Burton (22) draws the connection with broader strokes: Evgenii sees the "logical" link between his situation and imperial rule.

21. S. L. Frank calls attention to the theme of passions meeting implacable reality and the resulting madness, as well as Pushkin's fascination with demonic, life-threatening forces in "Svetlaia pechal'," *Etiudy o Pushkine* (Munich, 1957), 214; it is not unreasonable to link strongly felt emotions with irrational forces, the unknown within, and—when they have disastrous consequences—to associate them with the demonic. Terras too notes how Pushkin connected proud, "god-like" aspirations with diabolic forces (218).

22. A. D. P. Briggs, in his *Alexander Pushkin: A Critical Study* (Totowa, N.J.: Barnes and Noble, 1983), sees the most important theme of the poem as human impotence in the face of nature's enormous power (pp. 123–24); thus he identifies the poem's "saddest incident" as Alexander's recognition that even tsars cannot control God's elements.

23. Freud's definition of "melancholia" is remarkably apt:

> The distinguishing features of melancholia are a profoundly painful dejection, abrogation of interest in the outside world, loss of the capacity to love, inhibition of all activity, and a lowering of the self-regarding feelings to a degree that finds utterance in self-reproaches and self-revilings, and culminates in a delusional expectation of punishment.

Except for the fall in self-esteem, these features are characteristic of grief over loss as well. Freud's linking of profound mourning with loss of self-esteem, guilt, and suicidal tendencies provides an interesting perspective on Evgenii's reactions to his loss, suggesting how Evgenii might have died (the poem does not say). See "Mourning and Melancholia," in *A General Selection from the Works of Sigmund Freud*, ed. John Rickman (1917; Garden City, N. Y.: Doubleday and Company, 1957), 125.

24. Burton, without invoking Freud, talks of the Peter's "parental" wrath (22); seeing the tsar as a father figure gives additional suggestiveness to Evgenii's "identification," as well as his loss of his Parasha/mother.

For a discussion in psychoanalytic terms of the theme of the avenging statue in literature and myth, see Otto Rank, *The Don Juan Legend*, trans. and ed. David G. Winter (Princeton, N.J.: Princeton University Press, 1975); for discussions of the theme with reference to Pushkin's works, see Jakobson (4–10); and Andrej Kodjak (who expands the theme to include the "avenging playing card"), "'The Queen of Spades' in the Context of the Faust Legend," in Kodjak and Taranovsky, 112–14.

25. Another implication of this passage is that Alexander is no Peter.

26. Briggs, 130.

27. Erlich, 175.

28. D. S. Mirsky, *Pushkin* (New York: E. P. Dutton and Company, 1963), 166.

29. There seems to be little basis for Burton's statement that Peter persecutes Evgenii in a desire to "protect" his city against the "unleashed" forces of the humiliated. Peter disregards Evgenii (his back is turned toward him) until threatened, and then he becomes angry and pursues him. There is no evidence of higher motives here.

30. A Marxist perspective might focus on the interpenetration of economic values promoted by the state and attitudes of the populace toward the flood, or life-threatening disaster in general. The cold and unfeeling aura projected by the statue is clearly reflected in the behavior of the people of St. Petersburg following the flood. Soviet interpretations, following Vissarion Belinskii's lead, take a different tack, focusing on the conflict between state and individual with a view toward deter-

mining the victor in the conflict. One tradition, starting with Belinskii and rep-resented in our time by critics such as Blagoi, Gukovskii, and Reizov, comes down on the side of Peter and the statue, while another, led by Briusov and Merezhkovskii and followed by Makogonenko, Granin, Mezentsev, and others, sides with Evgenii and his protest. Yet another tradition, represented by Tynianov and later Timofeev (and Erlich: see above), takes the middle ground, emphasizing Pushkin's expression of the problem, not possible victors. Much depends, in this plethora of interpreta-tions, on choice of terms, perspectives, and level of abstraction.

31. "Cold apathy" is probably a more precise translation of *kholodnoe beschuvstvie*.

32. Lednicki (18–23 and 25–42) gives a detailed analysis of the poem as a polemical response to the Polish poet Adam Mickiewicz.

33. Not only is Pushkin to be identified with Peter, but the poem is to be consid-ered a work about the poet and poetry, about how Dionysian and Apollonian qual-ities come together in poetry; see Abram Tertz [Andrei Siniavskii], *Progulki s Pushkinym* (London: William Collins & Sons, and Overseas Publications Inter-change, 1975), 134–48. Briggs, too, speaks of affinities between the poet and Peter (129–30) when he notes how Pushkin unites sound and sense and imposes order with his rhyme scheme much in the way Peter ordered the elements in building his city.

34. Lednicki (72–84) explores the personal dimensions of the poem—particularly those aspects of Pushkin's final years (1833–1837) that suggest affinities between Pushkin's and Evgenii's goals, anxieties over losing loved ones, feelings of offense and aversion, eventual "humbling," and resignation. Corbet also covers the personal dimension, focusing on Pushkin's problems with Nicholas (139–44).

35. Briusov, 464.

36. See Blagoi (308–28) for a detailed analysis of the poem's Decembrist connec-tions.

The ambiguity of the statue's gesture was noted by Joseph de Maistre (Pushkin had in his library the 1831 edition of *Les Soirées de Saint-Petersbourg*): "On these deso-lated banks from which nature seems to have exiled life, Peter set his capital and created subjects for himself. His terrible arm is still extended over their descen-dants, who press around the august effigy; one looks at it and one does not know whether this bronze hand protects or whether it menaces" (cited in Lednicki, 36).

Pushkin's belief that the sovereign should show mercy is reflected in his poem "Feast of Peter the Great" (1835). The irony is that Peter is shown here to be merciful and forgiving—not vindictive. Pushkin apparently based his poem on Mikhail Lomonosov's reports of Peter's mercy toward those who had wronged him.

37. A. G. Mazour (204–5; 217) documents a strong case for this conclusion.

38. Cited in Mazour, 205.

39. Lednicki, 82–84.

40. Anna Akhmatova, "Pushkin i nevskoe vzmor'e," in *O Pushkine. Stat'i i zametki* (Leningrad: Sovetskii pisatel', 1977), 148–58. In this 1963 article, Akhmatova offers evidence establishing the depth of Pushkin's feelings over the providing of proper burial of his Decembrist friends and, in fact, over proper burial in general. As part of her argument, Akhmatova (155) uses one of Pushkin's unpublished poem fragments:

> Dva chuvstva divno blizki nam,
> V nikh obretaet serdtse pishchu:
> Liubov' k rodnomu pepelishchu,
> Liubov' k otecheskim grobam,
>
> . . . .
>
> Zhivotvoriashchaia sviatynia!
> Zemlia byla b bez nikh mertva

Kak   pustynia
I kak altar' bez bozhestva. (1830)

(Two feelings are wondrously close to us,
In them the heart finds nourishment:
Love for the native hearth,
Love for ancestral graves,

. . . .

Life-giving sacred thing!
The earth would be dead without them
Like a   desert
And like an altar without a divinity.)

This fragment is interesting not only because it testifies to Pushkin's feelings about respect for the dead (feelings with classical connections, as Akhmatova notes) but also because it helps to explain why no grass can grow where Evgenii is found and buried (lines 471–72). The gloomy ending of *The Bronze Horseman*, with the dead Evgenii buried in such a forlorn spot, and the open question of his unburied and unfound dear ones, acquires a mysterious depth when one considers the poet's futile search on the shores of the Neva for the graves of his Decembrist friends.

41. Documented by Mazour, 180.

42. There is no mention of *Antigone* in Pushkin's writings; we can assume Pushkin knew it, however, because of his classical education and his familiarity with A. W. Schlegel's *Lectures on Dramatic Art and Literature* (1809). To my knowledge, only Corbet (130) has pointed to the poem's kinship with *Antigone;* but he emphasizes only the clash between citizen and state, not the theme of proper burial, which is the basis for Antigone's revolt against state policies.

43. Briggs (131–32) notes how Evgenii's trip to find Parasha is analogous with crossing the River Styx on Charon's ferry. The manner in which the poem combines Christian and classical (pagan) elements is a topic deserving of further investigation. Jakobson notes, in this regard, that partially because of the Orthodox tradition in Russia, statues are associated with paganism, idolatry, and devilry—the antireligious and the supernatural (40).

D. S. Merezhkovskii explores pagan and Christian dimensions of the poem in his *Vechnye sputniki* (in *Polnoe sobranie sochinenii*, vol. 13 [Saint Petersburg, 1909], 456–65).

44. Antinomies are a basic feature of the poem; see Jakobson, 31: "The conversion of a sign into a thematic component is a favorite formal device of Pushkin's, and this is usually accompanied by exposed and pointed internal conflicts (antinomies) which are the necessary, indispensable basis of any semiotic world."

A semiotic frame of reference helps to account for the poem's suggestiveness, ambiguity, and referential power:

The relationship of the sign to the object signified, and especially the relationship of the representation to the object represented, their simultaneous identity and difference, is one of the most dramatic semiotic antinomies. It was precisely this antinomy that led to the bitter fights around iconoclasm; disputes about realistic art, which are constantly revived, are connected with precisely this antinomy, and the poetic symbolism exploits it. (Jakobson, p. 37)

45. Jakobson, 14.

46. *The Letters of Alexander Pushkin*, trans., with preface, introduction and notes by

J. Thomas Shaw (Madison: University of Wisconsin Press, 1967), 306–7. Blagoi (311–28) explores the theme of madness in Pushkin's works.

47. Walter Vickery, "Pushkin's 'Andzhelo': A Problem Piece," in *Mnemozina: Studia literaria in honorem V. Setchkarev* (Munich: Fink Verlag, 1974), 325–39; Vickery points out parallels, involving both the Decembrists and Pushkin's concerns over his own vulnerability, with other works by Pushkin in this period (333–35).

48. See Andrei Belyi, *Ritm kak dialektika i Mednyi vsadnik* (Moscow: Federatsiia, 1929), 266–79, for a discussion of Pushkin's psychological state and his relationship to Nicholas in the 1830s.

49. Vickery, 332. Much of what is said relating to *Angelo* can be applied to *The Bronze Horseman*. For example, B. S. Meilakh (in *Nedelia*, 6 December 1964, p. 16; cited in Vickery, 333) sees the central problem of *Angelo* as "the essence of tyranny, of the unlimited power of the despot, of the relationship of authority and the people, of the dogma of punitive law and the living logic of human feeling. . . ." Meilakh also draws attention to possible parallels in the work with the situation of the Decembrists and also with conditions in Russia under Nicholas. The crucial issue for *The Bronze Horseman*, I have argued, is the confrontation between the personalized and punitive law of the statue and the "living logic of human feeling" that Evgenii expresses. His anger functions as an emphatic message that is both biological and moral; see Joseph de Rivera, "A Structural Theory of the Emotions," in *Psychological Issues*, X, monograph 40 (New York: International Universities Press, 1977), for a discussion of the moral dimension of anger.

CHAPTER 3

1. I. Vinnikova, "Stat'ia 'Gamlet i Don-Kikhot' i demokraticheskii geroi v romane *Nakanune*," in *I. S. Turgenev v shestidesiatye gody (Ocherki i nabliudeniia)* (Saratov: Saratovskii universitet, 1965), 16.

2. As Turgenev expressed it, at the basis of the novel was the idea of the need for "consciously heroic nature"; I. S. Turgenev, *Polnoe sobranie sochinenii i pisem v dvadtsati vos'mi tomakh* 8 (Moscow-Leningrad: AN SSSR, 1964), 507. Here can be found valuable background material on the period and on topical issues in the novel (501, 520–21); also see Leonard Schapiro, *Turgenev: His Life and Times* (New York: Random House, 1978), 154; and Victor Ripp, *Turgenev's Russia: From "Notes of a Hunter" to "Fathers and Sons"* (Ithaca: Cornell University Press, 1980), 159–81.

The text of *On the Eve* used here is from vol. 8 of the complete works cited above (pp. 7–167). References to the text and annotations from this edition will be indicated by volume and page number. All translations are my own.

3. Petr Kropotkin, for example, indicated how important Turgenev's women were to his generation (8:522). For background information on prototypes and issues relating to women in the 1850s, see 8:517–18; 520; 522–23; also see Christine Johanson, "Turgenev's Heroines: A Historical Assessment," *Canadian Slavonic Papers* 26 (1984): 15–23; and Ripp, 160–73.

4. For views of Insarov, see 8:496–97.

5. Most critics of the novel have noted the central importance of character (e.g., Ripp, 162). Not all have been satisfied with the portrayal of Elena, however; Konstantin Leont'ev, for example, in "Pis'mo provintsiala k I. Turgenevu," in his *Sobranie sochinenii* 8 (Moscow: Izdanie V. M. Sablina, 1912)(1–14), is very critical of Turgenev's description of Elena, finding her pale and lifeless as a character (10).

The related issue—how Turgenev integrates political topics into his character studies—is also often studied. For discussions of the novel in terms of personal versus ideological, see, for example, Richard Freeborn, *Turgenev: The Novelist's Novelist, A Study* (Glasgow: Oxford University Press, 1960), 115; and Irving Howe, "Turgenev: The Virtues of Hesitation," *Hudson Review* 8 (1956): 540, who speaks of Turgenev's best work as a successful integration of two levels, the personal—where character reigns supreme—and the sociopolitical.

6. There are several studies of Schopenhauer's influence on Turgenev. One of the most obvious traces of the philosopher (noted by the editors of Turgenev's works, 8:543) is in Bersenev's distinction between love as pleasure and love as sacrifice (chapter 1). The question of Schopenhauer's influence is treated by A. Walicki, "Turgenev and Schopenhauer," *Oxford Slavonic Papers* 10 (Oxford: Clarendon Press, 1962), 1–17; Marina Ledkovsky (who concentrates on Schopenhauer's influence on Turgenev's view of the supernatural), *The Other Turgenev: From Romanticism to Symbolism* (Würzburg: Jal-verlag, 1973); and Vinnikova (see n. 1), 7, 20–22.

7. Contemporary critics from the political left and right, Nikolai Dobroliubov and Apollon Grigor'ev (8:538–39) appreciated the psychological subtleties (especially as revealed in the scenes in Venice). But the more politically oriented Dobroliubov complained that Insarov was not shown in action and that he was not one of "their own" (i.e., a Russian); thus he was not an ideal moral model, and the novel was not as politically significant as it might have been (8:533).

8. Freeborn (53) discusses structural patterns in the novels; also see Henry Gifford, "Turgenev," in *Nineteenth-Century Russian Literature: Studies of Ten Russian Writers*, ed. John Fennell (Berkeley and Los Angeles: University of California Press, 1973), 149.

9. The critic Mikhail Gershenzon noted the key ideological role of the first chapter in *Mechta in mysl' I. S. Turgeneva* (1919; Providence: Brown University Reprint, 1970), 84–85.

10. See Robert Dessaix's excellent study of the novel in his *Turgenev: The Quest for Faith* (Canberra: Australian National University Faculty of the Arts, 1980), 58–75. Elena and Insarov, he argues, were deeply imbued with Romanticism; thus Elena was predisposed to expect a Romantic hero in Insarov.

11. Ripp, 174.

12. Vinnikova, 25.

13. Dessaix, 62.

14. Dessaix, 62.

15. I think there is considerably more joy in their relationship than Ripp (176) sees; for example, Elena admits in Venice that for "weeks in a row" they were happy (8:156).

16. Dessaix, for example (64–65), uses this to build his case for Insarov's romantic individualism.

17. Ripp discusses the stay in Venice (179–80) but concentrates on its ambiguous role; while not completely disagreeing with his interpretation of the city's role, I would tend to go along with Dobroliubov and Grigor'ev in emphasizing the positive aspects of the city as Elena and Insarov experience them.

18. The influence of Schopenhauer may be in evidence here. It was his view that music, as the highest of the arts, represented a way of transcending anxiety over death (Ledkovsky, 46–47); he also associates it with the joys and sorrows of love (50).

19. Grigor'ev (as quoted in 8:538–39); originally from his article, "Iskusstvo i nravstvennost'," *Svitok*, no. 1, section 3 (1861), 12.

20. Changes not only magnify Elena's feelings of guilt; some also seem designed to

modify her "immodesty," which apparently offended contemporary norms of morality (8:508–9). Additional discussion of changes in various editions is given in 8:501–2 and 505–7.

21. Religion in Elena's life (and in Turgenev's as well) is taken up by Gershenzon, 81–82; and Dessaix, 68–69. In the end she abandons God as conventionally conceived.

22. Critics have sensed the cynicism beneath the surface as well as the nihilism; Dessaix (69–71) draws attention to biographical connections. Freeborn (115) notes the curious correlation of ideological optimism and personal pessimism and suggests that the two qualities are inversely related in the novel; I am not so sure that talk of optimism—in either the personal or ideological sphere—is justified.

23. Dessaix's explanation of Insarov's appeal is presented in the context of accounts provided by Turgenev's contemporaries (60–61). Nineteenth-century views, such as Dobroliubov's, tended to emphasize the quality of Insarov's idealism, the "greatness" of his ideal ("Kogda zhe pridet nastoiashchii den?"; reprinted in *Sobranie kriticheskikh materialov dlia izucheniia proizvedenii I. S. Turgeneva*, comp. V. Zelinskii, vol. II, part 1 [Moscow, 1899], 167). Modifications of this line included the suggestion of P. I. Basistov (in an 1860 review, 163–64) that Insarov realized her dream of action in behalf of the good. K. Chernyshev said Insarov was attractive to her because he was a living incarnation of an ideal, passionately committed to it and to action with all of his being; in *Lishnie liudi i zhenskie tipy v romanakh i povestiakh I. S. Turgeneva* (1896; quoted in *Sobranie*, 188–89). More recent critics continue along the same lines; Freeborn, for example, points to his appeal as the bearer of high ideals (92); S. M. Petrov suggests it is the "wholeness of his personality," his successful integration of words and action, that appeals to Elena (*I. S. Turgenev, Tvorcheskii put'* [Moscow: GIKhL 1961], 338); Ripp, however, offers something a bit different (174): Insarov represents sexual freedom as well as a chance to satisfy her intellectual quest; Insarov will help her "fulfill her desire to better the human condition." Ripp also offers an interesting account of Insarov's motivation—he willingly takes on the burden of Elena's love because it will inspire the best in him: he "equates" her with the "totality of experience" (176). Insarov's tragedy, according to Ripp, is that he mistakenly relied on someone outside himself, and not on himself. This reading is appealing, but it is not convincingly demonstrated.

24. Johanson's article is particularly informative on the limited possibilities for women; she notes how Elena's actions were especially serious when assessed in terms of Russian traditions and laws at that time (17–18). Because the legal code forbade marriage without parental consent, Elena's father was within his rights to divorce the couple and even to cloister her; this threat turns up in distorted form in her dream at the end of the novel.

25. The dark side of Insarov is examined from a moralistic (and disapproving) standpoint by A. I. Nezelenov, in his *Ivan Sergeevich Turgenev v ego proizvedeniiakh* (Saint Petersburg, 1903); see especially 206–11; Elena's fate is interpreted in terms reflecting the sexual morality of the time: she falls from purity, yields to (what Nezelenov considers) baser forces within her, and ends up betraying family and country. Coarse sensuality (represented by Insarov) leads to her downfall and unhappiness (215).

26. Another interesting possibility (within a frame that emphasizes Elena's interrelations with her family) is that Elena's choice of a foreigner as her sexual partner was modeled on her father's choice of Avgustina Khristianova.

27. Freeborn is undoubtedly correct in noting that Elena's sense of guilt was there long before she met Insarov, and that it was undoubtedly connected with personal emotions she regarded as self-indulgent (117). I have suggested that these feelings may have found an early manifestation in her relationship with Katia, in the strange-

ness she felt when she challenged her parents' values and authority. This relationship allowed Elena to vent feelings of hostility, dissatisfaction, and rebellion that were already there, waiting for an opportunity to be released; Katia represented more to Elena than a "vision of escape" (Freeborn, 116), and Elena's sense of dissatisfaction did not so much stem from but rather manifested itself in her relationship with Katia. Elena's remark in her last letter that she may have killed Insarov clearly indicates that she feels responsible and that her guilty feelings have greatly intensified. Ripp's interpretation of the remark (176–77)—it represents her realization that she served as the object of Insarov's misplaced reliance—seems unfounded.

28. As Ledkovsky notes (61), dreams have a special significance, connected with his reading of Schopenhauer, for Turgenev. Departed spirits can, for example, call the living, much as Katia and Insarov call out to Elena.

Elena frequently has dreams (she even dreams that Insarov has threatened her with a knife [8:80]). He too has dreams: of particular interest is his feverish dream following his visit to the businessman who is to procure a passport for Elena. The dream is laden with sexual imagery (including a knife) that makes sense in view of the fact that the meeting that preceded it was disturbing to him because it compromised Elena's virtue; see Ripp, 177–78.

Also see Eva Kagan-Kans, *Hamlet and Don Quixote: Turgenev's Ambivalent Vision* (The Hague, Paris: Mouton, 1975), 121–36; and Dessaix, 66–67, on dreams in the novel.

29. The "chaplet" (or *venok*) also connotes a marriage wreath. Thus, the episode with Katia hints at the future in yet another way.

30. Bird imagery is pervasive, as the excerpts suggest. See Gershenzon (74–86) for a discussion of Turgenev's use of bird imagery; generally speaking, the bird to Turgenev represented spiritual health, wholeness, and harmony.

31. Wasiolek, "Design in the Russian Novel," in *The Russian Novel from Pushkin to Pasternak*, ed. John Garrard (New Haven and London: Yale University Press, 1983), 55.

32. As Nezelenov (211; and Ripp, from a completely different perspective) noted, the second meeting (chap. 28) is very daring, for Elena offers herself sexually to Insarov (8:131).

33. The whole passage reads: "Elena did not know that the happiness of each person is based on the misfortune of another, and even profit and comfort require—as a statue requires a pedestal—the loss and discomfort of others" (8:157). This generalization lends itself easily to a Marxist perspective; as A. I. Batiuto notes (in *Turgenev—Romanist* [Leningrad: Nauka, 1972], 128–29), it also suggests the influence of Darwin.

34. According to Nezelenov (213–16), Elena's conscience was an indicator she ignored, the voice of inner truth, a moral guide. By not heeding it, she sacrificed her moral purity. Insarov was unworthy of his goal and for that reason died, for activity can only be fruitful when on the proper moral foundation.

35. Also see Vinnikova's article on the relation of Turgenev's essay, "Hamlet and Don Quixote," to the novel; Dessaix, too, refers to this essay. As he notes (63), self-delusion is a quixotic trait.

36. Dessaix, 64.

37. I agree with Dessaix's account, which emphasizes the novel's ambiguous representation of heroism (69), and also its "pessimistically mystical interpretation of life forces" (74).

38. Dessaix, 62.

39. Dessaix, 68–69; Freeborn expresses a similar view, though not in the same terminology of "suprahuman forces," when he states that destiny does not allow people happiness except as a kind of accident—and that when it is allowed, it is accom-

panied by guilt (120). In a similar key, human efforts to achieve "heroic self-suffi-
ciency" are also doomed, for destiny does not give people this right (121).

40. Gershenzon, 80.

CHAPTER 4

1. John Gardner, who praised the moral energy and commitment of Tolstoi's art,
was a notable exception; see his "Death by Art; or, 'Some Men Kill You with a Six-
Gun, Some Men with a Pen,'" in *Critical Inquiry* 3:4 (1977): 741–71.

2. "What Is Religion and in What Is Its Essence?", in *Polnoe sobranie sochinenii*
(Moscow: 1928–1958), 35:187–88. All textual citations refer to this ninety-volume
Jubilee edition; translations are my own, except where otherwise noted.

3. The topic of Tolstoi's religious views in his later years deserves special study.
As might be expected, his unorthodox thinking has generated considerable discussion and controversy. For a general account of how Russian philosophers have regarded Tolstoi's views, see George L. Kline, *Religious and Anti-Religious Thought in
Russia* (Chicago: University of Chicago Press, 1968), 28–34; also see V. V. Zenkovsky, *A History of Russian Philosophy*, trans. George L. Kline, vol. 1 (New York:
Columbia University Press, 1967), 392–96. George Steiner, in his *Tolstoy and Dostoevsky: An Essay in the Old Criticism* (New York: Vintage Books, 1961), 249–68, offers a fascinating discussion of the principal features of Tolstoi's religious
philosophy; he focuses on Tolstoi's anti-Platonistic view of the kingdom of God,
Tolstoi's attack on the theodicy of compensation, Tolstoi's chiliasm, his view of God
as "enclosed" in man, and his concept of Christ as a man.

4. Edward Wasiolek, *Tolstoy's Major Fiction* (University of Chicago Press, 1978),
109–12, 168–69, 199. Tolstoy has many characters in his fiction whose self-denial
and self-sacrifice are not virtues but empty abstractions impoverishing their lives.
Tolstoy's model is an "individualism" characterized by "at-one-ness with one's
being and the sensuous flow about one" (178).

5. In recent years readings have appeared that are more or less consistent with
Christianity in its conventional forms. James Olney, for example, in his "Experience, Metaphor, and Meaning: The Death of Ivan Ilych," *Journal of Aesthetics and Art
Criticism* 31 (1972): 101–14, emphasizes the power of Christ's example and the concepts of atonement, redemption, and grace (112); Olney's reading, complete with
quotations from the Vulgate, molds the story into an acceptable Roman Catholic
text. Robert Duncan adduces significant biblical allusions in the text to build a case
for the centrality of repentance and faith in God as conventionally conceived: "Ivan
Ilych's Death: Secular or Religious?", *University of Dayton Review* 15 (1981): 99–106.

6. Wasiolek explores the basic assumptions of Tolstoi's narrative style in efforts to
exonerate Tolstoi from the charge of being overbearing in "Tolstoy's *The Death of
Ivan Ilych* and Jamesian Fictional Imperatives," *Modern Fiction Studies* 6 (1960): 314–
24 (reprinted in revised form in *Tolstoy: A Collection of Critical Essays*, ed. Ralph E.
Matlaw [Englewood Cliffs, New Jersey: Prentice Hall, 1967], 146–56).

7. The quoted text ends by pointing up the difference between persuading by
logical demonstration and by artistic presentation: "And universal art, by uniting
the most different people in one common feeling by destroying separation, will educate people to union and will show them, not by reason but by life itself, the joy of
universal union reaching beyond the bounds set by life" *(What Is Art? and Essays on
Art*, trans. Aylmer Maude [New York: Oxford University Press, 1962], 288).

8. The powerful effect of Tostoi's imagery is examined by C. J. G. Turner,
"The Language of Fiction: Word Clusters in Tolstoy's *The Death of Ivan Ilyich*," *Modern Language Review* 65 (1970): 116–21; also see Robert Russell, "From Individual to

Universal: Tolstoy's 'Smert' Ivana Il'icha,'" *Modern Language Review* 76 (1981): 631.

9. See Gary R. Jahn, 231–33, in "The Role of the Ending in Lev Tolstoi's The Death of Ivan Il'ich," *Canadian Slavonic Papers* (September, 1982): 229–38.

10. Mythic connections of the story with the stories of Job, Orestes and the Eumenides, and Satan are suggested by William V. Spanos, "Leo Tolstoy's *The Death of Ivan Ilych:* A Temporal Interpretation," in *De-structing the Novel: Essays in Applied Postmodern Hermeneutics* (Troy, N. Y.: Whitston Publishing, 1982), 1–64; see esp. 6.

11. See, e.g., Gary R. Jahn, "The Death of Ivan Il'ič—Chapter One," in *Studies in Honor of Xenia Gąsiorowska* (Columbus, Ohio: Slavica Publishers, 1983), 37–43; also see Russell, 630–32; and Wasiolek (1978), 171.

12. L. P. Grossman, "Smert' Ivana Il'icha," 26: 679–91; text of the story, 26:61–113. For a history of the writing and a discussion of textual changes in successive editions, see L. D. Opul'skaia, *Lev Nikolaevich Tolstoi: Materialy k biografii c 1886 po 1892 god* (Moscow: Nauka, 1979), 7–16.

13. William B. Edgerton, "Tolstoy, Immortality, and Twentieth-Century Physics," *Canadian Slavonic Papers* 21 (1979): 293.

14. Mark Aldanov noted that Tolstoi first strove to "frighten the reader with death and then to reconcile him to it"; see his *Zagadka Tolstogo* (1923 Berlin; Providence, R.I.: Brown University Reprints, 1969), 60.

15. The importance of expressions referring to "pity" in the ideological fabric of the story is discussed by Russell, 631–32.

16. Thus I disagree with Spanos's pessimistic conclusion about the effects of Ivan's death on others: "What we discover—and are disturbed by—is that, despite the unspeakably terrible experience one of them has suffered, this 'community' has understood virtually nothing about it" (34).

Conclusions about Ivan's redemption also seem questionable: "Ivan, that is, has redeemed his life, but he has died a terribly lonely, as well as painful, death. Unlike the Christ he imitates, his crucifixion has not redeemed the world" (34). I argue that Ivan's death is neither "lonely" nor "painful" and is, in Tolstoi's view, probably much like Christ's in its potential effectiveness.

17. Several efforts have been made to approach Ivan's death with a perspective derived from Elizabeth Kübler-Ross's *On Death and Dying* (New York: Macmillan, 1969). It has been argued that Ivan's decline for the most part follows the pattern of denial, anger, depression, bargaining, and acceptance, with a final depersonalization and step-by-step withdrawal from the physical world ("decathexis"). According to Kübler-Ross, reaching this final stage marks a healthy and normal detachment—one achieved only by patients who have worked through their dying (170). Ivan's final joy may mark a departure from the norm, however; usually the acceptance stage is totally devoid of feelings (113), though moments of emotion may precede it.

For discussions using a thanatological perspective, see Y. J. Dayanada, *"The Death of Ivan Ilych:* A Psychological Study on Death and Dying," *Literature and Psychology* 22 (1972): 191–98; Walter Smyrniw, "Tolstoy's Depiction of Death in the Context of Recent Studies of the 'Experience of Dying,'" *Canadian Slavonic Papers* 21 (1979): 367–79; H. L. Cate, "On Death and Dying in Tolstoy's *'The Death of Ivan Ilych,'*" *Hartford Studies in Literature* 7 (1975): 195–205.

18. Kübler-Ross comments on the relationship of dying to early childhood experiences (112, 120). The complicated interconnections between deathbed regressions to childhood, feelings of rebirth, and immortality wish-formation recognized by psychoanalysis can easily be related to Ivan's story. For a discussion from a psychoanalytic perspective of experiences associated with dying and the feeling of

rebirth, see Richard S. Blacher, "Death, Resurrection, and Rebirth: Observations in Cardiac Surgery," *Psychoanalytic Quarterly* 52 (1983): 56–72; G. H. Pollock, "On Mourning, Immortality, and Utopia," *Journal of American Psychoanalytical Association* 23 (1975): 334–62. The connections of death and rebirth from a religious perspective are discussed by Duncan, 103–4.

19. Spanos, 38–48, gives a perceptive discussion of Ivan's replacement of one kind of language (his society's) by another, more authentic kind; language serves as a measure of the quality of Ivan's life: the more he rejects "public" language, the closer he comes to experiencing "the thing itself." While some may not agree with Spanos's ontological presuppositions and concerns, it is difficult to disagree with his perceptive observations on the relationship of various "languages" in the text.

20. As Kübler-Ross notes, "the harder they struggle to avoid the inevitable death, the more they try to deny it, the more difficult it will be for them to reach this final stage of acceptance with peace and dignity" (114).

21. Without denying the symbolic value of the black bag as womb or intestine, it is also possible to associate it with Ivan's ailment, as it was explained to him by doctors. Freud, in his *Introductory Lectures on Psychoanalysis* (New York: W. W. Norton, 1966) cites an 1861 study by K. A. Scherner which linked dreams with illness: "dreams seek above all to represent the organ that sends out the stimulus by objects resembling it" (95, 479). Also see Boris Sorokin's discussion of the image of the black sack in "Ivan Il'yich as Jonah: A Cruel Joke," *Canadian Slavic Studies* 5 (1971): 487–501, 503–4.

22. W. R. Hirschberg gives a concise and convincing demonstration of how the image of the womb makes for a coherent and reasonable reading: "Tolstoy's *The Death of Ivan Ilich*," *Explicator* 28, item 26 (1969). The link with excretion is discussed by Sorokin (see n. 19); Spanos too (20–28) refers to the theme of excretion, although he does not mention the black sack in this regard.

For Schopenhauer, whose works Tolstoi was familiar with, death is a natural part of the ongoing process of creation and destruction and does not differ in kind from excretion, which is also part of the process of creation and destruction within the body; something inessential is lost in both cases:

> The process of nourishing is a constant reproduction; the process of reproduction is a higher power of nourishing. The pleasure which accompanies the act of procreation is a higher power of the agreeableness of the sense of life. On the other hand, excretion, the constant exhalation and throwing off of matter, is the same as that which, at a higher power, death, is the contrary of generation. And if here we are always content to retain the form without lamenting the discarded matter, we ought to bear ourselves in the same way if in death the same thing happens, in a higher degree and to the whole, as takes place daily and hourly in a partial manner in excretion: if we are indifferent to the one, we ought not to shrink from the other. *(The World as Will and Idea,* trans. R. B. Haldane and J. Kemp [London: Routledge & Kegan Paul, 1883], 357)

Tolstoi's affinities with Schopenhauer are well known; especially relevant are his philosophical impersonalism (the moral order is attained by giving up the personal self), his emphasis on compassion and on denying the will to live, and his unconventional concepts of death and immortality; see Sigrid McLaughlin, "Some Aspects of Tolstoy's Intellectural Development: Tolstoy and Schopenhauer," *California Slavonic Studies* 5 (1970), 187–245, esp. 233; also Zenkovsky, 391–92.

23. Jahn (1982) points out how Tolstoi had used a similar metaphor of disorientation in describing his own conversion (in "What I Believe," cited on 232):

It happened to me as it happens to a man who goes out on some business and on the way suddenly decides that the business is unnecessary and returns home. All that was on his right is now on his left, and all that was on his left is now on his right; his former wish to get as far as possible from home has changed into a wish to be as near as possible to it. The direction of my life and desires became different, and good and evil changed places.

24. Tolstoi is promoting here an ethics of care, one that is "relational," emphasizing the universal need for compassion and care; see Carol Gilligan, *In a Different Voice: Psychological Theory and Women's Development* (Cambridge: Harvard University Press, 1982), 73, 98. This is the positive side of the socio-moral program suggested in the story—a side Spanos's "ontological" perspective underplays (34).

25. Duncan, 104, draws attention to the Christian parallel: Jesus said children and servants are ranked high in the kingdom of God (Matthew 18:3–4; Mark 10:14–16, 44–45). Ivan's final contact with Vasia, as well as his recollections of his own youth, underlines the theme of "innocent childhood" and suggests a biographical and subtextual dimension; see David Matual, *"The Confession* as a Subtext in *The Death of Ivan Il'ich," International Fiction Studies* 8 (1981): 25, 124–28.

26. Duncan and Jahn, for example, have conclusively demonstrated a biblical subtext, but how it relates to the story is still problematic.

27. Although it is true that Ivan's conversion does not have lasting results with respect to Praskov'ia, who continues to be caught up in the style of life of her class, for Vasia there is still hope: his father's conversion corresponds with the boy's incipient adolescence (the dark circles under his eyes are usually taken by critics to mean that he has begun to masturbate), and it was at approximately this age when his father first came under the corrupting influence of society. The force of Ivan's example, together with the boy's yet untainted sincerity and compassion, offer the only protection from the coercive pressure and mendacity that invariably accompany life led according to the pleasure principle. His father's rebirth and death serve as a rite of initiation as the boy enters the adult world. Thus it is not so clear that Ivan's death was a total failure as far as its effects on others are concerned; it has had an effect on Vasia, as well as on Peter Ivanovich: it indicates the "right" way, and now it is up to them to act on what they have learned.

28. Here critics part ways, depending on the significance they give to the power of the unconscious; most give prominence to Ivan's intention, not what he said, since it is a traditional request for forgiveness and suggests repentance (contrition) of a conventional sort. Hirschberg (and I) find a deeper meaning in Ivan's slip of the tongue: he is falling under the control of positive inner forces that will eventually direct him into the light. This reading has the advantage of coherence with what subsequently happens to Ivan, his passage from darkness into light: the expression *"propusti"* suggests that death will be a "transition" (see Edgerton, 298).

29. In his theological writing, Tolstoi emphasized not Christ as a savior, but as a man who lived and died in exemplary fashion. It is evil to strive for personal gain and pleasure, and the meaning of life will never be discovered by those who do. Living for others is the key to fulfillment and immortality. By showing compassion and by loving others one adds "something to the life and the salvation of others," and this loving spirit lives on in others long after one's own physical death. Tolstoi accumulates numerous examples of how organized Christianity has perverted Christ's simple and eminently practical message of love for one's neighbors and salvation through this love; salvation is not eternal and personal salvation (in a heavenly paradise) but liberation from lies and deceptions. It is also joy now on earth. Christ was not teaching salvation by faith or asceticism (which Tolstoi respectively labels "salvation by deceit of the imagination" and "by voluntary tortures in this life");

rather, he taught a way of life that would give people less suffering and more joy by saving them from the pain of a personal life *("V chem moia vera,"* 1882–1884, 23:401–2).

30. True life is beyond concerns of the flesh, beyond the limits of space and time; see "On Life" *("O zhizni"),* 26:401–9.

31. The structural properties of the story, including its temporal development, have been examined in great detail by Jahn (1982); Gunter Schaarschmidt, "Theme and Discourse Structure in *The Death of Ivan Il'ich," Canadian Slavonic Papers* 21 (1979): 356–66; Irving Halperin, "The Structural Integrity of *The Death of Ivan Il'ič," Slavic and East European Journal* 5 (1961): 334–40; and Spanos, 8–35, who focuses on the temporal dimension.

32. See, for example, discussions by Edgerton, McLaughlin, and Zenkovsky.

33. See Spanos.

34. Zenkovsky, 394.

35. Cited in Edgerton, 293.

36. Kline, 28–29, 33.

37. Temira Pachmuss, "The Theme of Love and Death in Tolstoy's *The Death of Ivan Ilych," American Slavic and East European Review* 20 (1961): 72–83.

38. Part of what makes Ivan's suffering seem so incommensurate with his sins is the assumption that the world is basically just and that life is fair. Tolstoi rejected this notion, replacing it with another: suffering does not vary with the quality of one's life; it is always there, sometimes very intense and sometimes less so. It can be minimized only by adopting the right attitude toward life (Tolstoi's comprehension). Adopting an alternative picture not dependent on our sense of balance and fairness is a tactic adopted by twentieth-century thinkers as well; for examples, see D. Z. Phillips, *Death and Immortality* (London: Macmillan, 1970), 52–55.

39. The issue of whether the story is secular or religious usually arises at this point. Duncan, for example, adduces the numerous New Testament parallels and allusions, together with Ivan's final "revelation," to prove that Tolstoi's vision is religious in the broad sense, and Christian besides. R. F. Christian, however, rejects the Christian conclusion (of Mirsky) that Ivan at the end "sees the inner light of Faith, renunciation, and love" and states that Ivan does not see at the bottom of the sack "God's love or immortality, but only a release from suffering" *(Tolstoy: A Critical Introduction* [Cambridge: Cambridge University Press, 1969], 237). Tolstoi thus, according to Christian, avoids a "facile 'religious' conclusion." While it is clear that Tolstoi avoids the "facile" solution, it seems equally clear that there is much more than "release" at the bottom of the sack: for Ivan, besides the absence of pain, there are the feelings of having vanquished death and of intense joy.

40. Duncan reads this differently; it is not a failure of conventional religion, represented by the priest and the rite of confession, but of Ivan, who is still clinging to his sinful ways and not yet ready to receive confession (102). This explanation will seem unsatisfactory, I suspect, to anyone who has read Tolstoi's vitriolic response to his excommunication, particularly his discussion of Church sacraments (34:245).

41. See Duncan, 103–4, for a discussion in biblical terms of the significance of "three," the connections between death and baptism, rebirth (the black sack as a "womb"), and Ivan's "change of mind," which to Duncan represents "repentance."

42. Tolstoi devoted considerable discussion to the matter of Christ's resurrection and "life after death" in the conclusion to his harmonization and translation of the Gospels (24:790–98); as might be expected, he was highly critical of conventional, and theologically official, understandings of this important part of Christian dogma.

43. Wasiolek (1978) suggests Marxist and psychoanalytic possibilities (169–70); also see his "Wanted: A New Contextualism," *Critical Inquiry* 1 (1975): 623–39. For a Marxist analysis of the story, see B. Tarasov, "Analiz burzhuaznogo soznaniia v povesti L. N. Tolstogo, 'Smert' Ivana Il'icha,'" *Voprosy literatury* 3 (1982): 156–76.

This approach seems particularly suitable for analyzing what was wrong with Ivan's life, viz., the constant flight from the facts of existence, such as birth, death, and love (171–72).

44. See Kenneth Ring, *Life at Death: A Scientific Investigation of the Near-Death Experience* (New York: Coward, McCann and Geoghegan, 1980).

CHAPTER 5

1. The two quotations are from *Detstvo (Childhood)*, in M. Gor'kii, *Polnoe sobranie sochinenii*, 25 vols. (Moscow: Nauka, 1972), 15:288–90. Other references to Gor'kii's works in this chapter are to this edition.

2. For a fine general discussion of Gor'kii's life and activity, see Irwin Weil, *Gorky: His Literary Development and Influence on Soviet Intellectual Life* (New York: Random House, 1966).

3. The text of the story is in Gor'kii's *Polnoe sobranie sochinenii*, 25 vols. (Moscow: Nauka, 1970), 5:7–21 (notes on 509–13); a translation may be found in *A Sky-Blue Life and Selected Stories of Maxim Gorky* (New York: New American Library, 1964), 111–28. All translations in this chapter are my own.

4. D. S. Mirsky, *A History of Russian Literature*, ed. Francis J. Whitfield (New York: Alfred A. Knopf, 1966), 381–82. This opinion is not universal (see, e.g., Vladimir Nabokov's sardonic critique in his *Lectures on Russian Literature* [New York and London: Harcourt Brace Jovanovich, 1981], 305–6; his fulminations against this story of a teenage girl who becomes the object of religious adoration are fascinating and ironic).

Studies referred to in this chapter included Jeffrey Bartkovich, "Maxim Gorky's 'Twenty-six Men and a Girl': The Destruction of an Illusion," *Studies in Short Fiction* 10 (1973): 287–88; N. Gekker, "'Dvadtsat' shest' i odna': Poema Gor'kogo," in *Kriticheskie stat'i o proizvedeniiakh Maksima Gor'kogo*, ed. S. Grinberg (St. Petersburg, 1901), 210–15; L. E. Obolenskii, "'Dvadtsat' shest' i odna': Poema M. Gor'kogo," in *Kriticheskie stat'i*, 233–35; L. Michael O'Toole, *Structure, Style and Interpretation in the Russian Short Story* (New Haven and London: Yale University Press, 1982), 128–41; A. I. Ovcharenko, "Obrazy rabochikh v rannem tvorchestve M. Gor'kogo," *O polozhitel'nom geroe v tvorchestve M. Gor'kogo 1892–1907: Stat'i* (Moscow: Sovetskii pisatel', 1956), 129–33; V. A. Kalashnikov, *Pisatel' i ego geroi: O polemicheskoi napravlennosti i nekotorykh drugikh osobennostiakh rannikh rasskazov M. Gor'kogo* (Minsk: Nauka i tekhnika, 1969), 170–71; F. M. Borras, *Maxim Gorky: The Writer* (Oxford: Oxford University Press, 1967), 86–88; Helen Muchnic, *From Gorky to Pasternak* (New York: Vintage, 1961), 70–72; and B. V. Mikhailovskii, *Tvorchestvo M. Gor'kogo i mirovaia literatura 1892–1916* (Moscow: Nauka, 1965), 185–86.

5. Mikhailovskii, Gekker, Ovcharenko, and Kalashnikov focus on the workers and the significance of their disillusionment. Several early interpretations (cited in the notes to the edition of the story used in this study) by A. A. Divil'kovskii (in 1905) and M. M. Filippov (1901) also give principal attention to the men.

6. The date of the story (1899) suggests its transitional status. It was written after the major "tramp" stories ("Chelkash" and "Makar Chudra") yet before Gor'kii's powerful dramatic treatment of the theme of "inspiring lies," *Na dne* (1902). The human longing for ideals, for something to worship, was a literary theme used by Gor'kii in a variety of forms throughout his literary and journalistic career.

7. The artistic function of the narrator is discussed by Ovcharenko, 182, and O'Toole, 133. Gor'kii talks of the Kazan' bakery and his experiences there in his autobiography, *Moi universitety*, in *Polnoe sobranie sochinenii*, 16:37–38 (English transla-

tion: *The Autobiography of Maxim Gorky* [New York: Collier Books, 1962], 537–39). Borras, 87–88, suggests a biographical dimension: the story represents a way for Gor'kii to express his disappointment over the ways humans (in particular, a woman he had idealized) fell short of his expectations.

8. See remarks on "reactionary criticism," especially the comments of F. Dobronravov (1902) and M. O. Menshikov (1900), in the 1970 edition, 511. Kalashnikov, 171, similarly speaks of the workers' superiority to Tania, who turns out to be *poshlaia* (vulgar) and insignificant in comparison with their image of her.

9. The psychologist Erik H. Erikson, in his *Childhood and Society*, 2d ed. (New York: W. W. Norton, 1963) offers a fascinating account of Gor'kii's biography ("The Legend of Maxim Gorky's Youth"); he gives particular attention to psychological patterns that may be peculiar to Russian society. In discussing the sadomasochistic temperament (related to the theme that suffering is "good" for salvation) of Gor'kii's grandfather, for example, he speculates that masochistic identification with authority has served as a "collective force" in Russian history and that the young Gor'kii rejects this pattern of response when his grandfather illustrates it (370–71).

10. Filia Holtzman, in *The Young Maxim Gorky: 1868–1902* (New York: Columbia University Press, 1948), 136, includes Tania in Gor'kii's early "heroes of protest and unrest"; she, like Loiko Zobar, Rada (from "Chelkash"), Chelkash, Konovalov, Foma Gordeev, and others, are "symbolic personifications of rebellion against all restrictions and prohibitions in Russian life." O'Toole (134–35, 139) also emphasizes Tania's vitality and individualism; Bartkovich (287), however, applies negative moral criteria in referring to Tania ("proclivity to evil"), as does Muchnic (72), who refers to the pathos of Tania's "fall" and her loss of "innocence and the respect of men."

11. See *Moi universitety (My Universities)*, in *Polnoe sobranie sochinenii*, 16:37–38.

12. For a discussion of this period in Gor'kii's life, see George L. Kline, *Religious and Anti-Religious Thought in Russia* (Chicago: University of Chicago, 1968), 112–16.

13. A similar image was used in "Suprugi Orlovy" (1897), in which a tavern is pictured as a beast's mouth, swallowing the Russian people. O'Toole also notes the personified inanimate forces ruling the pretzel makers (135).

14. The apocryphal story of the Virgin's visit to Hell *(Khozhdenie bogoroditsy po mukam)* is also a possible subtext.

15. Although there is no direct evidence of Gor'kii's familiarity with the poetry or philosophy of Vladimir Solov'ev, there is much to indicate that Gor'kii was well aware of the literary and cultural movements of his day. See Aleksandr Ninov, *M. Gor'kii i Iv. Bunin: Istoriia otnoshenii—problemy tvorchestva* (Leningrad: Sovetskii pisatel', 1973), 74–130; S. Elizarov, "Bor'ba M. Gor'kogo protiv reaktsionnykh tendentsii v literature," in *Stat'i o Gor'kom: Sbornik* (Moscow: GIKhL, 1957), 269–347; Mary Louise Loe, "Maksim Gor'kii and the *Sreda* Circle: 1899–1905," 44 *Slavic Review:* 49–66; and A. A. Volkov, *M. Gor'kii i literaturnoe dvizhenie kontsa XIX i nachalo XX vekov* (Moscow: Sovetskii pisatel', 1954). A discussion of Solov'ev's views, and in particular the concept of Sophia, may be found in Samuel D. Cioran, *Vladimir Solov'ev and the Knighthood of the Divine Sophia* (Waterloo, Ontario: Wilfrid Laurier University Press, 1977), esp. 42–63; the reference to Sophia at the "Entrances," which comes from Proverbs 8 and 9, is given on 18, n. 13. Just as Gor'kii seems to have given Sophia a concrete exemplification, so he would later give, as Ninov notes (83–84), the modernist motif of poet as smithy an expanded, more mundane ("social-revolutionary") meaning in his play *Meshchane* (1901).

16. See especially chap. 12 of *Detstvo (Childhood)*, in *Polnoe sobranie sochinenii*, 15:172–86.

17. These quotations are from Gor'kii's reminiscences of Tolstoi ("O Tolstom"),

in *Polnoe sobranie sochinenii*, 16:302–3.

18. Betty Forman notes that Nietzsche's "On the Prejudice of Philosophers" (a section of *Beyond Good and Evil)* appeared in Russian translation shortly before "Twenty-six and One" was published ("Nietzsche and Gorky in the 1890s: The Case for an Early Influence," in *Western Philosophical Systems in Russian Literature*, ed. Anthony M. Mlikotin [Los Angeles: University of Southern California Press, 1980], 163). She also notes (161) parallels between Gor'kii and Nietzsche in their glorification of strength, pride, and beauty in the exceptional individual and their preoccupation with inspiring and ennobling illusions (or "lies").

19. Muchnic, 72, sees this element of the story as an expresssion of "man's tragic inclination to destroy himself unwittingly, setting traps for what he lives and loves by." The psychological theory from which this observation springs is not elaborated.

20. Although *poema* designates a narrative poem, the term was also applied to prose works (by Gogol' and later writers). A. A. Volkov, *Put' khudozhnika: M. Gor'kii do Oktiabria* (Moscow: GIKhL, 1969), 55, associates the genre subtitle with the work's "poetic feeling" as well as its moral-heroic dimension; his focus, however, is on the workers, not Tania. Ovcharenko, 132–33, refers to the harmony of tone and genre, the story's "exalted essence," and musical qualities (which are analyzed in terms of syntactic parallelism, anaphora, contrasts, and rhetorical questions). O'Toole (136–37), using Roman Jakobson's concept of the "poetic function" of language, calls attention to metaphors, syntax, and phonetic patterning. The *Kratkaia literaturnaia entsiklopedia*, vol. 5 (1968), 934–35, indicates that the *poema* in the late nineteenth and early twentieth centuries had a mixture of lyrical and epic sources.

21. Gekker (214–15) saw hope for the twenty-six: they will keep looking for a better, more reliable, ideal, while Tania will discover disillusionment. Ovcharenko (131) observes in the ending an affirmation of the workers' bright future in the destruction of their illusions about Tania; the removal of an idol "pleases" the narrator because it improves the workers' chances for "renewing" life. This reading imposes an unsatisfyingly optimistic frame on the text.

22. Ovcharenko, again endeavoring to find hope for the workers, states that what is important is that they have found unanimity, have shown an ability to defend mutual ideals, and have indicated that they can live better through their common love for the *good*. Next time they will love what is truly good. Kalashnikov, 171, believes that they have retained their faith in the beauty of people. Muchnic, in contrast to critics with somewhat rosier pictures, can find nothing positive in the workers' lot (72); even with her lost innocence, Tania is in love, free, and healthy, while they are sick and imprisoned. O'Toole's view is similar: Tania (and the soldier) represent an assertion of the life force in individuals, while the workers illustrate "death in life of the collective consciousness" (140). Finally, Bartkovich, 288, sees the story as essentially nihilistic and thus fails to appreciate the positive model Tania provides.

CHAPTER 6

1. The poet Marina Tsvetaeva singled out Pasternak's optimism and hope as qualities he preserved under the most trying conditions; see her essay "Svetovoi liven': Poeziia vechnoi muzhestvennosti," in *Proza* (New York: Chekhov Publishing House, 1953), 353–71.

2. See, for example, Ronald Hingley, *Nightingale Fever: Russian Poets in Revolution* (New York: Alfred A. Knopf, 1981), 168–73. Antonina Filonov Gove discusses one of Pasternak's more outspoken lyrics, "Dusha" (which was published only in the

West); written in the fifties, after the death of Stalin, this indictment of the Soviet age does not present the same degree of risk that it would have in Stalinist times. See "The Poet's Self: Images of Soul in Four Poems of Pasternak," *Slavic and East European Journal* 27 (1983): 195–97.

3. The text used here is that included in Boris Pasternak, *Stikhotvoreniia i poemy* (Moscow, Leningrad: Sovetskii pisatel', 1965), 354–56; the poem was published in *Novyi mir*, 4 (1931): 63; and in the collection *Poverkh bar'erov* (Moscow, Leningrad; GIKhL, 1931), with a dedication to Irina Sergeevna Asmus; this dedication was omitted in the version printed in *Vtoroe rozhdenie* (Moscow: Federatsiia, 1932) and *Stikhotvoreniia v odnom tome* (Leningrad, 1933). A more important difference between the first printed texts of the poem is the omission of lines 33–36 in *Poverkh bar'erov* and *Stikhotvoreniia v odnom tome*. These lines refer, perhaps too transparently, to the prototypical (and thus contemporary) plague. The American edition, edited by Gleb Struve and Boris Filippov *(Boris Pasternak: Sochineniia,* 2 vols. [Ann Arbor: University of Michigan Press, 1961]), restores the dedication and prints the poem (1:331–33) so that lines 17–28 are divided into three quatrains instead of two sextains. This arrangement of the poem does not appear to affect my interpretation.

4. The poem is discussed by Dale L. Plank in *Pasternak's Lyric: A Study of Sound and Imagery* (The Hague: Mouton, 1960), 110–12; Johanna Renate Döring, *Die Lyrik Pasternaks in den Jahren 1928–34* (Munich: Otto Sagner, 1973), 91–95, 129, 150–51; and Krystyna Pomorska, in *Themes and Variations in Pasternak's Poetics* (Lisse: Peter de Ridder, 1975), 42–50.

5. See, for example, Nils Åke Nillson's excellent discussion and demonstration of this feature of Pasternak's poety in "Life as Ecstasy and Sacrifice," *Scando-Slavica* 5 (1959): 188–89. See also Andrei Siniavskii's "Predislovie" (31–32), in Boris Pasternak, *Stikhotvoreniia i poemy* (reprinted in translation as "On Boris Pasternak," in *Twentieth-Century Russian Literary Criticism*, ed. Victor Erlich [New Haven and London: Yale University Press, 1975], 235–46).

6. Samuel J. Kayser, in his article "Wallace Stevens: Form and Meaning in Four Poems," *College English* 37 (1976): 578–98, draws the same kinds of correlations between sound and meaning in the analysis of Stevens's poems.

7. Pomorska, 53.

8. Plank, 112; see also Plank's discussion and summary of scholarship on Pasternak's use of anagrams in the composition of his poetry (16–17).

9. Georgii Adamovich notes the poem's sudden shift from murkiness and vagueness to clarity in the ending; see his essay "Vladimir Nabokov," 229, in *Twentieth-Century Russian Literary Criticism*.

10. Siniavskii, 19–21.

11. I am endebted to Professor Herman Ermolaev of Princeton University for many useful suggestions concerning the poem's references to collectivization.

12. See Donald W. Treadgold, *Twentieth Century Russia*, 2d ed. (Chicago: Rand McNally, 1966), 269.

13. "Symposium," in *Plato: Selections*, ed. Raphael Demos (New York: Charles Scribner's Sons, 1955), 255.

14. A. S. Pushkin, *Polnoe sobranie sochinenii v desiati tomakh*, vol. 5 (Moscow: AN SSSR, 1964), 419.

15. The central position in Pushkin's play of Mary's concept of self-sacrificing love and concern for others (which is what the last stanza of "Summer" also emphasizes) is strongly advanced by I. D. Ermakov in his *Etiudy po psikhologii tvorchestva A. S. Pushkina* (Moscow, Petrograd: Gosizdat, 1923), 131–51.

16. Olga Ivinskaya, in her recollections of life with Pasternak, refers to experiences she had with him, as well as passages in *Dr. Zhivago*, in explaining the promi-

nence of hope, death, art, and resurrection in his worldview; see *A Captive of Time*, trans. Max Hayward (New York: Warner Books, 1979), 149–50. Pasternak's correspondence with Olga Freidenberg provides a biographical context for the experiences recorded in the poem; see Boris Pasternak, *Perepiska s Ol'goi Freidenberg* (New York: Harcourt Brace Jovanovich, 1981), 131–37.

17. Boris Pasternak, *Dr. Zhivago* (New York: Pantheon, 1958), 89–90. The poems Gove analyzes reinforce this theme—the close ties between art, love, and life, and the power of art, when it is united with love, to overcome death (198).

CHAPTER 7

1. Solzhenitsyn gives the publishing history of his novel, as well as some information on prototypes for his characters, in the 1979 edition of his works, Alexandr Solzhenitsyn, *Sobranie sochinenii*, 7 vols. to date (Vermont-Paris: YMCA-Press, 1979). Page numbers in the text refer to this edition; this quotation is from 4:36. Translations are my own.

2. Solzhenitsyn's publicistic work is discussed by John Dunlop, "Solzhenitsyn in Exile," in *Survey* 21 (1975): 133–54; and Edward E. Ericson, Jr., in his *Solzhenitsyn: The Moral Vision* (Grand Rapids, Mich.: William B. Eerdmans, 1980), 177–219.

3. See Georges Adamovitch, "Une Mise en garde," in *Soljénitsyne*, ed. Georges Nivat and Michel Aucouturier (Paris: L'Herne, 1970), 412–16. Stephen Allaback, in his *Alexander Solzhenitsyn* (New York: Taplinger Publishing Company, 1978), summarizes some of the critical discussion of Shulubin (169) and offers several reasons that Shulubin cannot be entirely trusted with the novel's moral significance. Discussions of the novel may be found in Francis Barker, *Solzhenitsyn: Politics and Form* (New York: Barnes and Noble, 1977); Lawrence L. Langer, *The Age of Atrocity: Death in Modern Literature* (Boston: Beacon Press, 1978); Kevin Windle, "Symbolism and Analogy in Solzhenitsyn's *Cancer Ward*," *Canadian Slavonic Papers* 13, nos. 2–3 (1971): 193–206; Christopher Moody, *Solzhenitsyn*, 2d rev. ed. (New York: Barnes and Noble, 1976); and Abraham Rothberg, *Aleksandr Solzhenitsyn: The Major Novels* (Ithaca, N.Y.: Cornell University Press, 1971).

4. See the chapter on Solzhenitsyn's experience in a cancer ward in Michael Scammell, *Solzhenitsyn: A Biography* (New York, London: W. W. Norton, 1984), 334–55.

5. For interesting comments on Vera Gangart in particular, see Georges Nivat, "On Solzhenitsyn's Symbolism," in *Solzhenitsyn: A Collection of Critical Essays*, ed. Kathryn Feuer (Englewood Cliffs, N.J.: Prentice-Hall, 1976), 54, 58.

6. Gary Kern discusses the symmetrical aspects of the ward in his "The Case of Kostoglotov," *Russian Literature Triquarterly* 11 (1975): 409–10.

7. For a discussion of Solzhenitsyn's use of material from the Russian literary tradition, see James M. Curtis, *Solzhenitsyn's Traditional Imagination* (Athens: University of Georgia Press, 1984); see 61–68 for the discussion of Tolstoi and *Cancer Ward*.

8. The text of the poem is from Aleksandr Pushkin, *Polnoe sobranie sochinenii v desiati tomakh* (Moscow: AN SSSR, 1963), 2:331.

9. Allaback has reservations about Shulubin's intellectualism, dogmatism, and lecturing tone (170–71).

10. See David A. Sloane, "*Cancer Ward* Revisited: Analogical Models and the Theme of Reassessment," *Slavic and East European Journal* 26 (1982): 403–18, for a discussion of the various levels of symbolism and analogous relationships in the novel.

11. Ericson (101–2) doubts whether Solzhenitsyn would subscribe to any kind of

socialism or to the notion (expressed by Shulubin) that "man is a biological type."

12. See Nivat's illuminating remarks (54) on Shulubin's philosophical sources.

13. Kern (423–26) gives an excellent discussion of the "animals" in the novel.

14. The "World Spirit" Shulubin refers to may be derived from other philosophical sources as well. Also see Nivat on Shulubin and Solov'ev (54).

15. John Schillinger, "Labor Camps and Other Malignancies in *Cancer Ward:* A Further Diagnosis," *Russian Language Journal* 37 (1983): 131–32.

16. For a summary of the controversy over Kostoglotov's health at the end of the novel, see Kern, 423.

17. Terence Des Pres, "The Heroism of Survival," in *Alexander Solzhenitsyn: Critical Essays and Documentary Materials*, ed. John B. Dunlop et al. (Belmont, Mass.: Nordland, 1973), 50.

BIBLIOGRAPHY

PRIMARY TEXTS

Gor'kii, Maksim [Aleksei Peshkov]. *Polnoe sobranie sochinenii.* 25 vols. Moscow: Nauka, 1968–80.

Pasternak, Boris. *Dr. Zhivago.* Translated by Max Hayward and Manya Harari. New York: Pantheon, 1958.

———. *Perepiska s Ol'goi Freidenberg.* New York: Harcourt Brace Jovanovich, 1981.

———. *Sochineniia.* Edited by Gleb Struve and Boris Filippov. Vol. 1. Ann Arbor: University of Michigan Press, 1961.

———. *Stikhotvoreniia i poemy.* Moscow-Leningrad: Sovetskii pisatel', 1965.

Pushkin, Aleksandr. *The Letters of Alexander Pushkin.* Translated, and with preface, introduction, and notes by J. Thomas Shaw. Madison, Wisconsin: University of Wisconsin Press, 1967.

———. *Polnoe sobranie sochinenii.* 10 vols. Moscow: AN SSSR, 1962–66.

———. *Pushkin Threefold.* Translated by Walter Arndt. New York: E. P. Dutton, 1972.

Solzhenitsyn, Aleksandr. *Sobranie sochinenii.* Vol. 4. Vermont-Paris: YMCA-Press, 1979.

Tolstoi, L. N. *Polnoe sobranie sochinenii.* 90 vols. Moscow, 1928–58.

———. *What Is Art? and Essays on Art.* Translated by Aylmer Maude. New York: Oxford University Press, 1962.

Turgenev, I. S. *Polnoe sobranie sochinenii i pisem v dvadtsati vos'mi tomakh.* Vol. 8. Moscow-Leningrad: AN SSSR, 1964.

SECONDARY SOURCES

Adamovitch, Georges. "Une Mise en garde." In *Soljénitsyn,* edited by George Nivat and Michel Aucouturier. Paris: L'Herne, 1970.

Adamovich, Georgii. "Vladimir Nabokov." In *Twentieth-Century Russian Literary Criticism,* edited by Victor Erlich. New Haven: Yale University Press, 1983.

Akhmatova, Anna. *O Pushkine. Stat'i izametki.* Leningrad: Sovetskii pisatel', 1977.

Aldanov, Mark. *Zagadka Tolstogo.* Berlin. 1923. Providence, R.I.: Brown University Reprints, 1969.

Allaback, Stephen. *Alexander Solzhenitsyn.* New York: Taplinger Publishing Company, 1978.

Arminjon, Victor. *Pushkin et Pierre le Grand.* Paris: Librairie des Cinq Continents, 1971.

Barker, Francis. *Solzhenitsyn: Politics and Form.* New York: Barnes and Noble, 1977.

Barthes, Roland. *A Barthes Reader.* Edited and with an introduction by Susan Sontag. New York: Hill and Wang, 1982.

Batiuto, A. E. *Turgenev—Romanist.* Leningrad: Nauka, 1972.

Bayley, John. *Pushkin: A Comparative Commentary.* Cambridge University Press, 1971.

Blacher, Richard S. "Death, Resurrection, and Rebirth: Observations in Cardiac Surgery." *Psychoanalytic Quarterly* 52 (1983): 56–72.

Blagoi, D. D. *Sotsiologiia tvorchestva Pushkina: Etiudy.* Moscow: Federatsiia, 1929.

Boothe, Wayne. "Freedom and Interpretation: Bakhtin and the Challenge of Feminist Criticism." *Critical Inquiry* 9 (1982): 45–76.

Borras, F. M. *Maxim Gorky: The Writer.* Oxford: Oxford University Press, 1967.

Briggs, A. D. P. *Alexander Pushkin: A Critical Study.* Totowa, N.J.: Barnes and Noble, 1983.

Briusov, Valerii. "Mednyi vsadnik." In *Pushkin,* edited by S. A. Vengerov. Vol. 3, pp. 470–72. St. Petersburg: Brokgauz i Efron, 1909.

Bugaev, Boris [Andrei Belyi]. *Ritm kak dialektika i Medyi vsadnik: Issledovanie.* Moscow: Federatsiia, 1929.

Burton, Dora. "The Theme of Peter as a Verbal Echo in 'Mednyj vsadnik.'" *Slavic and East European Journal* 26 (1982): 12–26.

Cate, H. L. "On Death and Dying in Tolstoy's *"The Death of Ivan Ilych."* *Hartford Studies in Literature* 7 (1975): 195–205.

Cavell, Stanley. *The Claim of Reason: Wittgenstein, Skepticism, and Tragedy.* New York: Oxford University Press, 1969.

Christian, R. F. *Tolstoy: A Critical Introduction.* Cambridge University Press, 1969.

Cioran, Samuel D. *Vladimir Solov'ev and the Knighthood of the Divine Sophia.* Waterloo, Ontario: Wilfrid Laurier University Press, 1977.

Corbet, Charles. "Le symbolisme du Cavalier de Bronze." *Revue des études slaves* 45 (1966): 129–44.

Curtis, James M. *Solzhenitsyn's Traditional Imagination.* University of Georgia Press, 1984.

Dayanada, Y. J. *"The Death of Ivan Ilych:* A Psychological Study on Death and Dying." *Literature and Psychology* 22 (1972): 191–98.

De Rivera, Joseph. "A Structural Theory of the Emotions." In *Psychological Issues* X (4), monograph 40. New York: International Universities Press, 1977.

Des Pres, Terence. "The Heroism of Survival." In *Alexander Solzhenitsyn: Critical Essays and Documentary Materials,* edited by John B. Dunlop et al. Belmont, Mass.: Nordland, 1973.

Dessaix, Robert. *Turgenev: The Quest for Faith.* Canberra: Australian National University Faculty of the Arts, 1980.

Döring, Johanna Renate. *Die Lyrik Pasternaks in den Jahren 1928–34.* Munich: Otto Sagner, 1973.

Duncan, Robert. "Ivan Ilych's Death: Secular or Religious?" *University of Dayton Review* 15 (1981): 99–106.

Dunham, Vera S. "The Strong-Woman Motif." In *The Transformation of Russian Society: Aspects of Social Change since 1861,* edited by Cyril Black. Cambridge, Mass.: Harvard University Press, 1960, pp. 459–83.

Dunlop, John. "Solzhenitsyn in Exile." *Survey* 21 (1975): 133–54.

Edgerton, William B. "Tolstoy, Immortality, and Twentieth-Century Physics." *Canadian Slavonic Papers* 21 (1979): 289–300.

Elizarov, S. "Bor'ba M. Gor'kogo protiv reaktsionnykh tendentsii v literature." In *Stat'i o Gor'kom: Sbornik*, Moscow: GIKhL, 1957, pp. 269–347.

Ericson, Edward E., Jr. *Solzhenitsyn: The Moral Vision*. Grand Rapids, Mich.: William B. Eerdmans, 1980.

Erikson, Erik H. *Childhood and Society*. New York: W. W. Norton, 1963.

———. *Gandhi's Truth*. New York: W. W. Norton, 1969.

Erlich, Victor. "Puškin's Moral Realism as a Structural Problem." In *Aleksandr Puškin: A Symposium on the 175th Anniversary of His Birth*, edited by Andrej Kodjak and Kiril Taranovsky. New York: New York University Press, 1976.

———. *Russian Formalism*. 3d ed. New Haven: Yale University Press, 1981.

Ermakov, I. D. *Etiudy po psikhologii tvorchestva A. S. Pushkina*. Moscow-Petrograd: Gosizdat, 1923.

Etkind, Efim. "Svoboda i zakon: zametki na temu 'Pushkin i nasha sovremennost.'" *Russian Language Journal* 35 (1981): 12–17.

Fanger, Donald. *Dostoevsky and Romantic Realism*. Harvard University Press, 1965.

Forman, Betty. "Nietzsche and Gorky in the 1890s: The Case for an Early Influence." In *Western Philosophical Systems in Russian Literature*, edited by Anthony M. Mlikotin. Los Angeles: University of Southern California Press, 1980.

Frank, S. L. *Etiudy o Pushkine*. Munich, 1957.

Freeborn, Richard. *Turgenev: The Novelist's Novelist, A Study*. London: Oxford University Press, 1960.

Freud, Sigmund. *Introductory Lectures on Psychoanalysis*. New York: W. W. Norton, 1966.

———. "Mourning and Melancholia." In *A General Selection from the Works of Sigmund Freud*, edited by John Rickman. Garden City, N.Y.: Doubleday and Company, 1957.

Gardner, John. *The Art of Fiction: Notes on Craft for Young Writers*. New York: Alfred A. Knopf, 1984.

———. "Death by Art; or, 'Some Men Kill you with a Six-Gun, Some Men with a Pen.'" *Critical Inquiry* 3 (1977): 741–71.

Gąsiorowska, Xenia. *The Image of Peter the Great in Russian Fiction*. Madison: University of Wisconsin Press, 1979.

Gershenzon, Mikhail. *Mechta i mysl' I. S. Turgeneva*. Moscow, 1919. Brown University Reprint, 1970.

Gifford, Henry. "Turgenev." In *Nineteenth-Century Russian Literature: Studies of Ten Russian Writers*, edited by John Fennell (Berkeley: University of California Press, 1973.

Gilligan, Carol. *In a Different Voice: Psychological Theory and Women's Development*. Cambridge: Harvard University Press, 1982.

Gove, Antonina Filonov. "The Poet's Self: Images of Soul in Four Poems of Pasternak." *Slavic and East European Journal* 27 (1983): 185–199.

Grossman, L. P. "Smert' Ivana Il'icha." In L. N. Tolstoi, *Polnoe sobranie sochinenii*, vol. 26. Moscow, 1928–58, pp. 679–91.

Gutsche, George. "Pushkin's 'Andrei Shen'e' and Poetic Genres in the 1820s." *Canadian-American Slavic Studies* 10 (1976): 189–204.

Halperin, Irving. "The Structural Integrity of *The Death of Ivan Il'ič*." *Slavic and East European Journal* 5 (1961): 334–40.

Hingley, Ronald. *Nightingale Fever: Russian Poets in Revolution*. New York: Alfred A. Knopf, 1981.

Hirschberg, W. R. "Tolstoy's *The Death of Ivan Ilich.*" *Explicator* 28, item 26 (1969).

Holquist, Michael. "The Irrepressible I: The Role of Linguistic Subjectivity in Dissidence." *Yearbook of General and Comparative Literature* 31 (1982): 30–35.

Holtzman, Filia. *The Young Maxim Gorky: 1868–1902.* New York: Columbia University Press, 1948.

Howe, Irving. "Turgenev: The Virtues of Hesitation." *The Hudson Review* 8 (1956): 533–51.

Ivask, George. "The Vital Ambivalence of St. Petersburg." *Texas Studies in Literature and Language* 17 (1975): 247–55.

Ivinskaya, Olga. *A Captive of Time.* Translated by Max Hayward. New York: Warner Books, 1979.

Izmailov, N. V. "*Mednyi vsadnik* A. S. Pushkina. Istoriia zamysla i sozdaniia, publikatsii i izucheniia." In A. S. Pushkin, *Mednyi vsadnik*, Leningrad: Nauka, 1978, pp. 147–265.

Jahn, Gary R. "*The Death of Ivan Il'ič*—Chapter One." In *Studies in Honor of Xenia Gąsiorowska*, edited by Lauren G. Leighton. Columbus, Ohio: Slavica Publishers, 1983, pp. 37–43.

———. "The Role of the Ending in Lev Tolstoi's *The Death of Ivan Il'ich.*" *Canadian Slavonic Papers*, September 1982, pp. 229–38.

Jakobson, Roman. *Puškin and His Sculptural Myth.* Translated by John Burbank. The Hague-Paris: Mouton, 1975.

Johanson, Christine. "Turgenev's Heroines: A Historical Assessment." *Canadian Slavonic Papers*, March 1984, 15–23.

Kagan-Kans, Eva. *Hamlet and Don Quixote: Turgenev's Ambivalent Vision.* The Hague-Paris: Mouton, 1975.

Kalashnikov, V. A. *Pisatel' i ego geroi: O polemicheskoi napravlennosti i nekotorykh drugikh osobennostiakh rannikh rasskazov M. Gor'kogo.* Minsk: Nauka i tekhnika, 1969.

Kayser, Samuel J. "Wallace Stevens: Form and Meaning in Four Poems." *College English* 37 (1976): 578–98.

Kern, Gary. "The Case of Kostoglotov." *Russian Literature Triquarterly* 11 (1975): 407–34.

Kline, George L. *Religious and Anti-Religious Thought in Russia.* Chicago: University of Chicago, 1968.

Knigge, Armin. *Puškins Verserzählung "Der eherne Reiter" in der russischen Kritik: Rebellion oder Unterwerfung.* Amsterdam: Adolf M. Hakkert, 1984.

Kodjak, Andrej. "'The Queen of Spades' in the Context of the Faust Legend." In *Alexander Puškin: A Symposium*, edited by Andrej Kodjak and Kiril Taranovsky. New York: New York University Press, 1976.

Kratkaia literaturnaia entsiklopediia. "Poema." Vol. 5. 1968.

Kübler-Ross, Elizabeth. *On Death and Dying.* New York: Macmillan, 1969.

Langer, Lawrence L. *The Age of Atrocity: Death in Modern Literature.* Boston: Beacon Press, 1978.

Ledkovsky, Marina. *The Other Turgenev: From Romanticism to Symbolism.* Würzburg: Jal-verlag, 1973.

Lednicki, Waclaw. *Pushkin's "Bronze Horseman": The Story of a Masterpiece.* Berkeley: University of California Press, 1955.

Leont'ev, Konstantin. *Sobranie sochinenii.* Vol. 8. Moscow, 1912.

Lincoln, W. Bruce. *The Romanovs: Autocrats of All the Russias.* New York: Dial Press, 1981.

Loe, Mary Louise. "Maksim Gor'kii and the *Sreda* Circle: 1899–1905." *Slavic Review* 44 (1985): 49–66.

Lotman, Iu. M. *Aleksandr Sergeevich Pushkin: Biografiia pisatelia*. Leningrad: Prosveshchenie, 1983.

McLaughlin, Sigrid. "Some Aspects of Tolstoy's Intellectual Development: Tolstoy and Schopenhauer." *California Slavonic Studies* 5 (1970): 187–245.

Makarovskaia, G. V. *"Mednyi vsadnik": Itogi i problemy izuchenii*. Saratov: University of Saratov, 1978.

Marcus, Steven. *Representations: Essays on Literature and Society*. New York: Random House, 1975.

Matlaw, Ralph. Introduction to *Tolstoy: A Collection of Critical Essays*, edited by Ralph E. Matlaw. Englewood Cliffs, N.J.: Prentice-Hall, 1967.

Matual, David. *"The Confession* as a Subtext in *The Death of Ivan Il'ich." International Fiction Studies* 8 (1981): 124–28.

Mazour, Anatole G. *The First Russian Revolution, 1825*. Stanford University Press, 1965.

Merezhkovskii, D. S. *Polnoe sobranie sochinenii*. Vol. 13. St. Petersburg: M. O. Vol'f, 1909.

Mikhailovskii, V. V. *Tvorchestvo M. Gor'kogo i mirovaia literatura 1892–1916*. Moscow: Nauka, 1965.

Mirsky, D. S. *A History of Russian Literature*. Edited and abridged by Francis J. Whitfield. New York: Alfred A Knopf, 1966.

———. *Pushkin*. New York: E. P. Dutton and Company, 1963.

Moody, Christopher. *Solzhenitsyn*. 2d rev. ed. New York: Barnes and Noble, 1976.

Muchnic, Helen. *From Gorky to Pasternak*. New York: Vintage, 1961.

Nabokov, Vladimir. *Lectures on Russian Literature*. New York: Harcourt Brace Jovanovich, 1981.

Nezelenov, A. I. *Ivan Sergeevich Turgenev v ego proizvedeniiakh*. St. Petersburg, 1903.

Nillson, Nils Åke. "Life as Ecstasy and Sacrifice: Two Poems by Boris Pasternak." *Scando-Slavica* 5 (1959): 180–98.

Ninov, A. M. *Gor'kii i Iv. Bunin: Istoriia otnoshenii—problemy tvorchestva*. Leningrad: Sovetskii pisatel', 1973.

Nivat, Georges. "On Solzhenitsyn's Symbolism." In *Solzhenitsyn: A Collection of Critical Essays*, edited by Kathryn Feuer. Englewood Cliffs, N.J.: Prentice-Hall, 1976.

Olney, James. "Experience, Metaphor, and Meaning: *The Death of Ivan Ilyich." Journal of Aesthetics and Art Criticism* 31 (1972): 101–14.

Opul'skaia, L. D. *Lev Nikolaevich Tolstoi: Materialy k biografii s 1886 po 1892 god*. Moscow: Nauka, 1979.

Ovcharenko, A. I. *O polozhitel'nom geroe v tvorchestve M. Gor'kogo 1892–1907: Stat'i*. Moscow: Sovetskii pisatel', 1956.

Pachmuss, Temira. "The Theme of Love and Death in Tolstoy's *The Death of Ivan Ilych." American Slavic and East European Review* 20 (1961): 72–83.

Petrov, S. M. *I. S. Turgenev, Tvorcheskii put'*. Moscow: Khudozhestvennaia literatura, 1968.

Phillips, D. Z. *Death and Immortality*. London: Macmillan & Co., 1970.

Plank, Dale L. *Pasternak's Lyric: A Study of Sound and Imagery*. The Hague: Mouton, 1960.

Plato: Selections. Edited by Raphael Demos. New York: Charles Scribner's Sons, 1955.

Pollock, G. H. "On Mourning, Immortality, and Utopia." *Journal of American Psychoanalytical Association* 23 (1975): 334–62.

Pomorska, Krystyna. *Themes and Variations in Pasternak's Poetics*. Lisse: Peter de Ridder, 1975.

Pumpianskii, L. V. "'Mednyi vsadnik' i poeticheskaia traditsiia XVIII veka." In *Pushkin. Vremennik Pushkinskoi komissii.* Vol. 4. Moscow-Leningrad: AN SSSR, 1939, pp. 91–124.

Rank, Otto. *The Don Juan Legend.* Translated, edited, and with introduction by David G. Winter. Princeton, N.J.: Princeton University Press, 1975.

Ring, Kenneth. *Life at Death: A Scientific Investigation of the Near-Death Experience.* New York: Coward, McCann and Geoghegan, 1980.

Ripp, Victor. *Turgenev's Russia: From "Notes of a Hunter" to "Fathers and Sons."* Ithaca, N.Y.: Cornell University Press, 1980.

Rorty, Richard. *Consequences of Pragmatism (Essays: 1972–1980).* Minneapolis: University of Minnesota Press, 1982.

Rosengrant, Sandra. "The Theoretical Criticism of Jurij Tynjanov." *Comparative Literature* 32 (1980): 355–89.

Rothberg, Abraham. *Aleksandr Solzhenitsyn: The Major Novels.* Ithaca, N.Y.: Cornell University Press, 1971.

Russell, Robert. "From Individual to Universal: Tolstoy's 'Smert' Ivana Il'icha.'" *Modern Language Review* 76 (1981): 629–42.

Rzhevsky, Nicholas. *Russian Literature and Ideology: Herzen, Dostoevsky, Leontiev, Tolstoy, Fadeyev.* Urbana: University of Illinois Press, 1983.

Sandomirskaia, V. B. "Poemy." In *Pushkin: Itogi i problemy izucheniia.* Moscow-Leningrad: Nauka, 1966, pp. 398–406.

Scammell, Michael. *Solzhenitsyn: A Biography.* New York, London: W. W. Norton, 1984.

Schaarschmidt, Gunther. "Theme and Discourse Structure in *The Death of Ivan Il'ich.*" *Canadian Slavonic Papers* 21 (1979): 356–66.

Schapiro, Leonard. *Turgenev: His Life and Times.* New York: Random House, 1978.

Schillinger, John. "Labor Camps and Other Malignancies in *Cancer Ward*: A Further Diagnosis." *Russian Language Journal* 37, Nos. 126–127 (1983): 123–38.

Schopenhauer, Arthur. *The World as Will and Idea.* Translated by R. B. Haldane and J. Kemp. London: Routledge & Kegan Paul, 1883.

Siniavskii, Andrei [Abram Tertz]. Introduction to *Stikhotvoreniia i poemy*, by Boris Pasternak. Moscow-Leningrad: AN SSSR, 1965, pp. 5–62.

———. *Progulki s Pushkinym.* London: William Collins & Sons, and Overseas Publications Interchange, 1975.

Sloane, David A. "*Cancer Ward* Revisited: Analogical Models and the Theme of Reassessment." *Slavic and East European Journal* 26 (1982): 403–18.

Slonimskii, Aleksandr. "Pushkin i dekabr'skaia dvizhenie." In *Pushkin*, edited by Vengerov. Vol. 2, pp. 503–28.

Smyrniw, Walter. "Tolstoy's Depiction of Death in the Context of Recent Studies of the 'Experience of Dying.'" *Canadian Slavonic Papers* 21 (1979): 367–79.

Sorokin, Boris. "Ivan Il'yich as Jonah: A Cruel Joke." *Canadian Slavic Studies* 5 (1971): 487–504.

Spanos, William V. *De-structing the Novel: Essays in Applied Postmodern Hermeneutics.* Troy, N.Y.: Whitston Publishing Co., 1982.

Steiner, George. *Tolstoy and Dostoevsky: An Essay in the Old Criticism.* New York: Vintage Books, 1961.

Tarasov, B. "Analiz burzhuaznogo soznaniia v povesti L. N. Tolstogo, 'Smert' Ivana Il'icha.'" *Voprosy literatury* 3 (1982): 156–76.

Terras, Victor. "Puškin's 'Feast during the Plague' and Its Original: A Structural Confrontation." In *Aleksandr Puškin: A Symposium*, edited by Andrej Kodjak and Kiril Taranovsky. New York: New York University Press, 1976.

Tomashevskii, B. V. "Peterburg v tvorchestve Pushkina." In *Pushkinskii Peterburg.*

Leningrad: Gazetno-zhurnal'noe i knizhnoe izdatel'stvo, 1949, pp. 3–40.
————. "Pushkin i Peterburg." In *Issledovaniia i materialy*. Vol. 3. Moscow-Leningrad: AN SSSR, 1960.
Treadgold, Donald W. *Twentieth Century Russia*. 2d ed. Chicago: Rand McNally & Company, 1966.
Tsiavlovskii, M. A.; Modzalevskii, L. B.; and Zenger, T. G., eds. *Rukoiu Pushkina*. Moscow-Leningrad: Academia, 1935.
Tsvetaeva, Marina. *Proza*. New York: Chekhov Publishing House, 1953.
Turner, C. J. G. "The Language of Fiction: Word Clusters in Tolstoy's *The Death of Ivan Ilyich*." *Modern Language Review* 65 (1970): 116–21.
Tynianov, Iurii. *Arkhaisty i novatory*. Leningrad: Priboi, 1929.
————. *Pushkin i ego sovremenniki*. Moscow: Nauka, 1969.
Vatsuro, V. E., and Meilakh, B. S. "Pushkin i deiatel'nost' tainykh obshchestv." In *Pushkin: Itogi i problemy izucheniia*. Moscow-Leningard: AN SSSR, 1966, pp. 168–97.
Vickery, Walter N. *Alexander Pushkin*. New York: Twayne Publishers, 1970.
————. "Pushkin's *Andzhelo*: A Problem Piece." In *Mnemozina: Studia literaria in honorem V. Setchkarev*. Munich: Fink Verlag, 1974, pp. 325–39.
Vinnikova, I. "Stat'ia 'Gamlet i Don-Kikhot' i demokraticheskii geroi v romane *Nakanune*." In *I. S. Turgenev v shestidesiatye gody (Ocherki i nabliudeniia)*. Saratov: University of Saratov, 1965.
Volkov, A. A. *M. Gor'kii i literaturnoe dvizhenie kontsa XIX i nachalo XX vekov*. Moscow: Sovetskii pisatel', 1954.
————. *Put' khudozhnika: M. Gor'kii do Oktiabria*. Moscow: GIKhL, 1969.
Walicki, A. "Turgenev and Schopenhauer." *Oxford Slavonic Papers*. Vol. 10. Oxford: Clarendon Press, 1962.
Wasiolek, Edward. "Design in the Russian Novel." In *The Russian Novel from Pushkin to Pasternak*, edited by John Garrard. New Haven and London: Yale University Press, 1983, pp. 51–63.
————. *Tolstoy's Major Fiction*. Chicago: University of Chicago Press, 1978.
————. "Tolstoy's *The Death of Ivan Ilych* and Jamesian Fictional Imperatives." *Modern Fiction Studies* 6 (1960): 314–24. Reprinted in revised form in *Tolstoy: A Collection of Critical Essays*, pp. 146–56.
————. "Wanted: A New Contextualism." *Critical Inquiry* 1 (1975): 623–39.
Weil, Irwin. *Gorky: His Literary Development and Influence on Soviet Intellectual Life*. New York: Random House, 1966.
Windle, Kevin. "Symbolism and Analogy in Solzhenitsyn's *Cancer Ward*." *Canadian Slavonic Papers* 13 (1971): 193–206.
Zenger, T. G. "Nikolai I—redaktor Pushkina." In *Literaturnoe nasledstvo* 16–18 (1934).
Zelinskii, V. *Sobranie kriticheskikh materialov dlia izucheniia proizvedenii I. S. Turgeneva*. Moscow: Balandin, Volkhonka, and Mikhalkov, 1899.
Zenkovsky, V. V. *A History of Russian Philosophy*. Translated by George L. Kline. 2 vols. New York: Columbia University Press, 1967.

INDEX